SHADOWS ON THE HORIZON

Shadows on the Horizon

The Battle of Convoy HX-233

W A Haskell

Foreword by Prof Dr Jürgen Rohwer

NAVAL INSTITUTE PRESS
Annapolis, Maryland

First published in Great Britain in 1998 by Chatham Publishing,
61 Frith Street,
London W1V 5TA

Published and distributed in the United States and Canada by the Naval Institute Press,
118 Maryland Avenue, Annapolis, Maryland 21402-5035

A Library of Congress Catalog Card No. is available on request.

ISBN 1 55750 887 9

Printed and bound in Great Britain.

Contents

Of the events of the war, I have not ventured to speak from any chance information, nor according to any notion of my own. I have described nothing but what I saw myself, or learned from others of whom I made the most careful and particular inquiry. The task was a laborious one because eyewitnesses of the same occurrence gave different accounts of them as they remembered, or were interested in, the actions of one side or the other. And very likely the strictly historical character of my narrative may be disappointing to the ear. But, if he who desires to have before his eyes a true picture of the events which have happened and of the like events which may be expected to happen hereafter in the order of human things shall pronounce what I have written to be useful, then I shall be satisfied.

THUCYDIDES, *PELOPONNESIAN WAR*, 1.22
(JOWETT TRANSLATION)

Foreword

In the last forty years many books and articles have appeared about the convoy battles of the longest campaign of The Second World War, the Battle of the Atlantic. Many have been written by participants of the battles: U-boat captains, officers of the escort groups or merchant seamen; others have been published by journalists or by historians from one side or the other. But there are few stories available looking at both sides of the battle based on eyewitness accounts and memories of the participants and documents from the Allied *and* German archives.

Winthrop A Haskell has selected for his book a convoy, neglected until now, from the critical turning tide of the Battle of the Atlantic in April 1943: the Convoy HX-233. Having participated in many convoys on the North Atlantic and the Murmansk routes, this convoy interested him not only because he was there, but also because it was a convoy well defended by a joint British/American/Canadian escort group assisted by a British support group, against a few German U-boats sent to intercept it, reported by chance by a U-boat going on a special mission.

The author, now living in Germany, was able not only to search through the documents in the Bundesarchiv-Militärarchiv at Freiburg, the Traditionsarchiv Unterseeboote at Cuxhaven, the Public Records Office in London, the National Archives in Washington, and the National Archives in Ottawa, but he also had contact with the military/naval historical research institutes in Germany, Great Britain, the United States and Canada. And he established close personal relations with surviving members of the participating German U-boats, especially the sunk *U-175*, as well as the US, Canadian and British escort and support vessels and some of the participating merchant ships. He has been able to correct many of the errors and mistakes in earlier accounts and to present a painstaking analysis of this battle, combining his research of the documents with a great amount of 'oral history'.

So now we have to thank the author for one of the very best convoy histories of the Second World War, which adds enormously to our understanding of the conflict in the North Atlantic.

Stuttgart, 1998

PROF DR JÜRGEN ROHWER
Chairman of the 'Curatorium' of the
Foundation, 'Library of Contemporary
History' at Stuttgart

Acknowledgements

The unstinting help of a number of very generous people was essential to bring the following events onto paper, and it seemed right that participants tell their own stories as far as possible.

I am most grateful to *U-175* survivors Peter Wannemacher, Gustav Brückmann, Dieter Wolf, Werner Bickel, Karl Kempf, Gerhard Winkler, Walter Schröder, Herbert Schwarze, Phillip Labs, Werner Siegert, Rudolf March, and Jean Bamberg for sharing memories. I extend unreserved thanks also to Fregatten Kapitän a D Heinz Franke, Ritterkreuzträger (*U-148, U-262, U-3509, U-2502*) for his contributions.

Eyewitness' accounts from Convoy HX-233 participants added significantly to official reports, including those of former USMMA Deck Cadets Robert D Mattox, James E Bentley, and Perry Jacobs, with thanks to James Hoffman for putting us in contact. Thanks are due to cousins Revd Stanley R Haskell, for memories of Barbados, and Stanley James Haskell DSM and Harry K Rawlings for memories of HMS *Bryony* as well as other ex-crew members of that vessel, HMS *Offa* (especially William Robertson), HMS *Daniella*, and HMS *Bergamot* (especially T F J Rogers, Peter Bowen, Vic Whitely and J C Morris). To ex-DEMS gunner on *Fort Rampart* Charles Collis, for his still vivid memories of 17 April 1943. I am also grateful that former, long-valued shipmate Arthur Timmons added his own recollections, as well as members of the *Spencer* Association Jim Tierney, G S Hall and H D Walker, and members of the USCG Cutter *Duane* Association Albert Viau, R C Golec, Earl L Hyde and Bruno Vendramin.

For supplying invaluable data sincere thanks to Horst Bredow of Stiftung Traditionsarchiv Unterseeboote, Korvetten Kapitän d R Hans Köbberling, (*U-1022*), Fregatten Kapitän a D Gerd Thäter (*U-466, U-3506*), Kapitän zur See a D Adolf Oelrich (*U-92*), Wolfgang Kaufmann, Hans Krekelmann, Dr Maierhöfer of the Bundesarchiv-Militärarchiv, Philip Dutton of the Imperial War Museum, and to ex-Merchant Navy radio officer James P Derriman for tracking down vital British documents. For vital input from Yves Trembley and Deborah Shaw of the Canadian History Directorate, R D Squires MBE of the North Russia Club, and E R Allan of the Russian Convoy Club, also my debt of thanks.

To Prof Dr Jürgen Rohwer, O D Cresswell, Ian A Millar, Captain Charles Dana Gibson, and Captain Harold D Huycke, deep gratitude for constructive suggestions. Very special thanks must go to USCG historian Scott Price for his unflagging support and encouragement, providing priceless details of operations, contacts to former crew and tracking down invaluable documents and photos. And last, a special debt of gratitude to my wife for her unfailing patience in revising and correcting the typescript, entering endless changes and providing encouragement, without which none of this would have been possible.

Acknowledgement and thanks are due to the following for permission to use copyright, or personal, material and illustrations: Adolf March, Peter Wannemacher, Fregattenkapitän a D Heinz Franke Ritterkreuzträger, Gustav Brückmann, S J Haskell DSM, Revd Stanley R Haskell, Werner Bickel, Public Records Office by permission of the Controller of Her Majesty's Stationery Office, Imperial War Museum, National Archives of Canada, US Coast Guard, US Navy, US National Archives, Steamship Historical Society Collection of University of Baltimore, Jim Morris, T F J Rogers, and Stuttgart Library of Contemporary History.

This study is dedicated to those who gave their all on both sides. There are no tombstones on sailors' graves.

Introduction

The Merchant Navy, with Allied comrades, night and day, in weather fair or foul, faces not only the ordinary perils of the sea but the sudden assaults of war from beneath the waters or from the sky. Your first task is to bring to port the cargoes vital for us at home and for our armies abroad and we trust your tenacity and resolve to see this stern task through.
                                    SIR WINSTON CHURCHILL, 1941

I consider the protection of our trade the most essential service that can be performed.
            ADMIRAL NELSON TO CAPTAIN BENJAMIN HALLOWELL, 1804

It was clear to both Germany and the Allies from the outset, that without constantly replenishing Great Britain's civilian and war *materiel*, the Allies stood only a slim chance of surviving, and no chance at all of winning, the Second World War. The Battle of the Atlantic, the longest running battle over the largest single battlefield in world history, was focused on the Allied supply lines. Beginning with the sinking of the *Athenia* and loss of 112 lives ten hours after the opening of hostilities on 3 September 1939, this battle did not end until 7 May 1945, five years, eight months and four days later with the sinking of S/S *Avondale Park*, torpedoed one mile southeast of May Island in the Firth of Forth, by *U-2336* (Kptlt Emil Klusmeir).

The heavy losses suffered by British, US and Allied merchant navies have all too rarely been addressed. Seven thousand British Merchant Navy men lost their lives in 1941 and eight thousand in 1942. Although seldom achieved, U-boat commanders tried to take prisoner the captains and chief engineers of the merchant ships they sank, to further deplete the Allies' experienced personnel.

During 1941 Germany sank 717 British ships, amounting to a loss of 2,824,056 tons, and resulting in acute food shortages in Britain. Between 1939 and 1941 Britain lost twenty big refrigerated ships and, in just the last nineteen days of January 1942, thirty-nine ships, including sixteen tankers, were hit. During the first six months of the same year U-boats sank sixty-eight British tankers in the Atlantic, sixteen off the US coast and seventeen in the Caribbean. U-boats sank 609 vessels, amounting to 3,122,456 tons, between December 1941 and August 1942 in American waters alone.

In January 1942 the much-touted U-boat operation, 'Paukenschlag' ('drum roll'), began devastating Allied shipping off the East Coast of the United States, doing no more damage, however, than its less publicised counterpart, 'Operation Neuland' in the Caribbean. The latter, beginning a month later, lasted till year's end, accounting for 36 per cent of Allied shipping losses for the year world-wide. Unfortunately, the

US Navy was no better prepared to meet the German onslaught here and no more effective than off its own coastline. U-boats in the Caribbean rampaged unchecked, even entering brilliantly lit harbours to torpedo ships moored to the docks. Ninety-seven German U-boats and seven Italian submarines operated 146 patrols in Caribbean waters to sink a staggering 400 ships and damaging 56 more. With only seventeen boats lost, Germany had executed her most effective U-boat campaign of the War. In May and June the campaign reached its climax when 70 per cent of 109 Allied ships sunk world-wide were sunk by U-boats in the Caribbean. In July, in the same theatre, U-boats sank seventy-six ships and severely damaged three more, for 60 per cent of the world total. Sixty-seven invaluable tankers were sunk and twelve badly damaged between May and July 1942, representing a loss of more than double the number of replacement tankers which the Allies could build, launch, and put into service during those three months.

Although Japan never seriously threatened America's West Coast or industrial production, Admiral King and the US Navy focused their attention on the Pacific, ignoring the serious danger to Allied cargoes, not least among them oil, sugar, and the bauxite ore so vital to the burgeoning aircraft industry, flowing from Central and South America and the West Indies. U-boats sailing directly from European bases constituted an entirely separate and highly effective offensive against those supply lines, reflecting the genius of the U-boat commander Admiral Dönitz. Had Dönitz received the number of U-boats he wanted, the War's outcome might well have been very different.

No record of any official US concern about the bloody losses of 1942 has been found, but the British Ministry of War Transport was gravely concerned about its high casualty rate of nearly eight thousand experienced seamen in one year, and justifiably apprehensive about morale. It is not generally known that the pay of a merchant seaman stopped and his leave began at the moment of the loss of his ship. Falling bombs and shells, and the threat of mines and torpedoes were his common lot, and it was not unusual for survivors to become survivors again when the rescuing vessel was also lost to enemy action. Yet, despite this, British morale remained generally unfaltering, with courage and *esprit* supported by the unfailing British sense of humour, and the strong sense of comradeship amongst seamen, gunners and officers.

On the other side, the U-boat men were the elite of the German armed forces, chosen for ability, intelligence, strength, stamina and their equanimity under stress in crowded, cramped quarters. They were protected from politics by their highly respected commander, Admiral Karl Dönitz.

Hitler complained frequently, 'I have a reactionary army, a Christian navy, and a National Socialist air force'. Naval personnel were not even permitted to join the NSDAP. The Nazi salute, not normally used by the navy, was almost studiously avoided by submariners. Naturally there were political views of all persuasions among military personnel, as among civilians, but the Kriegsmarine was the least political of all forces.

*   *   *

The U-boat war was a tonnage war for the Germans, with the Americans simply able to build more ships than the U-boats could sink. If the struggle in the North Atlantic came within a hair's breadth of German victory, that in the Caribbean came at least as close to severing the trade routes to the United States, and, ultimately, to Britain. Known popularly on the German side as the 'Second Happy Time', the sinkings during this period were far more serious than the Pearl Harbor debacle but were

The Second World War poster by the artist Charles Wood emphasising the importance of the Merchant Navy and their role in the North Atlantic. *(PRO)*

swept under the rug of wartime secrecy. The same inability to recognise and estimate a threat was responsible for the dispatching of unarmed, or under-armed, ships to North Russia.

Submarines accounted for 2,828, or well over half, of the 5,150 Allied merchant ships sunk or badly damaged during the War. Over 50,000 Allied merchant seamen and merchant ship gunners lost their lives, the majority to German submarines which also sank 148 Allied warships including three battleships and two aircraft carriers.

Kelshall wrote in his Foreword to *The U-boat War in the Caribbean*:

> During World War II seventeen U-boats were sunk in the Caribbean – two percent of the total U-boat losses for the entire war. But for each U-boat sunk the Allies lost 23.5 merchant ships. For the German navy, the Caribbean U-boat campaign was the most cost-effective campaign fought by Germany anywhere during World War II.

Even Morison, otherwise fulsomely praising the US Navy, commented:

> This writer cannot avoid the conclusion that the US Navy was woefully unprepared, materially and mentally, for the U-boat blitz on the Atlantic coast.

He further believed that, apart from the want of air power which was due to prewar agreements with the Army, this unpreparedness was largely the Navy's own fault.

German statistics show that of 1,131 U-boats entering service, 863 were deployed against the enemy. Of 785 boats lost, 754, over 85 per cent, were sunk. From a force of 39,000 men, the U-boat Memorial at Möltenort overlooking Kieler Förde, Germany, has engraved in bronze the names of the 28,728 men who lost their lives. Some 18,897 lives were lost and 458 boats sunk in the Atlantic theatre alone, representing some 74 per cent loss of personnel and 70 per cent of operational boats. These losses were proportionately far higher than in any other service in the world. Only around five thousand men were taken as POWs. United States Coast Guard (USCG) Captain John M Waters observed that the number of lives lost on both sides was greater than the combined deaths in all naval battles over the preceding five hundred years.

Curiously pleading lack of suitable escorts, the United States all but withdrew its navy from North Atlantic mercantile convoy protection soon after entering the War. The Atlantic Fleet, commanded by Vice Admiral Royal E Ingersoll, had seven battleships including four newly commissioned, three cruiser divisions, eight aircraft carriers with four tenders, nine destroyer squadrons of seventy-seven destroyers with five tenders, fifteen patrol squadrons totalling some 180 Catalina aircraft, fifteen tenders, forty-five minelayers and five destroyers converted to high speed minesweepers, eighteen fleet oilers, and thirty-eight Coast Guard vessels designated as the 'Greenland Patrol', all under naval control as late as 5 August 1942. With its imposing array of massive strength the US Navy was dispersed in the North Atlantic where U-boats were *not* operating in 1942 although it had been active and conspicuous in provocative circumstances *before* 7 December 1941. For example, Convoy HX-150 with fifty ships under Rear Admiral E Manners RN sailing 16 September 1941, included four US destroyers in its Escort Group. Afterwards the heavy burden of convoy protection fell on the British and Canadian navies supplemented by a handful of Allied vessels from Norway, Poland, Belgium and the Free French. When the Americans withdrew completely, two escort groups had to be disbanded at a time of mounting crises that already threatened Britain's lifeline. They did not return in force to the Atlantic theatre until late 1943, well after the crisis had passed, with the advent of the so-called 'Hunter-Killer' groups, centred around merchant ships converted to small escort aircraft carriers. The first of these, the USS *Bogue* (CVE 9), operated as part of 6th Support Group, but her deployment was largely nullified by being placed in the centre of Convoy HX-228 where she had no room to manoeuvre.

Only one American unit was still operational, the joint US and Canadian Group A-3 which included the nearly-new, 1940-built, US *Benson* class destroyer *Gleaves* (DD-423), with Cdr J B Heffernan USN, formerly commander of Destroyer Division 60. Other ships in the group were US Coast Guard cutter *Spencer* and RCN corvettes *Algoma, Arvida, Shediac* and *Bittersweet*. Despite extensive group training, however, including night practice prior to sailing, when Group A-3 escorted Convoy ONS-92, the convoy ran into U-boat patrol line 'Hecht' and lost five ships the first night out on 12 May 1942, and ultimately two more ships. Inept handling of the Escort Group was considered responsible and Heffernan later candidly admitted he had not known what was happening. But the failure of A-3 was complete. Senior Officer Heffernan, commanding a group for the first time, wrote: 'The COs of all the escorts are entitled to credit for a highly satisfactory performance', which only brought a storm of protest from all quarters including the convoy commodore and the master of the attached rescue ship. The latter noted that the failure of the senior officer to act on HF/DF bearings may well have contributed greatly to the loss of valuable lives and ships. The commodore noted sardonically that *Gleaves* was never there when the convoy was under attack.

The Western Approaches command and RCN Headquarters in Ottawa, Canada, were stunned, even though the earlier devastating losses in US coastal waters had already undermined their faith in the US Navy. The Senior American Officer in Londonderry, Captain H T Thébaud USN, passed the word along about Allied reactions to the mishandling of Convoy ONS-92 and Heffernan was quickly and quietly posted to another command. Unfortunately, the Merchant Navy as usual paid a heavy price.

Henceforth, the meagre US protection of North Atlantic convoys fell on a handful of the US Coast Guard's superb 327-foot 'Treasury' class cutters *Campbell, Ingham, Bibb, Hamilton* (lost 1942 off Iceland), *Spencer* and *Duane*. Roomy and comfortable, and incorporating hospital facilities, they were sea kindly vessels. They also had a long range (7,000 miles at 13 knots), were heavily armed, well-equipped and fast enough (SHP 6200 = 19.5 knots) to catch a surfaced U-boat. Manned mostly by prewar professional and experienced crews, they filled a vital niche in the desperate North Atlantic battle.

Replacing Heffernan was Cdr Paul R Heineman USN, lately in command of the *Porter* class destroyer USS *Moffett* (DD-362) as escort to Convoy WS-12X, the ill-starred convoy that successfully transported 20,000 British troops from England to

Singapore, only to arrive on 9 December 1941 just in time for them to be taken as Japanese POWs.

From December 1941 to April 1942 Cdr Heineman commanded the destroyer USS *Benson* (DD-423), sistership of Heffernan's *Gleaves*, and escorted Convoy HX-183 which managed to avoid attack. Shortly thereafter he was promoted to captain and succeeded Heffernan as senior officer of Escort Group A-3 aboard USCG cutter *Spencer*, commanded by Cdr Harold S Berdine USCG. This Escort Group sank two U-boats and damaged others during the aptly named 'Bloody Winter' of 1942–43.

Probably the true turning point of the North Atlantic battle came shortly after the U-boat struggle around three east-bound convoys, SC-122, HX-229 and HX-229A, consisting of over 150 merchant ships and escorted by B-4, B-5 and 40th Escort Groups. Three U-boat groups attacked them: 'Gruppe Raubgraf' of eight boats, 'Gruppe Stürmer' of eighteen, and 'Gruppe Dränger' of eleven, plus eight unattached boats. The three convoys lost twenty-two ships, amounting to 146,596grt, to U-boats, while one ship went missing, one sank in collision with an iceberg and one escort, the brand new 'Isles' class trawler HMS *Campobello* foundered under ice and weather damage. The casualty list, the majority being merchant seamen, totalled 372 men of whom 68 were military personnel. A naval escort lost one man overboard from HMS *Mansfield*, ex-USS *Evans* (DD-78), an old four-stacker transferred to Britain in September 1940.

The Germans dubbed the U-boat battles around HX-229 and SC-122 in March 1943 'The Greatest Convoy Battle of All Time' ('Die größte Geleitzugsschlacht aller Zeiten') and the story has been well documented in two fine books: *Convoy* by Martin Middlebrook and *The Critical Convoy Battles of March 1943* by Prof Dr Jürgen Rohwer. Succeeding convoys marked the gradual decline, and finally Germany's withdrawal, of her U-boats from the Atlantic.

The latter part of March 1943 saw wild North Atlantic weather with winds of up to Force 11. Abominable as it was, however, it 'saved' three convoys – ONS-170 (west-bound, UK to New York), SC-123 and HX-230 – when approximately thirty U-boats in the area were able to sink only one ship, a straggler; another, the commodore's ship in one convoy, capsized and went down with all hands.

The experienced Lieutenant Commander (later Vice Admiral) P W Gretton RN escorted the next convoy, HX-231, with B-7 Escort Group. Although fewer U-boats were being sent to sea because only one U-boat refuelling tanker was available, twenty-two U-boats found HX-231 and managed to sink three ships, a straggler and two rompers (a ship which ran ahead of a convoy by virtue of her greater speed), and damage two others, but lost two of their own boats in the process. HX-232 was also heavily attacked and lost several ships to *U-563* and *U-706*, but the Battle of the Atlantic had turned a corner, unrecognised at the time.

Many of the merchant ships that left New York early in April in Convoy HX-233 were battle-tested veterans of hard-fought bouts with U-boats and North Atlantic weather. Just a month earlier eleven of them had been intercepted by thirteen U-boats while in Convoy ON-170 west-bound in ballast for New York. These were the British *Devis*, *Empire Pakeha*, *Kaituna*, *City of Khios*, the Belgian *Ville d'Anvers*, the

US Coast Guard cutter *Spencer* passing cutter *Duane* (foreground) at
sea during Convoy HX-233 operations in April 1943. *(US National
Archives)*

Norwegian *Villanger* and *John Bakke*, the American *Alcoa Cutter*, *Axel Johnson*, *Maya*
and *Atenas*, an ancient banana carrier built in 1908 for the United Fruit Company of
New York. Despite encounters with U-boats, Convoy ON-170 as well as the two
following, ONS-171 and ONS-172, reached Newfoundland without loss among over
one hundred merchant ships. The majority of available U-boats had been diverted to
attack the heavily-laden convoys SC-122 and HX-229 in what became one of the most
bitterly-fought convoy battles of the war.

   HX-233, sailing a more southerly route than usual, was detected early. Although
eight outward-bound U-boats homed in, including *U-175*, only one merchant ship

was lost, proving the effectiveness of an adequate, armed escort and sufficient air cover.

Admiral Dönitz wrote regarding these battles:

> In the big convoy battles in March most of the U-boats engaged had exhausted their supplies of both fuel and torpedoes and were forced to return to base. As a result, at the beginning of April there was a 'U-boat vacuum' in the North Atlantic, and it was not until the middle of the month that there was once again a group, code-named 'Meise', deployed north-east of Cape Race, Newfoundland. Towards the end of April there were also a number of U-boats on passage from Biscay ports to the North Atlantic. One of these [NB: *U-262*, Franke] sighted an east-bound convoy, which had been routed on a somewhat unusually southerly course, 400 miles north of the Azores. This was HX-233, which had taken this circuitous southerly route in order to be sure of avoiding the U-boat groups which were thought to have been concentrated on the northern route.
>
> Four more boats sailing independently to their operational areas were directed on to the convoy and came up with it, one after another, within the space of a day. In the calm and windless weather of these southern latitudes all the boats were at once detected by the radar [sic] of an exceptionally strong escort and subjected to continuous attack with depth charges. The normal convoy escort had been reinforced by the ubiquitous *Offa* Support group. One ship of 7,487 tons [sic] [NB: *Fort Rampart* actually 7134 tons] was sunk, and *U-176* [sic] under Commander Bruns was lost.

On the Allied side Captain Roskill noted that a total of ninety-eight U-boats sailed during the month of April 1943 to become

> . . . almost a flood . . . coming out of Germany by the northern route, or leaving the Biscay bases. . . . The first attempt made by the enemy's new concentration was against HX-233 in the middle of April . . ., and the attack on it was not at all a success. The escort received a timely reinforcement in the shape of the *Offa*'s support group [NB: and timely air cover], and only one ship was lost and *U-175* was sunk.

If HX-231 can be considered the 'crisis convoy', certainly battles around the two subsequent convoys reveal the growing technical superiority of the Allies' anti-submarine forces. Exploiting the decrypts of the German Enigma codes HF/DF radio intercepts, radar, asdic, and providing adequate air and sea support, the Battle of the Atlantic, in retrospect, was now clearly moving towards the Allied side. Escorts of HX-237 in mid-May detected eleven U-boats and drove them off. Unfortunately, three ships were lost, but at a cost of three U-boats, an unacceptable rate of loss for the Germans. Aircraft around the convoy kept the U-boats down and sank two, marking their decisive defeat.

Roskill wrote of this encounter:

> After forty-five months of unceasing battle, of a more exacting nature than posterity may easily realise, our convoy escorts and aircraft had won the triumph they had so richly merited.

In this vital sea battle, perhaps the most vital of this global war, the action surrounding the passage of Convoy HX-233 in April 1943 was a microcosm. HX-233 was a fairly typical convoy in the bridge of ships from the New World to the Old that delivered in all some 100,000 merchantmen and their cargoes. HX-233 was untypical, however, because its passage demonstrated that the tide of advantage had turned in the Allies' favour.

The United Kingdom appropriately held its Fiftieth Anniversary Commemoration of these convoy battles from 26 to 31 May 1993 at Merseyside in Liverpool, recalling that the climax of U-boat successes had passed by April–May 1943, and that those convoy battles marked not only the turning point in the Battle of the Atlantic, but also that of the War itself. Without success in the Atlantic an Allied victory two years later would not have been possible.

Witnessing on 17 April 1943 the loss of another fine ship to a torpedo, then shortly afterwards the sinking of a U-boat, which he has only recently learned was within seconds of turning his own ship into a fireball, and finally developing a warm friendship with survivors of that U-boat, led this author directly to the present study. A survey of pertinent literature revealed numerous factual errors, so research has relied heavily on original official records and documents in the Public Records Office, London, the National Archives of Canada and the US National Archives, Washington, as well as eyewitnesses' and participants' accounts from both sides. Here, too, contradictions or omissions required a certain amount of interpretation, so the author must accept responsibility for any continuing errors included in this major effort to clarify the events of over fifty years ago and emphasise their historical importance.

The German Armed Forces used only Middle European time, so these are the times given for them unless otherwise noted. Allied vessels' times are local or, where specified, Greenwich Mean Time.

1

The Convoy System and Convoy HX-233

According to *The Oxford Dictionary* a convoy is 'an escort with armed force, usually merchant or passenger vessels', also 'a company supply of provisions, etc, under escort'. Whether armed or unarmed, merchant vessels sailing alone in wartime are highly vulnerable to attack, whereas convoys with naval escorts can frequently ward off attack, a fact which was not fully appreciated until towards the end of the First World War. Despite recognising its island nation's extreme dependence on imports, the British Admiralty waited until the 'five-minutes-to-midnight' deadline of 1917 to adopt a convoy system during the First World War. When war came again in September 1939, however, the Admiralty immediately instituted the convoy system, but only to 300 miles off the UK coast. There the escorts left the merchant vessels to reach North America as best they could. The first convoy from North American shores with escort for part of the crossing was HX-133 which lost eight ships and 102 lives to torpedoes. Fully-escorted transatlantic convoys did not begin until 1941 and only after 1942 did support groups of heavily-armed destroyers briefly reinforce the convoy escorts at critical times.

The typical Allied mercantile convoy of 1943 consisted of fifty to sixty ships steaming in a standard formation of nine to twelve columns, five to six ships deep. In the case of HX-233, twelve columns were later reduced to eleven. Columns were numbered from the port side, Column No 1 being the port hand, and each column of ships was numbered from No 1 from the head. The first number would be the column and the final number the vessel's position with the column; thus, No 11 was the lead ship of the first column to port and No 12 the second ship in the first column. Columns were 1,000 yards apart and ships in a column 800 yards apart, presenting a broad, compact front to allow signals to be seen from all ships, while offering a smaller flank target to U-boats. A convoy such as HX-233 with over fifty ships covered more than five square miles of sea, with a four to five-mile frontage and a one to one-and-a-half mile depth.

Convoy escorts varied according to what was available: armed trawlers, corvettes, destroyers or even battleships were employed. Convoy HX-233 had an escort of two powerful US Coast Guard cutters, a Canadian destroyer and six corvettes, and later a support group of four heavily-armed British fleet destroyers. It was well-protected,

Typical North Atlantic convoy weather, 1942/43 *(US Navy)*

indeed, in comparison with earlier convoys and reflected the growth and improvement of the Allies' anti-submarine forces in the North Atlantic.

In overall charge of a convoy was either a British 'escort commander' or a US 'senior escort officer', who had complete responsibility for the convoy's safety and defence. According to British policy the escort commander also commanded his ship: according to US policy the senior officer and his small staff were responsible for the convoy only. HX-233 under US command embarked the senior escort officer, a US Naval officer, on the US Coast Guard cutter *Spencer*, with a US Coast Guard officer commanding the ship. The US Coast Guard constitutes part of the military forces, presently under the Department of Transportation in peacetime and as an integral part of the Navy in time of war.

The convoy commodore, usually a retired senior Royal Navy officer recalled to duty, or an experienced merchant officer with a commission in the Royal Naval Reserve, held responsibility for the internal discipline of the convoy and always embarked in a large, well-equipped merchant ship at the head of a central column within view of all ships in the convoy. His staff comprised five signallers from the Royal Navy, since constant communication between ships was essential for efficient convoy operations. Communication at night by wireless telegraphy was a tedious and slow business as each message had to be encoded and decoded. During daylight, signalling was visual with use of Aldis Lamp light or flag hoists based on the Merchant Navy code book 'Mersigs'. In the case of HX-233, Commodore Dawson was in the Lamport & Holt Company's 6054-ton *Devis*, built 1938, speed 14 knots, Position 71.

The operating agent with the US Navy for convoy routing in New York was the Port Director's office, which handled as much as 60 per cent of the total shipping from the US. By 24 July 1943 the port of New York had cleared no fewer than 12,276 ships, which came close to overtaxing its port facilities and anchorages.* Every ship entering the port was a candidate for a departing convoy. War Shipping Administration agents' dispatches from departure ports kept the Port Director informed of pending arrivals, and tentative future convoy sailings were prepared from these lists. Subject to constant changes due to failure to arrive or load on schedule, or to engine or crew problems, the list required constant updating.

If repairs were required in New York, these were often made during the vessel's loading to save time. Once repaired and loaded, the ship was shifted to an anchorage assigned to outbound vessels in upper New York Bay to free the loading berth for another ship. Meanwhile, the vessel's master had to report to the convoy routing office, where he would have relinquished his old instructions and confidential documents. He also had to provide details regarding his ship, such as cargo, draft, destination, speed, armament, any special convoy equipment, crew, gun crew, and any other pertinent information requested. This information was then examined, classified and the vessel's fitness for inclusion in the next scheduled outbound convoy determined, thereby placing her in the convoy best suited to her capabilities to take her to her port

* Bureau of Naval Personnel Information Bulletin, Port Director's Office, Third Naval District, New York, December 1943.

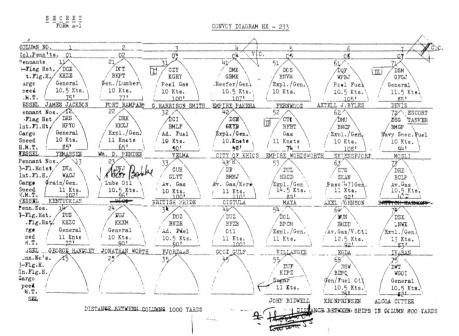

of destination. With this the convoy and routing officer established the convoy formation, size, and the location of every ship to be included therein.

Prior to sailing, usually the day before, the master of each vessel, accompanied by his senior radio officer, attended a Convoy Sailing Conference held in the local naval authority headquarters for what was essentially a briefing of procedures to be followed at sea under various conditions. Presided over by the New York Port Director, Third Naval District, it was attended by the convoy commodore who was responsible for the manoeuvering and internal discipline of the convoy as well as the escort commander responsible for the convoy's safety. In New York these meetings were held at Third Naval District Headquarters, 17 Battery Place, and chaired by a senior American naval officer. One experienced British master recalled succinctly:

> There was a considerable number of 'brass hats'. It was typical of all US conferences which, in my opinion, were always overloaded with officers, each having something to say. There was an atmosphere of tension as though something sensational was about to happen at any moment. At the UK conferences the atmosphere was that of calm; you were told the facts without any window dressing and you left the conference feeling all would go well during the voyage.*

The vice commodore, appointed at the pre-sailing conference, was a well-experienced merchant vessel master who would take over convoy responsibility should the commodore or his ship be lost. The vice commodore of HX-233 was the master of the *Empire Pakeha*, 8,115grt, Captain H C Smith, in Convoy Position 41. The divisional commodores were Captain W S Stein in *Fort Rampart*, Position 21; Captain P W Barry in *Empire Wordsworth*, Position 52; Captain W Pittman in tanker *Robert F. Hand*, Position 111.

Each master was given a sealed envelope containing sailing orders, the names of all ships in the convoy, the departure schedule, a diagram of the order of steaming,

* Captain W Luckey, M/V *Luculus* as quoted in *Convoy*, p94.

Order of steaming. The official convoy diagram for Convoy HX-233. *(PRO)*

communication plan, stragglers' procedure if a ship became separated from the convoy, and a description of ports the vessel was scheduled to enter. A vital operation also covered during the conference was the departure-plan which had to be carefully coordinated due to the vast expanse of New York Harbour. Each ship was given a specific time for undocking or weighing anchor and, to aid masters and pilots to reach the ocean rendezvous for forming up, reference points were designated en route with the time each vessel was scheduled to pass, so as to arrive in proper order.

Aircraft and surface vessels meanwhile patrolled offshore to check that there were no enemy lurking to attack before the vulnerable ships of that convoy could assemble and the escort deploy. Once the convoy had formed up, with each ship flying her numeral pennants showing her assigned convoy position, the commodore would give the signal to proceed at the designated course and speed. The communications system for both convoys and independently routed ships permitted vessels to observe radio silence yet receive the most complete coverage possible of enemy activity. Routing was based on a number of factors including the latest reported enemy submarine activities, weather, ice conditions and hydrographic information, the objective being to route convoys away from known enemy presence, while including diversion routes should the need arise.

US Coast Guard cutter *Spencer*. She is shown here as she appeared in 1943. Commissioned in 1937, she carried a complement of 250. *(US Coast Guard)*

US Coast Guard cutter *Duane*. This postwar photograph shows her with her Coast Guard number and a 5in gun mounted in a turret. *(US Coast Guard)*

The convoys were designated 'fast', the HX (Halifax-UK) and ON (UK-Halifax) series, capable of at least nine knots, and 'slow', the SC and ONS series capable of six-and-a-half knots. Convoy speed was calculated at the speed of the slowest ship. The HX convoys sailed approximately eight days apart, the SC convoys twelve days apart, ensuring that a convoy reached United Kingdom's Western Approaches every three to four days. A true bridge of ships, it was the very lifeline of civilian Britain. In September 1942 convoys began forming in New York rather than Halifax, and convoy numbers indicated the order of departure, with HX-233 departing New York being the 233rd in one series that by war's end totalled nearly four hundred convoys.

If the convoy cycle was inexorable, so was the U-boat menace. Fast Convoy ON-170 departed Liverpool on 3 March 1943 with fifty-two ships accompanied by Escort Group B-2. Among the escorts were the new sloop *Whimbrel* (on loan from Second Escort Group then forming, under Lt Cdr J W Moore), HM Destroyers *Vanessa* and *Whitehall*, and HM Corvettes *Gentian, Heather* and *Sweetbriar* of the 'Flower' class. Escort Commander Donald Macintyre DSO, RN, embarked in *Whimbrel* while his own ship, the destroyer *Hesperus*, was undergoing repairs after ramming and sinking *U-357*. Weather for ON-170 was extreme even by the standards of the North Atlantic, with an endless series of gales and blizzards in which at least two ships suffered heavy weather damage. The British *Karamea* had her deck cargo smashed and the US freighter *Steel Traveller* had her topmasts carried away due to heavy rolling.

HMCS *Skeena*, destroyer Flotilla leader, commissioned in 1937. This photograph was taken in Halifax, 1944. *(National Archives of Canada)*

Several U-boat groups had formed patrols across potential convoy routes, and on 11 March BdU (*Befehlshaber der Underseeboote* – U-Boat High Command) ordered the 'Raubgraf' group to patrol a line northeast of Newfoundland. The Allies, having broken the German radio code, detected BdU's message and ordered ON-170 on an evasive course change. However, bad weather having made it impossible to replenish from accompanying tankers, the convoy escorts were short of fuel, and ON-170 was compelled to remain on course. On 13 March *U-603* sighted the convoy, whereupon BdU ordered 'Raubgraf' to deploy against it. Repeated D/F bearings by *Whimbrel* and skilful counter-attacks kept the U-boats at bay, and miraculously ON-170 passed through a gap created by a U-boat's failure to get into position. Air cover arrived on 16 March, and no successful attack was made.

The American flush deck, four-stacker destroyer *Upshur* (DD 144), dispatched earlier to reinforce ON-170's escort, was ordered back to her original convoy on 14 March. Based on their B-Dienst interception that day, the Allies had learned that BdU had re-deployed 'Raubgraf' against Convoy SC-122. The re-deployment came too late, however, as SC-122, two hours ahead of schedule, had already passed the position given. 'Raubgraf' then operated against HX-229 during the night of 17 March, sinking a number of ships before being forced to break off due to a fuel shortage. Meanwhile, ON-170 ships arrived at their various destinations to commence loading before joining HX-233 and the next convoy cycle.

There were fifty-two ships in HX-233, including twenty tankers which was an unusually high proportion. The eighteen American vessels included nine new Liberty ships and four tankers. Of the twelve British vessels, five were tankers. Fifteen Norwegian ships included eight tankers, and there were one Dutch and one Panamanian tanker. Twenty-two freighters completed the convoy, sailing under either one of the above or Belgian, Honduran, Greek, or Swedish flags.

Spencer and her consorts joined HX-233 at Westomp (Western Ocean Meeting Place) at sunset on 12 April, relieving the local escort. Instead of taking the usual, shorter Great Circle convoy course, HX-233 was routed well to the south where the weather could be expected to be better and the waters calmer. Although described as American, the escort was a mixed force consisting of two USCG cutters, *Spencer* and *Duane*; the Canadian destroyer *Skeena*; two Canadian corvettes, *Wetaskiwin* and *Arvida*; and three British corvettes, *Dianthus*, *Bergamot* and *Bryony*, all experienced, seasoned, North Atlantic veterans. Convoy escorts were subject to Operation Plan No 5–43, under US Atlantic Fleet (CTU 24.1.3, A4-3 [3]/FF13, Serial No 007), dated 11 April 1943, St Johns, Newfoundland, 23pp.

The convoy had originally consisted of fifty-seven ships. One, *Hannibal Hamlin*, a new US Liberty ship, became a straggler and proceeded independently to arrive safely.

HMCS *Skeena* in convoy in 1943. Note the twin Lewis AA guns mounted at left and the depth charge thrower, right. *(National Archives of Canada)*

HMS *Byrony*, a Flower class corvette, pennant No 192, built Harland & Wolf, commissioned 1941. She had a complement of 83. (*Imperial War Museum*)

Two had to return to St Johns (*Cape Howe* and *William R Keever*) and one was lost to U-boat attack while in convoy (the freighter *Fort Rampart*). Several others did not sail for various reasons, including the escort HMCS *Rosthern*, but fifty-one ships were delivered. HMS *Dianthus* delayed her departure from St Johns until 12 April and overtook the convoy at 1800hrs on 14 April.

With a mean course of east, it is not surprising that almost due west of the U-boat base at Lorient, eight outbound U-boats homed in on the convoy. The interception of four radio transmissions on 15 April revealed the imminent danger of U-boat attack but the escort commander judged them too distant, ignoring them to the potential peril of the convoy.

Of the eight U-boats identified as operating against Convoy HX-233, namely *U-262* (Franke), *U-268* (Hasenschar), *U-226* (Borchers), *U-358* (Manke), *U-264* (Looks), *U-382* (Koch), *U-614* (Sträter) and *U-175* (Bruns), only four played any significant role in the battle and only their activities have been traced in detail.

At 0805hrs on 16 April 1943 USCG Cutter *Duane* sighted a westbound vessel sailing independently and was dispatched to investigate and challenge. She proved to be the fast (16 knots) Norwegian motorship *Elizabeth Bakke*, bound from Glasgow to New York, Knut Knutsen of Haugesund, Norway, owner. Almost new (built 1937, 5,450 tons × 133m × 17m × 7m), this vessel's consort M/V *John Bakke* (built 1929, 4,718 tons × 119m × 16m × 7m) was by coincidence in Convoy HX-233, Position 23, second vessel astern of *Fort Rampart*. The two *Bakkes* had an interesting experience earlier, worth briefly describing here. At the outbreak of war a number of Norwegian vessels had been trapped in Sweden, in Göteborg on the Kattegat, and arrangements were secretly made, presumably through the Royal Naval Attaché in Sweden, Captain Henry Denham RN, for five of them to break out through the Skagerrak to the North Sea, between the 23 and 28 January 1941, to be met and escorted over the North Sea by units of the British Home Fleet. Among these were *Elizabeth Bakke* and *John Bakke*. The breakout was successful and, despite enemy air attacks and a near brush with German battlecruisers on 'Operation Berlin' in the Kattegat, the five vessels arrived safely at Scapa, escorted by Home Fleet cruisers and destroyers as arranged. A later breakout by the remaining vessels proved disastrous, with most lost to enemy action en route.

On 16 April 1943 *Elizabeth Bakke* passed safely through the U-boats around Convoy HX-233. Earlier she had participated in convoys to Malta, including MW-11 in

HMCS *Arvida*, a Flower class corvette, pennant No K-113, built by Morton, Quebec, and commissioned in 1940. A typical example of the improved design, with single mast mounted forward of the bridge and 'lantern' 271m radar above the bridge structure.
(National Archives of Canada)

the eastern Mediterranean between 11 June and 12 July 1942 on operations 'Harpoon' and 'Vigorous'. She survived the War to return home to her owners for more peaceful operations. Throughout the War a number of vessels with superior speed, i.e., 14 to 16 knots or more, were dispatched alone across the Atlantic but their loss rate was double that for ships in convoy.

Before the War was over, twenty-one commodores, twelve admirals RN, and nine captains RNR had lost their lives. The two commodores who escorted the record number of convoys during the war were Rear Admiral Sir E Manners, with fifty-two convoys to his credit, and Rear Admiral E W Leir with forty-eight. Signal men had the highest percentage of fatalities of any special branch, with 138 men losing their lives.

2

British Air Support and Escorts

*It will comfort you to know that my role in this war has been of the
greatest importance. Our patrols have helped keep the trade routes clear
for our convoys and supply ships.*

FLYING OFFICER V A W ROSEWARNE RAF*

The most serious delay to Allied ascendancy over the North Atlantic was the reluctance to commit aircraft to support of the trans-oceanic convoys. This was a blunder and was paid for by the lives of merchant seamen.

Scientific Advisor to British Coastal Command, Professor Patrick M S Blackett, set up an Operational Research Unit together with four research colleagues to analyse Coastal Command's anti-submarine efforts. In January 1942 the unit moved to the Admiralty, where their statistical analysis of battle reports produced some startling results. For instance, by increasing the size of convoys from an average of thirty-two to fifty-four ships, thereby reducing the number of convoys, they calculated that losses would drop by a projected 56 per cent, while increasing the number of escort vessels from six to nine would reduce convoy losses by 25 per cent. Air cover eight hours a day would, by itself, reduce losses a very substantial 64 per cent!

Dr Blackett's results ultimately created an organisational revolution within the convoy system. Donald Macintyre writes in *The Battle of the Atlantic*:

> The startling forecast of 64 per cent . . . was not, however, given its due weight. The limited number of Liberator aircraft, adaptable for the very long range work, . . . were coveted by Bomber Command with the backing of the Air Staff in their (mistaken) belief that priority had to be a maximum bombing effort on Germany.
>
> Furthermore, a number of those [planes] available to Coastal Command were employed on unproductive patrolling of the U-boats' transit areas. . . . at the turn of the year [1942–3] there were still no more than ten VLR Liberator aircraft able to operate in mid-Atlantic. Yet this handful of aircraft was time and again to intervene decisively in convoy battles . . .

---

* From a letter to his mother, printed in *The Times*, 18 June 1940. He was posted missing on 30 May 1940.

Professor Blackett wrote in an article in *Brassey's Annual* for 1953.

From the figures . . . it could be calculated that a long-range Liberator, operating from Iceland and escorting the convoys in the middle of the Atlantic, *saved* at least a half dozen merchant ships in its service lifetime of some thirty flying sorties. If used for bombing Berlin, the same aircraft . . . would . . . kill not more than a couple of dozen enemy men, women and children and destroy a number of houses.

No one could dispute that the saving of six merchant ships and their crews and cargoes was of incomparably more value to the Allied war effort than the killing of some two dozen enemy civilians, the destruction of a number of houses and a certain very small effect on production.

The difficulty was to get these figures believed. But believed they eventually were, and more long range aircraft were made available to Coastal Command.

The United States put its first Atlantic B-24 Liberator bomber into service on Christmas Day 1942. Its range was an impressive 2,400 miles, but not until later was the US Navy to have fifty-two, and Coastal Command eighteen, of these aircraft at their disposal as invaluable reinforcements to convoy protection. The Mark III, a revised version of the Liberator, had radar capable of detecting a U-boat at 12 miles and a convoy at 40 miles.

In early 1943 the Battle of the Atlantic was at a critical juncture, with the Allies facing potential defeat. They therefore dismissed earlier misgivings about inflicting French civilian casualties and launched the raids on French U-boat bases. These destroyed French seaport residential areas but had no detrimental effect whatsoever on the U-boat repair facilities.

Air Marshal Sir Arthur Harris, head of Bomber Command, himself wrote a strong letter of protest, pointing out the futility of bombing the U-boat shelters, overlooking the earlier, greater mistake of not having bombed the pens while they were under construction behind watertight caissons and particularly vulnerable. Once the U-boats were in their concrete shelters, it was too late. On the day the Allied Casablanca Conference opened, 19 January 1943, Air Marshal Harris, much to his consternation, received a directive to make his biggest contribution so far to the Battle of the Atlantic. It read in part as follows:

> . . . to subject the following [U-boat] bases to a maximum scale of attack by your Command at night with the object of effectively devastating the whole area in which are located the submarines, their maintenance facilities and the services, power, water, light, communications, etc. and other resources upon which their operations depend.

The order of priority of the bases showed Lorient topping the list for many priorities.

Bomber Command went that very night, 19–20 January 1943, and the following three nights, delivering 1,000 tons of bombs. The planes returned again on the night of 29–30 January and the following four nights in February. The heavily defended U-boat facilities at Lorient fairly bristled with anti-aircraft guns: over two hundred 20mm, nine 75mm, eighteen 88mm, forty-three 105mm, twelve twin-105mm, and five

128mm guns. Of the more than four hundred aircraft deployed by Bomber Command some thirty-eight were shot down and an additional nine lost in accidents.

In March 1943 the British Anti-U-boat Committee arrived at a compromise, increasing the number of available VLR aircraft from ten to forty, which amounted to only about a dozen aircraft operational at any one time. The real stumbling blocks were in England when Harris still insisted that all heavy bombers be allocated to the campaign over Germany, and in the United States when Fleet Admiral E J King deployed his allocation of VLR aircraft to the Pacific theatre. As Marshal of the Royal Air Force John C Slessor wrote:

> The whole story . . . is one of misunderstanding, argument, procrastination and delay, bedevilled throughout by inter-service controversies in Washington and [Admiral] King's determination, *pace* Casablanca, to give priority to the Pacific . . . King's obsession with the Pacific and the Battle of Washington cost us dearly in the Battle of the Atlantic.

This, despite the plenary meeting of the combined Chiefs of Staff of 23 January at Casablanca, at which the first sentence of their report read that 'The defeat of the U-boat must remain a first charge on the resources of the United Nations.'

Convoy HX-228 with sixty ships, sailing the southern route in March 1943, was attacked by thirteen U-boats. HMS *Harvester* was torpedoed by *U-432* (K Eckhard) on 11 March, and four other ships were sunk and two damaged. By the time of the passage of HX-233 the coverage by VLR aircraft had increased, and there were no further attacks once air cover arrived over the convoy at 1335hrs on the afternoon of 17 April.

Admiral Dönitz wrote:

> . . . Our whole method of conducting submarine warfare, which was based on mobility and operations on the surface, reached its culmination in the wolf pack tactics we had evolved. In areas where air cover was strong our most successful method of waging war would no longer be practical. The aircraft had suddenly become a very dangerous opponent.

U-boats feared aircraft perhaps more than any other single factor and the appearance of air cover forced a U-boat under, where, with its slow underwater speed and restricted visibility, it soon lost contact with the convoy. As Captain Roskill commented, 'The aircraft . . . became a decisive factor in the defeat of the U-boat'.

Land-based air support first reached Convoy HX-233 in the form of a Sunderland aircraft, at 40°N 21°W. At 1730hrs a VLR Liberator arrived over the convoy and reported a U-boat submerging 4 miles from the convoy, bearing 315°, at 2304hrs. Just before midnight aircraft on a patrol sweep ahead of the convoy observed a U-boat submerging 3.5 miles ahead at 040°, possibly Sträter (*U-614*), no doubt driven down by the aircraft. All escorts were ordered to drop two deterrent depth charges set at 150ft, and 33 minutes later each escort dropped one further depth charge, also set for 150ft.

Aircraft undoubtedly played a major role in suppressing the surrounding U-boat menace and seeing the convoy through without further losses. Just after noon on 18 April a Flying Fortress arrived, joined by a Sunderland in the late afternoon. Thanks to air cover it was reckoned that by afternoon of the 18th U-boats were no longer in contact with the convoy. Since BdU ordered breaking off the attack at noon, 18 April, it may have received reports of air coverage. Some seven aircraft were providing cover by then, and it was continuous thereafter.

At night aircraft were reported using recognition lights, occasionally navigation lights, and communicating with a red Aldis lamp. It is noteworthy that no further attacks were made on the convoy and one is left pondering the earlier cost in lives, ships and cargo. In the words of the escort commander, 'Plane coverage was of inestimable value in spotting submarines on the surface, and driving and keeping them down.'

The Anti-Submarine Warfare Division of the Admiralty summarised all U-boat incidents occurring on 17 April 1943 as a total of fourteen. Of these eleven were aircraft sightings and/or attacks, highlighting the efficacy of adequate aircraft coverage.

In 1956 Captain Roskill wrote:

> For what it is worth, this writer's view is that in the early spring of 1943 we had a very narrow escape from defeat in the Atlantic; and that, had we suffered such a defeat, history would have judged the main cause to have been the lack of two more squadrons of VLR aircraft for convoy escort duties.

Ocean Escorts

Derby House was established in Liverpool, February 1941, and Admiral Sir Percy Noble appointed as Commanding Officer of Western Approaches in complete charge of all convoy operations. Sir Max Horton took charge of Western Approaches in November 1942, about four months before the crisis battles of the Atlantic convoys began, and six months before the Allies gained the upper hand.

With the UK depleting its reserves, consuming 750,000grt more oil and military equipment than were arriving in 1941-42, the protection of convoys became a priority and the Royal Navy was doing 50 per cent of the escort work and the Royal Canadian Navy 46 per cent, with America's minimal involvement represented by Coast Guard cutters and the few Naval Armed Guards stationed on merchant ships.

The bulk of the escorts available at this time were the 'Flower' class corvettes, originally intended for inshore defence. It was built at a large number of yards and was based on the design of the successful whale catcher, the 582grt *Southern Pride*, built 1936, by Smith's Dock, Middlesborough. There were 262 corvettes built in all, 111 of them in Canada. Their crews consisted of a smattering of regular navy men and petty officers, with 'hostilities-only' crew trained at the Royal Navy's training base in HMS *Ganges* near Ipswich. The crews saw long, hard service and performed the lion's share of rescue work in convoys, with three corvettes alone saving 1,242 men in 1941-42. The first corvette to sail was HMS *Gladiolus*, K34, in April 1940, from

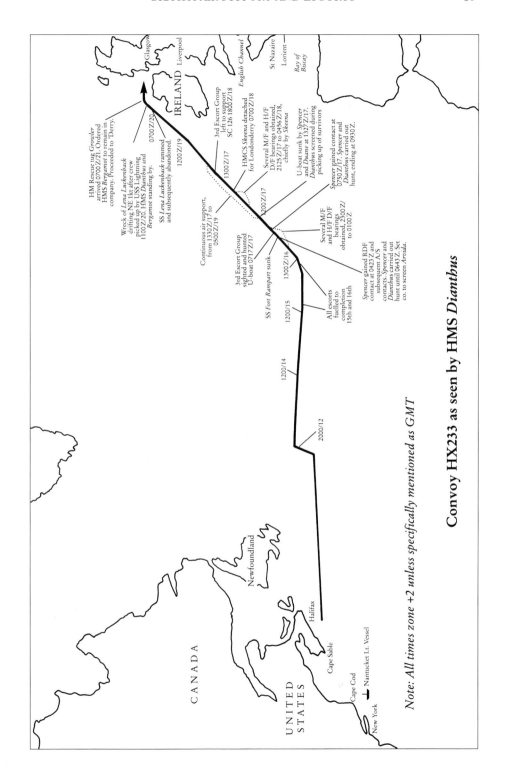

HM Rescue tug *Growler* arrived 0700 Z/21. Ordered HMS *Bergamot* to remain in company. Proceeded to Derry.

Wreck of *Lena Luckenbach* drifting NE 1 kt after crew picked up by USS Lightning 1100 Z/20. HMS *Dianthus* and *Bergamot* standing by.

0700 Z/20

SS *Lena Luckenbach* rammed and subsequently abandoned.

1200 Z/19

3rd Escort Group left to support SC 126 1800 Z/18

1300 Z/17

HMCS *Skeena* detached for Londonderry 0700 Z/18

Several M/F and H/F D/F bearings obtained, 2125 Z/17 to 0456 Z/18, chiefly by *Skeena*.

1200 Z/17

Continuous air support, from 1330 Z/17 to 0500 Z/19

U-boat sunk by *Spencer* and *Duane* at 1327 Z/17. *Dianthus* screened during picking up of survivors.

Spencer gained contact at 0750 Z/17. *Spencer* and *Dianthus* carried out hunt, ending at 0930 Z.

3rd Escort Group sighted and hunted U-boat 0717 Z/17

1300 Z/16

Several M/F and H/F D/F bearings obtained, 2300 Z/ to 0100 Z

SS *Fort Rampart* sunk

1200/15

All escorts fuelled to completion 15th and 16th

Spencer gained RDF contact at 0423 Z, and subsequent A/S contacts. *Spencer* and *Dianthus* carried out hunt until 0643 Z. Set co. to screen *Arvida*.

1200/14

2000/12

Glasgow

Liverpool

IRELAND

English Channel

St Nazaire

Lorient

Bay of Biscay

Newfoundland

Halifax

CANADA

Cape Sable

Cape Cod

Nantucket Lt. Vessel

UNITED STATES

New York

Note: All times zone +2 unless specifically mentioned as GMT

Convoy HX233 as seen by HMS *Dianthus*

Smith's Dock, and her first 'kill' was *U-26* (Kptlt Scheringer), sunk on 1 July 1940, southwest of Ireland. She was torpedoed and sunk only 13 months later, possibly by *U-558*, while escorting SC-48. All hands were lost.

After Britain's coastal air and ship patrols drove the U-boats away from her shores, the corvette became exclusively an ocean-going, anti-submarine, convoy escort vessel, a task ill-suited to her design. Although extremely seaworthy, the corvette was too small and slow for her new role, even after modifications were made. In moderate seas she pitched and rolled violently, and most men spent their first weeks desperately ill. Extremely lively in only a light sea, she reportedly would 'roll on wet grass', and the author well remembers in heavy seas seeing under the keel of corvettes, while only the screw remained in the water. Corvette sailors, uncomfortable in the extreme and perpetually wet at sea, all recall their ships as a source of numbing fatigue and indescribable discomfort. Conditions were aggravated by over-crowding, when by 1941 the little ships carried twice the crew allowed in their original plans, and sometimes survivors as well. Men slept where they could: on lockers, tables or in some dark, special place that offered a little warmth. For all that, Vice Admiral Sir Peter Gretton described the 'Flower' class corvette as the workhorse of the convoy escort force, and Captain Roskill maintains that 'it is hard to see how Britain could have survived without them'.

Support Groups

In February 1943 Convoy SC-118, although heavily defended by Escort Group B-2 (three British destroyers, two US Coast Guard cutters, and four Free French corvettes), lost eleven ships to U-boats, a devastating blow which led directly to the formation of Support Groups to reinforce the convoy escorts. Facing the bitter reality of mounting shipping losses, in early March an escort was withdrawn from each Western Approaches Escort Group, freeing sixteen ships to form four Support Groups, supplemented by a half-flotilla of Home Fleet destroyers posted as a fifth Support Group. Convoy SC-118's heavy losses also revealed the urgent need for adequate air support in mid-ocean, but the Americans and Bomber Command steadfastly refused to release VLR aircraft.

Support groups, with highly trained crews, consisted of four to six anti-submarine vessels, usually Royal Navy destroyers or sloops, that could rush like cavalry to the convoy's aid as soon as U-boats were sighted. They were free to disregard the convoy and pursue a U-boat, whereas escort vessels had to relinquish pursuit to maintain their assigned function of directly protecting the convoy. By the end of March 1943 five support groups were operational and very quickly proved their worth. Captain Roskill wrote;

> At the end of 1943, when the Admiralty cast their eye backward to the crises of the previous spring, they recorded that 'the Germans never came so near to disrupting communication between the New World and the Old' . . . In the first ten days [of March] in all waters we lost forty-one ships; in the second ten days fifty-six. More

than half-a-million tons of shipping were sunk in those twenty days . . . and what made those losses so . . . serious . . . was that nearly two-thirds of the ships sunk during the month were in convoy. It appeared possible . . . we should not be able to continue [to regard the convoy as an effective system of defence].

This was tantamount to admitting defeat by the U-boats. If Britain's aid was effectively cut off, there could be no continued US build-up, no invasion of North Africa or Europe, and the UK would face starvation. The future of the War and ultimate victory, everything, hinged on the firm bridge of merchant ships and their crews. Fortunately, with the advent of Support Groups and finally more VLR aircraft, the tables turned on the U-boats with astounding suddenness. Convoy HX-233, with eight U-boats directed against it, survived almost intact because the escorts were able to prevent them from gaining the initiative, and the timely arrival of the Third Support Group and air support ended the battle 50 hours after it had begun.

3

The US Navy Armed Guard and DEMS

The right of a merchant vessel to defend herself has been recognised for hundreds of years; and in Europe, until the seventeenth century, merchant and fighting ships were virtually interchangeable. Great Britain was an island nation, dependent on overseas trade and imports, with centuries of experience in bitterly fought sea warfare, and the first duty of the Royal Navy was the protection of merchant shipping. The US Navy's original purpose was the same.

In Britain in 1798 His Majesty's Government passed the Compulsory Convoy Act, giving the Admiralty authority to require all seagoing merchant vessels to sail in convoy, as single sailing ships who took their chances were snapped up by enemy warships. The surrender of Napoleon in 1815 ushered in a century which was to experience no wars on a global scale and the Compulsory Convoy Act was repealed in 1872 as redundant. By 1914, according to the accepted international law of the Hague Convention, a belligerent power could seize or destroy certain well-defined war materials if they were intended directly or indirectly for the enemy, and the sinking of the merchant vessel was allowed, provided passengers and crew were given an alternate place of safety.

> For this purpose the ship's boats are not regarded as a place of safety unless the safety of the passengers and crew is assured in the existing sea and weather conditions by the proximity of land or the presence of another vessel which is in a position to take them aboard.

On 19 September 1914, shortly after the outbreak of the First World War, the US Department of State forwarded a memorandum to the belligerent governments, addressing the question of armed merchant vessels, stating that: 'A merchant vessel of belligerent nationality may carry armament and ammunition for the sole purpose of defence without acquiring the character of a ship of war'.* It should be noted that submarine warfare did not yet play a role.

---

* Department of State file 763, 72111/226a; 1914 Supp. 611–12

By September 1917 all British vessels up to 7,000grt had been armed with two 4.7in guns and those over this tonnage with two 6in guns; many carried depth charges as well, although the latter were not strictly defensive armament. What was more important was that by 15 April 1915 the British Admiralty had issued secret instructions that: 'If a submarine is obviously pursuing a ship by day, and it is evident to the master that she has hostile intentions, the ship pursued should open fire in self-defence, notwithstanding the submarine may not have committed a definite hostile act, such as firing a gun or torpedo.'‡ This clearly put British merchant vessels outside the realm of 'fire only when fired on' and altered the charade of 'defence' to one of belligerent action, as when the unarmed British steam packet *Brussels* attempted to ram the German submarine *U-33*. The master, Captain Fryatt, was later seized and shot for this as not being a combatant, therefore not entitled to take any offensive action.

By 1916 a restricted campaign by German U-boats against merchant shipping was beginning to take effect, and the submarine potential had been recognised by Admiral Henning von Holtzendorf, chief of the German Admiralty Staff. Admiral von Holtzendorf advocated unrestricted U-boat warfare, despite the likelihood of bringing America into the War on the side of the Allies. This inevitably happened on 6 April 1917 following President Woodrow Wilson's 1916 successful re-election campaign based on the slogan: 'He kept us out of war!'.

On 26 February 1917 the US House of Representatives passed the Armed Ship Bill, which was blocked by the Senate, whereupon President Wilson bypassed Congress and ordered the Navy to provide guns, gunners and ammunition to all US flag vessels bound for European ports. Not surprisingly, the first hostile action against an armed US flag vessel occurred 3 April 1917, just three days before a formal declaration of war, when the S/S *Aztec* was torpedoed and sunk off the English coast with one man lost. In this 'war to end all wars', US Naval Armed Guard served on 384 merchant ships, 126 of which were lost to enemy action and an additional six to marine hazards, with 58 armed guards losing their lives.*

The British did not forget the lessons learned in that earlier war and began arming their merchant vessels the day war began, 3 September 1939. Lieutenant John Hamilton, Training Development Officer at the Naval Gunnery School in HMS *Excellent*, Gosport, developed the idea of a 'Defensively Equipped Merchant Ship' (DEMS), and Admiral Sir Frederick Dreyer, Retired, Inspector of Merchant Navy Gunnery, recruited its gunners from the Royal Navy and the Royal Artillery. By the end of the year more than 1,500 guns had been mounted and gunners embarked.

By 1943, of the 26,000 lives lost at sea, 2,713 had been DEMS gunners. Their ranks consisted at that time of six regiments of Maritime Royal Artillery who saved an estimated 1.25 million tons of shipping while earning 841 naval awards, including 263 DSMs and 110 BEMs. By 1944 the organisation had expanded worldwide, and over 35,000 gunners were serving in DEMS.

‡ International Law Situations, 1930, Naval War College (Washington 1931)
* *Merchant Vessels of the US, 1917, 1918, 1919, 1920*, US Department of Commerce (GPO Washington)

While President Roosevelt was assuring the parents of America in 1941 that '. . . your boys are not going to be sent into foreign wars', he was busy circumventing the Neutrality Act. Professor E B Potter in his *Illustrated History of the U.S. Navy*, summarises what he calls the 'devious means' of steering the country into another war, including arming US merchant ships and embarking US Navy armed guards, although Congress had denied approval. The Lend-Lease Act of 11 March 1941 established the duty of the armed guard as defending the ships carrying war supplies to the Allies. When it was officially reactivated on 17 November 1941, the US Navy was as woefully unprepared as in the previous war to take on this duty, and one can only wonder how the professional 'brass' could have been so taken by surprise. As late as June 1942 the Navy continued to dispatch unarmed or underarmed merchant ships out of US coastal ports, even to northern Russia, loaded with vital cargoes of military equipment, explosives, fuel, gasoline and ores. During the same period, it should be noted, guns and ammunition were supplied to foreign vessels, even to those sailing at times in convoys that included their own unarmed American flag vessels.*

When a merchant vessel was under naval routing, master and crew were under direct naval control and authority. At the close of every voyage the armed guard commander on each vessel was required to submit a 'Voyage Report' to the US Navy Chief of Naval Operations, reporting contacts with the enemy, if any, and whether the master and officers of the ship had carried out 'Instructions for Naval Transportation and US Merchant Vessels in Time of War'.

In early 1942 all pretence of 'defensive fire only' went by the board and orders were issued to armed guard units to 'fire on sight' and the ship's master was ordered to 'ram' if possible.

The first armed ships carried a handful of antique weapons and a few ill-trained gunners commanded by an almost equally inexperienced petty officer. However, as the programme moved into high gear ships were better armed with one 3in forward, one 4in astern and up to eight 20mm anti-aircraft guns. A signal man and a radio man, plus gunners commensurate with the number of weapons, were supplemented by members of the merchant ship's crew. All were commanded by a hastily trained naval officer, usually an Ensign or Lieutenant junior grade.

There has been considerable distortion of the problems and friction between naval gun crews and merchant ship crewmen, the inference being that problems were generally the fault of the merchant seamen. However, disciplinary problems *within* the Armed Guard sometimes made the post of Armed Guard Commander a vexing one. Indeed, the dedicated service of the armed guards through repeated, prolonged, heavy enemy attacks was particularly commendable in view of often deficient training.

Every US Navy Armed Guard on every American flag vessel in Convoy HX-233 was awarded a bronze battle star for the action between 16 and 18 April 1943, to be worn on his European-African-Middle Eastern medal ribbon, according to a letter from US Navy Bureau of Personnel to the Commanding Officers of Armed Guard

* *History of the Arming of Merchant Ships and the Naval Armed Guard* (unpublished US Navy, no date, Washington).

Centres dated 25 September 1944. Merchant seamen in the same ships received no commendation whatsoever, and were not regarded as veterans of the battle.

By early 1943 the armed guard programme was in full swing, and the new ships had received their full complement of modern weapons and gun crews. In Convoy HX-233 the gun crew commanders consisted of eight ensigns and three lieutenants junior grade, whose written reports to the Chief of Naval Operations are in Record Group 38, Naval Transportation Service, Armed Guard Files, in the US National Archives.

These reports constitute an interesting insight into the officers' abilities to observe and report, from the terse: 'No contacts with the enemy', to detailed reports running to several pages. Pertinent sections seem worth quoting for their historical value and for sometimes conflicting observations of the battle around Convoy HX-233 and can be found in Appendix 1.

4

On Board U-175

*I don't think it is even faintly realised the immense, impending revolution
which the submarines will effect as offensive weapons of war.*
ADMIRAL SIR J A FISHER, 20 APRIL 1904

The German historian Michael Salewski, in a section in Günther Buchheim's *U-Boot
Krieg* entitled 'U-Boot Krieg Historisches', recommends 'for a proper understanding
of the complexities of the 69-month-long, unending Battle of the Atlantic, on which
battlefield more than any other depended the outcome of WWII, one could most
profitably study a single, heavily-engaged U-boat which . . . mirrored at the same
time the overall strategy of the war and its every day horrors.' *U-175* was such a
submarine.

The sinking of the *U-175* became probably the most widely publicised of any
sinking because each of the US Coast Guard cutters involved had an expert cameraman on board, Jack January on *Spencer* and Bob Gates on *Duane*, who recorded the
entire action in a dramatic series of photos on that grey day in the North Atlantic, 17
April 1943. Months later when censors had cleared the films for release, the US news
magazine *Life* published the more sensational ones and the author realised the
significance of the electrifying events he had witnessed. Of the two photographers,
Chief Bosun's Mate Jack January, formerly a professional photographer with the *St.
Louis Post Dispatch* newspaper, obtained some of the most spectacular pictures to
come out of the Battle of the Atlantic and they have accompanied much subsequent
literature.

U-175, a type IXC, long-range submarine, 1,102 tons, built by Deschimag, Bremen,
was commissioned on 10 December 1941. Her commander, 29-year-old Kapitänleutnant Heinrich Bruns, was a career naval officer of the class of 1931, formerly in
command of the new torpedo boat, *T-3*. Following her loss in September 1940 he was
posted to U-boats, and after serving one U-boat patrol as prospective commanding
officer, he was sent to the Perisher Course ('Lehrgang für Sterben'), the U-boat
Commanding Officers' course. He was posted aboard *U-175* from before her commissioning until her loss in April 1943.

U-175 crew members were assigned piecemeal to 'stand-by' during construction and housed in Bremen, two to a room, in a North German Lloyd Shipping Company building. *U-175*, lying between *U-174* and *U-176* at the wharf, took nine months to complete. All three boats were lost in the same year, 1943, *U-174* off Newfoundland to aircraft and *U-176* off Cuba to a combination of surface ships and aircraft.

U-175's U-Boat Acceptance Command (UAK) trials took place at Kiel from 23 December 1941 until 6 January 1942, in company with four other U-boats. Following trials and acceptance, *U-175* was posted to Gydnia for torpedo exercises where she found herself ice-bound until the end of April, with her crew's accommodation shifted to the depot ship, the 3,184-ton *Frida Horn*. Torpedo exercises lasting fourteen days were completed off Hela in May, supervised by Kapitänleutnant (Ing.) Müller. In June, during ten days of tactical exercises off Gydnia with four other U-boats, *U-175*'s periscope fouled the bottom of a cutter on surfacing, and she had to return to Danzig for a replacement. Silent-running tests off Bornholm Island revealed her to be an exceptionally noisy boat.

At the end of June 1942 *U-175* was sent to the Stettin 'Oderwerke' for six weeks of final adjustments, and there the ship's company lived in the Bredower Naval Barracks and had leave by watches. In company at Stettin was the Type IXC *U-512* and another boat, probably *U-181*, commanded by FK Wolfgang Lüth. After final adjustments were completed on 25 July, *U-175* fuelled and embarked a full complement of torpedoes, fifteen electric and eight air-propelled, before returning to Kiel on 27 July where she remained until 10 August 1942.

*   *   *

All recruits first completed three months of the arduous, intensive basic training (Grundausbildung) given all naval recruits regardless of subsequent postings. This general infantry training instilled iron discipline, accustomed the men to military service and familiarised them with the use of weapons. It took place at naval training detachments (Schiffsstammabteilungen) scattered along the coast. Mech Obgefr Peter Wannemacher from Ludwigshafen/Rhein and Matr II Werner Bickel of Zela-Mehlis, Thüringen, both went to Schiffsstammabteilung Breda in Holland, where both simply recall having been 'always tired'. Bickel well remembers the 'vierter Zug der achter Kompanie' (fourth platoon, eighth company) from 5 February to 27 March 1941 commanded by Bootsmaat Knoll, who was popularly known as the 'Terror of the North Sea'. Drill, more drill, inspections, guard duty, severe punishment for even the most minor infractions, and one day a week 'Sportstag', with running 100m, 200m and 400m, jumping, handball or football, all culminating in a 10km march to a target range for live firing practice, and then the return march to the barracks, which was marked by an aircraft alarm drill. During this the column was required to dive into roadside ditches, which was welcomed by the recruits as an unexpected break, or rest period. All gear had to be clean and in perfect condition at all times.

Final training and graduation included a review and address by Großadmiral Raeder and Konteradmiral Dönitz, followed by a parade march-past. Recruits were then posted to advanced training units. In March 1941 50 per cent went to U-boat training after passing final examinations. Those posted to U-boats then went to special schools to learn U-boat routine, their own special skills, and escape procedures via a water tank, using the 'Dräger Tauchretter', a U-boat escape apparatus. Recruits were subjected to a rigorous physical examination before entering U-boat training and only the very best were accepted.

Peter Wannemacher was dispatched to the torpedo school at Flensburg, whereas Werner Bickel packed his seabag and took the train for the 'erste U-bootlehrdivision' (First U-boat training division) in Pillau (now Baltijsk) facing the Baltic Sea, not far from Königsberg (now Kaliningrad) on the Danzig Bight. He was housed aboard the luxury liner *Robert Ley*, 27,288grt, built 1938 as a cruise vessel of the 'Deutsche Arbeitsfront GmbH' for German workers. He was assigned to the technical division commanded by Korvettenkapitän Zerpka and known as 'Zerpka's fast troops', under the overall command of Fregattenkapitän Ibbeeken. Living in comparative luxury (for the Navy), Bickel's specialist U-boat training lasted from 28 March until 10 September 1941. After the successful completion of the final examinations and then graduation, he was dispatched to a 'front boat' under construction, the *U-175* at Deschimag AG Shipyard, Weser, in the old Hanseatic city of Bremen.

It was deliberate German naval policy to assign newly graduated U-boat trainees, if possible, to a boat when under construction to familiarise them with their submarine, literally from the keel up. Each crew was divided into two groups, the 'seemännische', or seaman's, and the 'technische', or technical divisions, with torpedo specialists and radiomen assigned to the latter. On 10 December 1941, *U-175* was placed in commission after a brief ceremony in which the commandant accepted the boat from the builder, the naval ensign was hoisted, and a celebratory champagne party and dinner followed. The number '175' was the subject of considerable discussion regarding the selection of an insignia, until 80 per cent of the company voted in favour of the double paragraph sign, for Paragraph 175 of the German law code.

Until 1939 U-boats were identified by numbers, but after the outbreak of war the numbers were no longer displayed on the outside, and radio signal traffic addressed the boat only by the commander's name. For secret visual identification a chosen symbol was painted on the conning tower, many quite ingenious and usually related to some recognisable factor aboard the ship, such as a horse shoe on *U-99* after one was found on her anchor. *U-201* chose a snowman symbolising her commander's name, Schnee, meaning snow. Other examples were *U-108* with the coat-of-arms of Danzig, *U-537* with the Olympic Rings, and *U-333* with three little fish. Probably only *U-175* was able to disguise its number so adeptly from the enemy, while displaying it so perfectly to fellow countrymen. The German double paragraph sign, §§, signified to Germans the familiar paragraph 175 of their legal code, which forbade homosexual activity. Originating in 1871, when the country was unified under Bismarck, the paragraph remained valid until repealed in 1969. Its use as a U-boat

The commissioning of *U-175*, Type IX C, at Bremen on 10 December 1941. *(Adolf March)*

symbol was, and still is, an 'inside joke' to the Germans and, after the final battle, a conundrum to the US Coast Guard.

By the time *U-175* departed Bremen for Kiel Naval Base on her first training/shake down and trial cruise, her crew had been trained as well as could be expected under wartime conditions. By late 1941 most prewar crews and commanders had been lost, either killed or taken as POWs, and the crew of *U-175* reflected this. Veterans were promoted to petty officers and a senior one, Ob Masch Karl Keutken, aged 27, had already survived thirteen patrols in other boats. The commander wisely instructed his inexperienced crewmen to heed Keutken, an outstanding engineer and strict disciplinarian, at all times.

When *U-175* departed on her third and final patrol, her complement of fifty-four officers and men had changed dramatically despite Bruns' continuing efforts to retain his crew relatively intact. Some sixteen, or about 30 per cent of her original crew had been transferred for a variety of reasons, from Lt z See Heinz Ehrich, First WO, for his frivolous attitude, to Fk Gefr Karl Kempf for chronic seasickness. Obergefreiter Peter Wannemacher, who completed his technical training in record time, was a latecomer who boarded *U-175* on her first patrol just as she was sailing out of Kiel's naval base.

Some personnel data for those who went on her final patrol is revealing. Of forty-seven officers and crew with known addresses, the majority, or fourteen, were from the Rhineland, six from Lower Saxony, five were Prussians and five Bavarians, four came from Saxon Anhalt, three from Baden, two each from Saxony and Thüringen, and one each from Mecklenburg, Brandenberg, Silesia, Saarland, Sudetenland and Austria. The average age of the crew on her last patrol was 23, with four over 30- and three 29-year-olds, each of the latter being an officer or senior petty officer.

The 'most important man' aboard was 'Smutje' (the cook), Matr Gefr Alfred Tepke from Hamm, Westfalen, who presided over the galley, a tiny cubicle-like compartment, a mere 59in by 23.5in, containing an electric stove and two small ovens, a small refrigerator and a tiny sink with running hot and cold distilled seawater. Utensils had to be stowed in a bulkhead locker in the adjacent officers' wardroom. Tepke prepared meals for the entire crew and kept coffee available at all times, in accordance with a very carefully developed menu, intended to provide an adequate and balanced diet at sea, insofar as circumstances allowed.

A Type IXC U-boat such as *U-175* was normally victualled for a twelve-week patrol, embarking almost 14 tons of food, listed below, or 16 tons according to survivors of *U-175*, stowed in every conceivable nook and cranny and suspended overhead, with careful consideration given to the boat's trim.

In 'Die Ernährung des U-bootsfahrers im Kriege', Jobst Schaefer listed the food embarked on a Type IXC U-boat.

494lbs fresh and cooked meats	2,365lbs other fruits
238lbs sausages	551lbs butter and margarine
4,808lbs preserved/tinned meats	611lbs soup ingredients
334lbs preserved fish	408lbs marmalade and honey
3,858lbs potatoes	309lbs fresh and preserved cheese
397lbs dried potatoes	1,728lbs milk
3,428lbs other vegetables	441lbs fruit juice
1,226lbs bread dough	154lbs coffee
2,058lbs preserved breads	205lbs other drinks
463lbs rice and noodles	441lbs sugar
595lbs fresh eggs	132lbs salt
917lbs fresh lemons	108lbs chocolates

*   *   *

Little has been written about the problems associated with navigating a U-boat, perhaps because, from the trackless wastes of the often wild, stormy North Atlantic to the tropics, U-boats seemed to have found their way without serious difficulty, although certainly never easily.

Their basic navigational equipment consisted of a superior Plath sextant, a gyro compass, a chronometer and a stopwatch. These were the charge of the Obersteurmann (Chief Quartermaster), an expert and experienced navigator and one of the most important men aboard, vying with the cook for first place. Due to the steady loss of U-boat navigators as the War progressed, skilled navigators from German merchant ships were reassigned to the U-boat arm, and this was the case with *U-175*.

Navigating from the low, wet conning tower of a U-boat, pitching and rolling in heavy seas, was difficult but had, nonetheless, to be accomplished. A shout down the conning tower hatch, 'Sun's out' ('Chance zum Sonnenschiessen') or 'Chance for a star sight' ('Chance zum Sternschiessen') brought the navigator rushing topside, sextant in hand. Despite the probability of a madly heaving horizon, he had to use every opportunity to fix the boat's position by celestial sights. For the remainder of the time the commander and navigator relied on very careful, albeit potentially inaccurate, dead reckoning based on speed, engine revolutions, time and estimated distance of travel. The chart in use was kept up to date on the German grid system imposed on a normal sea chart.

The U-boat Commander's Handbook (U Kdt Hdb), paragraph 320, emphasised the importance of 'faultless navigation' as a 'decisive factor' in U-boat operations and it was the duty of the commander to ensure efficient navigation. The handbook stressed the importance of repeated reckonings during the day and of cultivating a 'feeling' for speed and drift in varied sea conditions. It further required that if errors in position were discovered, they were rectified at once.

When a celestial sight was obtainable, a seaman stationed in the control room (Zentralmaat) awaited, stopwatch in hand, for the Obersteuermann's inquiry 'Stop-watch ready?' ('Stoppuhr klar?'). On affirmative response the navigator took his sight while the seaman watched the chronometer. On the navigator's shout 'Null' (zero), the seaman took his reading of the chronometer and the navigator his sextant, record-ing both. By using the readings just obtained in combination with data from the

Lines drawings of a Type IXC, 1941. *(Werner Bickel)*

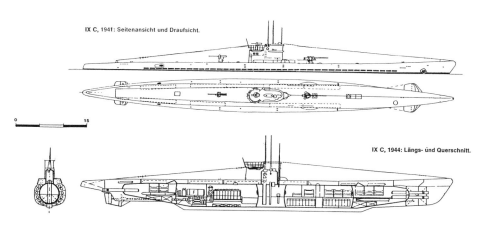

IX C, 1941: Seitenansicht und Draufsicht.

IX C, 1944: Längs- und Querschnitt.

almanac, navigation tables, course and speed, a position was plotted on the chart. The Grid Chart, or 'Marinequadrat', was merely a field of squares drawn over a Mercators' projection of the ocean's surface. Each square had two identifying letters assigned to its total area as coded, universally numbered subdivisions that could be further divided to give a coded position without revealing the actual location.

Radio communication from U-boats to BdU, and vice versa, formed a vital link in BdU's overall command of operations. The signals were transmitted by wireless telegraphy only. The telegraphy enabled boats, however, to make an immediate, coded response to a convoy sighting, and BdU to order additional U-boats quickly to its vicinity.

The U-boat Commander's Handbook of 1943 Section I C, 'Means of Communication of the Submarine', stated unequivocally that '. . . of decisive importance for the development and success of the attack is wireless telegraphy', and in 'Rules of communication in Permanent War Service Orders of the Commander in Chief, Submarines (BdU)', 'Equipment must be kept up to date in accordance with the latest information', asserting that greatest care must be taken to ensure that every submarine picks up each message promptly. The radio room on board a U-boat had to be manned continuously around the clock to receive incoming traffic. *U-175* typically carried four radio men ('Funker' or 'Puster') who doubled as sound men or hydrophone operators when required.

Paragraph 67 went on to state that 'When transmitting a wireless message, the U-boat always exposes itself to the danger of being located by direction finders'. In the next paragraph, however, it stressed the overriding importance of some messages defined as:

- enemy reports that make it possible to send other submarines into action,
- warnings of enemy submarines or minefields,
- situation reports including (enemy) traffic and description of patrols,
- weather reports,

The emblem, or badge, of *U-175* which was noted on the conning tower by the members of the boarding party from *Spencer. (Peter Wannemacher)*

U - 175

Crew members of *U-175* during training.
(Adolf March)

- enemy ship movements, especially to allow BdU to assess them, and
- reports ordered by BdU.

It further instructed that every message include the U-boat's grid position, followed by a paragraph again emphasising the danger posed by the enemy's Direction Finding equipment. BdU continued to demand almost endless reports from U-boats at sea, and no less a commander than top tonnage ace Otto Kretschmer of *U-99* complained bitterly of BdU's constant insistence on reports about weather, fuel and torpedoes remaining when interviewed for the film 'The Battle of the Atlantic' (Pendragon 1995).

From the winter of 1939/40, in order to avoid DF intercepts insofar as possible, BdU began using a 'Short Signal' code in which a series of coded signals could be transmitted in seconds, reducing the exposure of a full-length signal. These sentences and phrases compressed into single words or syllables were then coded for

Kapitänleutnant Heinrich Bruns, Commanding Officer of *U-175*.
(Peter Wannemacher)

transmission on the appropriate channel and prefixed by two Greek letters. However, by 1943 the British DF stations had become so efficient and sophisticated they could pinpoint a U-boat's location within minutes, allowing timely convoy diversion. When the HF/DF was seaborne on the escorts, it provided local interception, thus giving immediate warning that the convoy was being shadowed and an estimate of the position of the shadower. The Germans never knew of the existence of HF/DF which, in combination with radar, quickly made it too hazardous for single U-boats to attack convoys at all, as their best weapons, the cloak of invisibility and the element of surprise, were eliminated. It must be kept in mind that a submarine of the period was, in fact, a surface vessel capable of diving rather than a truly underwater attack craft.

U-boats were equipped with very efficient hydrophones (Horchgeräte), underwater sound detection devices. Since sound travels much farther underwater, a U-boat could often dive and, using the hydrophones, detect and obtain a bearing on a nearby convoy which was invisible from the low U-boat conning tower. The U-boat logbooks (KTB) show numerous instances of such 'Horchtauchen', or diving to listen on hydrophones for a sound bearing. *U-226* actually located Convoy HX-233 through the use of hydrophone bearings on the morning of 17 April 1943, and they eventually enabled her to close in, as described in Chapter 8. Sound bearings were also vital after a U-boat had been detected and submerged, to enable it to keep track of the counter-attacking escorts, and often facilitating a timely evasion.

*   *   *

U-175 frozen in at Gotenhafen during the winter of 1940/41. *(Adolf March)*

On 8 April 1943 *U-175*, in the wet dock at Lorient, received a number of last-minute crew replacements before departing two days later on a northwesterly course with orders believed to be for North America. On 11 April BdU radioed *U-175* to steer for Grid Square AK75 and the following day for AL15. When *U-262* (Franke) sighted and reported Convoy HX-233, BdU ordered Bruns to report on the weather and then pursue the convoy forthwith. At 2330hrs, in Grid Square BE4542, *U-175* sighted and reported a 'destroyer' (possibly *Spencer*) but apparently remained undetected as there was no reaction from the vessel. *U-175* then sighted and reported the convoy from astern. It was the last message Bruns was to send.

5

U-175's First Patrol: The Caribbean Theatre

In August 1942 BdU ordered *U-175* to the Trinidad area, where she joined *U-201, U-202, U-332, U-512, U-514, U-515* and *U-516* as part of the fourth wave of U-boats in the Caribbean. Earlier boats there had already departed for home base, but their eight replacements continued the campaign that covered two-and-a-half million square miles of sea, with Bruns' operational area being off the Guianas. By this time convoys of a sort had been instituted, reinforcements had begun to arrive and resistance to stiffen, so BdU concentrated on vessels sailing independently, with eight U-boats accounting for more than 127,000 tons of Allied shipping.

U-175 departed from Kiel in company with *U-179*, a Type IXD2 commanded by FK Ernest Sobe, on the forenoon of 10 August 1942 escorted by a 'Speerbrecher' ahead and a mine sweeper/anti-aircraft vessel astern. After passing through the Kattegat and Skagerrak, the boats arrived on 12 August at the submarine base in Kristiansand, Norway, to top up fuel and water. On the following day *U-175* separated on orders to act independently and proceeded north along the Norwegian coast to approximately the latitude of Bergen, seven to eight miles offshore, in position 60°N, 03°E. She then advanced at an economical speed of seven to eight knots on a course of 325° until reaching position 64°30'N 03°60'W, with the Faeroe Islands 35 miles to port. Her first dive, aside from daily practice, came when an aircraft appeared on 20 August in the vicinity of the Faeroes. Despite reckoning that the aircraft had not spotted them, Bruns remained submerged for several hours for safety's sake.

U-175 then passed into the North Atlantic between the Faeroes and Iceland, sighting numerous drifting mines, along a course of 245°, to position 62°N 15°W. Shortly thereafter she again sighted an aircraft, forcing her to remain submerged for some time, as the aircraft could be seen through the sky-search periscope still circling overhead. After the plane finally departed, *U-175* surfaced and resumed her speed and mean course of 225° to position 45°12' N 43°W, altering course to 202° to bring her to Barbados in keeping with orders to operate in the Windward Passage,

West Indies.* BdU, however, changed her operational area, instructing Bruns to patrol along the 100 fathoms isobath off the South American Coast from Trinidad to the mouth of the Orinoco River.

On arrival off Barbados at 0740hrs two days later, 13 September, *U-175* cruised around the island, having received a report on 11 September 1942 that another U-boat had sunk 'two tankers' off Bridgetown. The following day she sighted 'two wrecks' in Carlisle Bucht,† one with its stern still projecting above the surface. Lingering briefly in the vicinity of Barbados, *U-175* saw only a 500grt fishing vessel depart Bridgetown, which Bruns deemed an unworthy target. As no other ships presented themselves, *U-175* departed south-bound for her assigned patrol, leaving Tobago about 12 miles to port and Trinidad to the west, arriving in her operational zone for one of the final, most successful U-boat forays in the Caribbean.

Though Allied air cover had been vastly improved and convoy routeing instituted, the configuration and large number of the Caribbean islands forced ships to sail along well-defined routes. It was here, in the remote waters east of Trinidad, that U-boat Command discovered the focal point where east-west shipping to and from Trinidad and the north-south coastal traffic intersected. Here the U-boat scored most successes in 1942. In September twenty-nine ships (143,000grt), in October seventeen ships (81,742grt), and in November twenty-five ships (150,132grt) were sunk. Victims of an average of eight patrolling U-boats, the majority were vital bauxite carriers and oil tankers, independently routed.

By the time *U-175* arrived on station, her crew were suffering from oppressive heat and humidity on a boat without air-conditioning and experiencing temperatures above 47°C. Her first attack came in the early morning of 18 September 1942. The crew manned battle stations. The air was still, the horizon hazy, the moon visible above the cloud and a slight drizzle played on the water as the U-boat prowled the surface.

Bruns sighted a shadow that proved to be a steamer and fired a single torpedo from Tube I. It missed, as high phosphorescence allowed the vessel to observe its approach and alter course in time to avoid it. From the bridge Bruns noted the vessel turning hard about, heading for the coast. His charts were inadequate to risk following her, but he suspected the attack had forced the steamer to seek shallow water. As the ship's wake flattened out, he followed her cautiously until only three meters of water were under his keel, three miles offshore. As the ship was still visible, he ordered the deck gun to be fired but after two shots called a halt as the steamer was barely visible on the darker, hazy, western horizon, and Bruns recognised the danger of staying on the surface as dawn approached. A radio message from the steamer was overheard as *U-175* dived and proceeded seaward.

* She probably replaced *U-94*, Oberleutnant zur See Otto Ites, Ritterkreuz; sunk off Kingston, Jamaica, on 28 August 1942 by corvette HMCS *Oakville* and aircraft.

† Carlisle Bay in the area of Bridgetown, Barbados. Eyewitnesses do not recall two wrecks.

Allied sources report that the Norwegian freighter *Sørvangen* (built 1929, owner Gørrissen & Co, Oslo, 2,400grt) ran aground 18 September 1942 after a torpedo and gunfire attack. Apparently, *U-175* did hit the *Sørvangen* though, according to some sources, the ship's bauxite cargo absorbed the shell fire, accounting for the minimal damage. In the end she ran herself aground in the mouth of the Waine River off the South American coast in position 08°25'N 59°35'W, but was subsequently refloated and restored to service.

Less than an hour later Bruns' lookouts sighted a twin-engine, land-based bomber, which failed to sight him as the submarine crash dived. Proceeding seaward to the 25 fathom isobath, *U-175* altered her course to the south. At noon German time lookouts sighted a smoke plume, and by 1352hrs Bruns was at periscope level in attack position. He fired a single torpedo from Tube II just as the ship filled his attack periscope, a '. . . tanker in ballast, painted light grey, showing no flag or exterior markings . . . in grid square E01815 (08°36'N 58°13'W)'. The steamer sank within two minutes. With the threat of enemy aircraft Bruns remained submerged and departed the area as quickly as possible. The Allied vessel was the British Canadian freighter *Norfolk*, (built 1923, owned by Canada SS Line, Montreal, 1,901grt) with funnel and engines aft, hence the mistaken description 'small tanker'.

Later, at 1453hrs, the smoke of a vessel appeared, bearing 060°, but Bruns man-oeuvred in vain to reach an attack position. An aircraft circled about 500m overhead and the steamer behaved oddly, keeping her bow pointed towards the U-boat while zig-zagging but without really moving forward. Bruns described her as a 'normal appearing freighter of about 5,000grt with two masts, one funnel, painted black with a white ring on the single funnel' but was suspicious of her. *U-175* crept away on course 070° and resurfaced at 0034hrs in Grid Square E01831. Bruns reported to BdU that he strongly suspected a U-boat trap, possibly a Q-ship.

Two days later, off British Guiana, the sudden appearance of an aircraft again forced *U175* to crash dive, and again she was not sighted. The following day, 21 September 1942, still off the British Guiana coast and astride the bauxite ore traffic route, *U-175* sighted a shadow at 0515hrs in Grid Square EO1864, bearing 296°. Moving closer, the U-boat submerged for attack while keeping the target in the bright moonlight. At 0639hrs Bruns launched a single torpedo from Tube III and one minute later another from Tube II. The first shot missed but the second, after a run of 80 seconds smashed into the small Yugoslav freighter, *Predsednik Kopajtic*, under her bridge. Bruns described her as a 'freighter, about 6,000grt, three island type, straight bow, normal stern, two masts, afire forward'. She was in fact only 1,798grt (built 1928, Jadranska Plov, Split, owners) and sank in position 08°30'N 59°30'W. Her survivors were later picked up. She sank seven minutes after being hit. Although about 150 miles southeast of Trinidad's Galeota Point and well within range of patrolling aircraft, *U-175* remained undetected. She was operating in the same general area as *U-512, U-514, U-515* and *U-516.*

U-175 surfaced at 0651hrs and, apparently finding no trace of the vessel, set a course of 030° under both engines. Bruns informed BdU of his success and reported

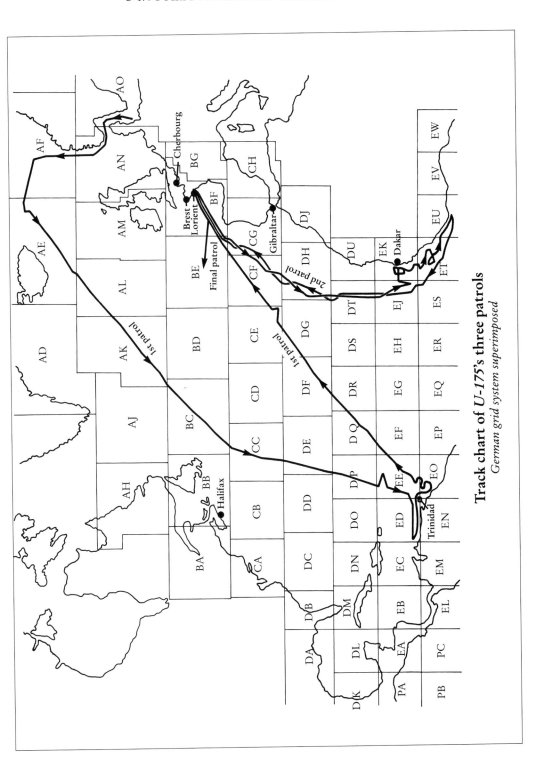

Track chart of _U-175_'s three patrols
German grid system superimposed

128cbm of fuel remaining.

At 0853hrs, in Grid Square EO1836, lookouts sighted a small target, bearing 290°, and travelling fast, but then it suddenly vanished. Bruns concluded that it was probably another U-boat, which would have been likely given that five boats were operating in so small and crowded a sea area.

View through the attack periscope of *U-175*. *(Peter Wannemacher)*

Kelshall reports *U-175* remained undetected during this period. Not quite. Bruns' entry in the logbook for that afternoon at 1340hrs in Square EO1532 reports sighting an aircraft amid rain showers at 600m, bearing 230° and coming directly in to attack. It dropped three bombs close aboard, two close enough to shake them severely and do serious damage. Bruns crash-dived and remained submerged while the crew began to repair damage as far as was possible. At 2157hrs the boat resurfaced to continue repairs. Damage to flood valves and other equipment was considerable and despite repeated attempts was scarcely repaired by the third day after the attack when another aircraft, described as a 'twin-engine land bomber', appeared. *U-175* submerged and either the aircraft failed to notice the boat or was simply out of bombs, for none fell and Bruns prudently remained submerged until twilight to avoid any subsequent aircraft patrols.

By the following morning, 24 September, the U-boat was about 100 miles north of Georgetown, British Guiana, and 250 miles southeast of Trinidad in Square EO1358, when a shadow, bearing 226°, was identified at 0457hrs as a large freighter. She proved to be the US flag freighter *West Chetac* (built 1919, Los Angeles, Seas Shipping Co NY, owner, 5,627grt). Due to a bright, full moon and the presence of an aircraft circling the ship, Bruns had to submerge in order to attack. The variable weather conditions in the area with, typically, heavy rain squalls alternating with clear visibility, were an added strain for commanders. By 0924hrs Bruns was able to launch a single torpedo from Tube IV at 1800m, submerged. Aimed forward of the bridge, the torpedo hit the port side at No 2 hatch, and the vessel sank by the bow in six-and-a-half minutes.

The freighter, sunk in position 08°45'N 57°00'W, according to Bruns' logbook, was en route from Norfolk, Virginia, to Basra, Iraq, by way of Trinidad with 6,100grt of war supplies. She had been in convoy TAW-14 (Trinidad-Aruba-Key West) until it had dispersed a few hours earlier, leaving all vessels to proceed independently. When *U-175*'s torpedo blew out her No 2 hatch beams and covers, the vessel settled quickly by the head. The crew abandoned ship immediately in the four boats, but a choppy sea and the turbulence generated by the sinking vessel combined to capsize all the boats and the only survivors were those who managed to swim to the liferafts. Twenty-two crew and nine naval armed guard were casualties including the master, Captain Frank Matthew Jasper. Seventeen merchant crew and two naval personnel were rescued from the liferafts by the American destroyer *Roc* (DD-418) almost a week later, around 1000hrs on 1 October, and taken to Port of Spain, Trinidad where six of the crew and both armed guards were hospitalised.

At 2240hrs on 24 September *U-175* spotted another U-boat, steering easterly in Grid Square EO1554. Although BdU never confirmed it, Bruns identified her as *U-512* (Ktlt Wolfgang Schultze), who had sunk two ships, including the neutral Spanish *Monte Gorbea*, 3,720grt. She also delivered the *coup de grâce* to the wreck of the Waterman Line freighter *Antinous*, 6,034grt, under tow during a vain attempt at salvage after her crew gallantly reboarded but failed to get the badly-damaged vessel under way. On 2 October 1942, exactly a week after her probable sighting by *U-175*, *U-512* was bombed and sunk, in 06°50'N 52°25'W, north of Cayenne, by a B-18 whose pilot, Lt Lehti of US Army Bomber Squadron 99, was based in French Guiana. There was only one survivor from the U-boat.

During the night of 26 September Bruns surfaced and got under way on one diesel to minimise fuel consumption. At 0500hrs local time, southeast of Trinidad, he sighted a shadowy vessel and in early dawn's light dived for an underwater approach and attack. At 0625hrs a single torpedo from Tube I travelled for 47 seconds before hitting the little *Tambour*, 1,827grt, beneath her mainmast. Bruns described her as a 'normal 3–4,000grt freighter in ballast'. She sank by the stern after three minutes about 100 miles southeast of Galeota Point on Trinidad's coast, in position 08°50'N 59°50'W. The *Tambour*, owned by the US Maritime Commission and sailing under the Panamanian flag, was sunk on passage from Paramaribo to Trinidad, heading west for the Serpent's Mouth entrance to the Gulf of Paria, Trinidad. Twenty-four survivors were rescued out of a crew of thirty-two. Because of the constant threat of air attack, *U-175* submerged to clear the area, steering a course of 090° before surfacing to run slow ahead on both diesel engines for battery recharging, and then, after 0410hrs on one diesel to cut fuel consumption.

On 28 September, two days later, at a few minutes past midnight, *U-175* surfaced in Grid Square EO1468 and set a course of 320° in bright moonlight, with a light breeze and a visibility of about eight miles. Lookouts sighted shadowy steamer bearing 296° and Bruns dived for attack some 20 miles off the mouth of the Orinoco River about 100 miles southeast of Trinidad. At 0149hrs the crew launched a torpedo from Tube II. It missed. An alert naval armed guard on lookout on *Alcoa Mariner* had sighted the torpedo approaching port and shouted a warning. Captain John Martino promptly ordered the helm hard to starboard and the torpedo passed about 15ft astern. Two minutes later Bruns ordered a second torpedo from Tube IV, which after a running time of 2mins 17secs hit the target at the break of the poop, at Number 5 hatch.

Bruns, watching from periscope depth, observed that the ship had stopped, but though her four boats were leaving the badly damaged ship, she was not sinking. Twenty minutes later, with the lifeboats now well clear, he fired a third torpedo, this time from Tube V. Another miss, this one attributed to a defective steering mechanism in the torpedo. A fourth shot, from Tube VI, scored a direct hit in the engine-room on the port side, after which the old ship quickly sank. Bruns fairly accurately described her as a 'freighter with passenger facilities, 4,500grt, in ballast, five hatches, armed with two anti-aircraft machine-cannon mounted on the foc'sle, four machine guns on the bridge and one 7.5mm deck gun on a mounting on the stern'.

Allied records note that at 1531hrs, 28 September 1942, the US freighter, *Alcoa Mariner* (ex-*New Windsor*, built 1919, Newburgh, NY, Alcoa Steamship Co NY, owner, 5,590grt), sank about 90 miles SE of Trinidad and 20 miles off the Orinoco River, at 08°57'N 60°08'W, en route from Trinidad to Georgetown, British Guiana, in ballast to load bauxite ore. Her complement of thirty-eight crew and thirteen naval armed guard all survived. The master, Captain John Luther Martino, had previously been master of the *Alcoa Cadet*, 4,823grt, when a German air-laid mine sank her in Kola Inlet, Murmansk, North Russia, on 21 June 1942.* Thus, Captain Martino lost two ships to enemy action in the space of three months.

According to *Alcoa Mariner*'s report, at 0547hrs on 28 September she sighted a torpedo to port and the Master ordered the helm hard to starboard, so that the torpedo passed about 15ft astern. Three minutes later a second torpedo hit the port side aft in way of Number 5 hatch, destroying the poop deck interior and almost breaking the stern off at a 30° angle. The stern remained attached to the vessel mainly by the shaft, but there was extensive flooding of the engine-room via the shaft tunnel. The crew

---

* The author's cousins, Captain Arthur C Haskell and Captain Randall Haskell served as young officers with Captain Martino. Captain Martino lost his brother, Captain William Mack Martino, in the sinking of the four-masted schooner *Albert F Paul* by *U-332* (Liebe) on 13 March 1942 en route from Turks Island to Baltimore with a full load of salt. There were no survivors.

Onboard *U-175* in the Carribean during her first patrol.
(Peter Wannemacher)

abandoned ship immediately in four lifeboats, except for the armed guard commander and the after gun crew who, isolated by the structural damage, left in a small raft. *U-175* fired a final torpedo once the crew had abandoned ship. The lifeboats picked up the crew members and armed guard from the raft, and later that morning a US Army air patrol sighted the boats and signalled that help was en route. Just after noon the Canadian *Turret Court*, (McNaughton, Montreal, owner, 1,879grt) picked up the survivors and landed them at Georgetown, British Guiana, that evening.

U-175 had now expended her torpedo supply inside the boat and had to surface to transfer the eight torpedoes from the deck storage containers. This had to be done at night, without lights, and involved six to seven hours of heavy, arduous and dangerous labour. The crew accomplished their task without disturbance and within the assigned patrol area. The boat then cruised on both diesels in order to fully recharge the batteries, and at midnight altered course to 260° in the direction of the South American coast. On the last day of September seven U-boats were operating from the Barbados area south to the Brazil frontier. Of these *U-175, U-202* (Linder) and *U-332* (Liebe) were working east of Trinidad.

On 1 October 1942 at 0200hrs lookouts sighted a shadow that materialised into a blacked-out steamer. An hour later Bruns dived for a submerged attack, approaching on a course of 310°. At approximately 0330hrs, while surfaced, lookouts sighted an aircraft patrolling overhead. Three minutes later the plane had left, and Bruns launched a torpedo from Tube I, hitting the steamer midships after a run of 15 seconds.

An explosion towering 100m high, laced with flame, was visible through the periscope, and Bruns saw the ship lowering her boats and launching rafts while lights flashed about the decks. The steamer continued on her course before turning abruptly to avoid a shot from Tube III. At 0400hrs a torpedo from Tube IV also missed, and immediately the steamer turned directly toward the periscope. The boat crash dived to 20m and, by seconds, avoided being rammed.

Fifty minutes later, at 0451hrs Bruns returned to the surface, according to his log book 'between boats and rafts where, due to the language problem, understanding each other was very difficult. The steamer's name was something like *"Empire Ten-esse"*, estimated 6,000grt, length 140m, a turbine ship'.* Allied sources report the British freighter *Empire Tennyson* (built 1942, Murrell Steam Ship Co, owner, 2,880grt) was sunk 1 October 1942 in position 09°27'N 60°05'W, 70 miles southeast of Trinidad. A single torpedo had caused the explosion, but the crew were able to man the lifeboats. The U-boat surfaced and interrogated the crew of the port lifeboat, going away without properly understanding her name. The freighter managed to send a distress signal, despite going down quickly, to alert short-based aircraft.

Apparently, Bruns saw no evidence of aircraft, as he makes no mention of it in his logbook, but he did sight another steamer less than an hour later, and after he dived to attack, waited nearly two hours to reach attack position. At 1308hrs in Grid Square E01455 a torpedo from Tube I took 39secs to travel some 800m and hit a stationary steamer. An unusually powerful explosion followed and Bruns concluded the ship must have been carrying explosives or ammunition. After the column of smoke receded, there was no sign of the ship and Bruns was therefore unable to identify her; he could only give the time and location of her sinking, apparently with all hands, southeast of Trinidad. There is no confirmation of this attack from Allied sources, and the ship may already have been abandoned and derelict.

On 2 October 1942 southeast of Trinidad, *U-175* was herself a target but suffered no damage from two air attacks. A VP-74, PBM-5, gull-winged Martin 'Mariner' patrol bomber caught *U-175* on the surface and bombed her heavily but with minimum damage.

At 0430hrs Bruns saw a shadow and dived in preparation for a submerged attack in bright moonlight. Thirteen minutes later a single torpedo from Tube II took 43 seconds to travel 900m, and hit below the mainmast of a steamer. The U-boat surfaced and picked up the steamer's coded radio message: 'MIB III NVA 2 MINS', issued twice, and *U-175* dived again, anticipating patrolling aircraft. Six minutes later the steamer sank by the stern, and Bruns estimated she was a freighter, 4,500grt and 120m long, with turbine engines. He proceeded underwater, having sighted no survivors and no further targets in the area.

On 2 October the freighter, *Aneroid*, 5,074grt, under the Panamanian flag, went

---

* There was in fact no ship named *Empire Tennessee*. The British freighter *Tennessee*, 2,342 tons, was sunk, out of convoy SC-100, by *U-617* (Brandi) on 23 September 1942 in position 58°40'N, 33°41'W.

Onboard *U-175* in the South Atlantic during her first patrol.
(Peter Wannemacher)

down in position 08°24'N 59°12'W, 140 miles southeast of Trinidad. Although reportedly two torpedoes hit her, she did not sink at once, as aircraft found the wreck
abandoned and drifting some twelve hours later. However, she presumably sank later
that night, since she was never seen again. Although this data conflicts with some
U-175 KTB entries, it is certain *U-175* sank her.

Next morning, 3 October, at 0438hrs local time and still on the northeast coast of
South America, lookouts sighted a shadow and Bruns dived, as his boat was surfaced
on the bright eastern horizon at approaching sunrise. The steamer apparently did not
sight the U-boat and continued on course, out of range. Through the periscope Bruns
sighted two freighters and a tanker, both also out of range.

At 0511hrs local time on 4 October, at break of dawn, lookouts again saw a shadow
on the horizon and Bruns submerged to attack. One torpedo, launched from Tube I,
struck a freighter after 2 mins 16secs but seemed to have done little damage. The
vessel, estimated at 3,500grt, length 110m, had stopped and was emitting 'white
smoke' possibly steam. Bruns struck again, this time from Tube III. The torpedo,
porpoising along the surface, struck the vessel near the mainmast and she sank by
the stern, hitting bottom at between 16m and 18m so that her bow remained out
of the water.

According to Allied reports, on 4 October, off the mouth of the Orinoco River,
Venezuela, in position 08°35'N 59°37'W, the German *U-175* had sunk the American
laker *Carib Star* (ex-*Lake Fanquier*, ex-*Guayaquil*, 2,592grt × 77m × 13.3m, built 1919,

Lorain, Ohio; Stockard & Co, NY, owner; Alcoa SS Co, operator; Captain Fred Gomez Valez). She was en route in ballast from Trinidad to Georgetown, British Guiana, when a torpedo struck her port side and exploded in the boiler room, destroying the boilers, bursting the steam lines and killing three men. A second torpedo hit the starboard quarter causing a huge explosion, probably detonating the ship's magazine, and the vessel began to sink rapidly stern-first. The bow remained visible for about three hours before finally sinking beneath the surface. Seven officers, twenty-two men and six armed guards abandoned ship after the second torpedo, getting away in one lifeboat (the other being wrecked) and two liferafts. The men on the liferaft were later taken aboard the lifeboat. Fourteen hours later the American Navy's *PC-469* rescued six officers, nineteen men and six armed guards, and landed them at Port of Spain, Trinidad. One crewman died aboard the *PC-469* and the second assistant engineer died in the US Army hospital at Docksite, Trinidad, both casualties of the scalding steam from exploding boilers.

At 1132hrs local time Bruns had a 4,000grt steamer in ballast in his sights, but two torpedoes failed to hit their target, and he sensibly left the scene to avoid the danger of air attack.

On the day following, 5 October, at 0410hrs a shadow proved to be another blacked-out steamer, and a single torpedo from Tube IV, after running 1min 32secs, hit the vessel between the funnel and the bridge. An estimated 100m high column of smoke shot into the air, and the steamer stopped and sank slowly by the stern, losing a large amount of fuel. After the crew abandoned ship, Bruns used his deck gun to hasten the vessel's end. Firing had to cease after about twenty hits when a shell lodged in the gun barrel. Suddenly planes came in to attack with bombs and depth charges, and the U-boat crash-dived to safety. From periscope depth Bruns observed six flares hit the surface and the steamer burning her entire length (estimated 120m, 4,000grt) while a plane played a red searchlight over the surface of the water.

At 08°35'N 59°37'W, about 50 miles east of Corocoro Island, Venezuela, *U-175*'s last torpedo had hit the American collier, *William A McKenney* (built 1916, Newport News, Virginia; Mystic SS Co, Boston, owner; Captain James Franklin Lusby, master; Alcoa SS Co, operator, 6,153grt) she was en route alone from Georgetown, British Guiana, to Mobile, Alabama, carrying 3100 tons of bauxite ore, with a crew of thirty-one plus four armed guards. It is worth noting that the fact that coastwise colliers had been pressed into a service to transport urgently needed ore is an indication of the havoc U-boats had already wrought. The torpedo struck the port side just aft of the engine room bulkhead, creating a huge 20ft hole in the waterline, blowing off the massive, solid steel hatch covers on Number 3 hold, wrecking the steering engine, and bringing down the antennae. Because the ship was sinking slowly, *U-175*, having expended all her torpedoes, had surfaced and begun shelling the wreck with her 4.1in deck gun, firing six to eight rounds into the vessel and setting her afire. All hands abandoned ship except Captain Lusby, the radio operator and one crewman, who were attempting to rig an emergency antenna to radio an SOS. However, all hands finally got away in two lifeboats, after which *U-175* resumed shelling the wreck with

U-175 flying her victory pennants, one for each boat sunk, on her return to Lorient, 28 October 1942. *(Adolf March)*

eight to ten more rounds. The vessel finally sank after about four hours.

That evening an RAF Hudson aircraft patrol located the sinking *William A McKenney*, still in flames and only ten miles offshore. Noting the overcrowded lifeboats of survivors nearby, the pilot guided rescuers to the scene. The American destroyer *Blakely* (DD 150) picked them up that evening and landed them at Port of Spain, Trinidad.

With no more torpedoes and a 'respectable' 33,428grt of nine enemy ships destroyed and one damaged, *U-175* was ordered on 7 October to return to the U-boat base at Lorient. By next day she had reached the Little Antilles and on 9 October began her eight-day journey across the Atlantic to the southern Azores.

On 14 October headquarters ordered Rosenberg (*U-201*) and Bruns to report their positions, and estimate how much fuel each could spare in an extremity. Bruns replied he was in Square DR1368 and could probably spare 10cbm of fuel. Headquarters ordered him to continue on course. On 20 October, approximately 28 miles off Point Castello in the eastern Azores, lookouts sighted a sea plane at 800m overhead in bright moonlight, whereupon *U-175* crash dived to the safety of the Atlantic depths.

Off Cape Finisterre on 23 October *U-175* came up twice in the one night whilst entering the dangerous Biscay area to recharge the batteries, and during the next night in the Bay of Biscay, three surfacings were necessary to recharge. This time an unexpected sea plane, flying 100m overhead, briefly interrupted the urgent work in progress.

On 27 October, after a successful patrol of 78 days, *U-175* reached 'Punkt Laterne' ('lantern point'), and on 28 October a victorious crew arrived in Lorient to a welcoming committee, a band, girls, flowers, fresh food, beer and a bath.

Top: U-175 entering Lorient at the end of her first patrol, approaching the mooring hulk. *(Peter Wannemacher)*
Above: The welcoming committee for *U-175* at Lorient. *(Peter Wannemacher)*

6

U-175's Second Patrol: West Africa

Almost immediately after the Germans had captured Lorient on 21 June 1940, engineers began working to clear the port for U-boats. Vizeadmiral Hans Stohwasser was appointed 'Oberwerftdirector' and the first boat to use the new facility, *U-30* under Kptlt Fritz-Julius Lemp, arrived on 7 July for re-supply. In November 1940 Admiral Dönitz set up his headquarters at nearby Kerneval, a foreland facing Lorient. By the time *U-175* reached Lorient in 1942, the base was the largest, most intricate and important of all U-boat bases in France, providing technical assistance to all others despite having only two flotillas: the 2nd U-Flotille, 'Saltzwedel'*; and 10th U-Flotille‡. Even a few Japanese submarines visited Lorient, including *I-29* and *I-30*, the latter lost four days after her return to Malaya on 9 October 1942. Following the British commando raid on St Nazaire in March 1942 Hitler ordered Admiral Dönitz and BdU to Paris.

Meanwhile, in the two ensuing years, Lorient had become a fortress with bomb-proof submarine bunkers and a unique, remarkably engineered, land-based, protected slipway containing a U-boat transport system described as a 'moveable transverser'. The bunker roofs, 3.5m thick topped by a bomb trap ('Fang Rost') of pre-cast U-beams, had been designed to absorb the shock waves of bombs detonating on them. The largest RAF bombs of 12,000lbs high-capacity explosive were ineffective, and even the specially designed 'Tallboys' of 12,030lbs dropped from 40,000ft, although they penetrated the roofs of the bunkers at Brest, failed to do much else there and at Lorient nothing at all.

Not until the approach of the American Army in 1944 were Lorient's dock workers evacuated, and the last U-boat to depart the base was *U-155* under Oberleutnant zur See Ludwig-Ferdinand v Friedeburg on 5 September 1944. The 10th U-Flotille was

---

* Named after Reinhold Saltzwedel, WWI U-boat commander and recipient of Germany's then highest award, the *Pour Le Mérite*, for 150,000grt destroyed; lost in *UB-81* in 1917.

‡ Created in Lorient January 1942 with fifty U-boats, but reduced to thirty-two by April 1943. Among the most successful U-boats and captains based in Lorient were Aces KK Günther Prien (*U-47*), Kptlt Otto Kretschmer (*U-99*), and Kptlt Joachim Schepke (*U-100*), each of whom departed Lorient on his last patrol. The seven U-boats with largest tonnage sunk (*U-37, U-48, U-99, U-103, U-124, U-107,* and *U-123*) all operated from Lorient, destroying 313 Allied ships between them.

disbanded in October when all U-boat activity in Lorient ended, but the 'Festung', under the command of General Wilhelm Fahrnbacher, held out until 8 May 1945.

On arriving in Lorient on 27 October 1942, *U-175* first moored alongside a hulk near the Saltzwedel Barracks but was shifted that evening into No 1 Pen in the vast Scorff Shelter. She remained in Lorient from 28 October until 1 December, her crew living in Hundius Barracks. While *U-175* was in drydock between 31 October and 28 November her ship's company had three-week home leaves by watches. On the first two days in port the boat was cleared out and all apparatus tested. A few days later she was moved to Pen 17 in the Keroman shelter to have her periscope removed and replaced, electric motors overhauled, and compressors removed, checked and rebuilt. A Metox R 600 A GSR radar impulse detector was also fitted. By 16 November all major work and some minor repairs and adjustments had been completed.

Towards the end of November twenty-three torpedoes, fifteen electric wakeless and eight air-driven, ammunition and provisions were embarked in Scorff Shelter. On 29 November the test run began, on the 30th corrections were made, and on 1 December 1942 *U-175* started on her second patrol. She departed Lorient at 1648hrs seen off by Korvetten Kapitän Günter Kuhnke, Commanding Officer of the 10th Flotille, and in company with a Type VIIC U-boat from a Brest-based flotilla. Because of the risk of mines a 'Sperrbrecher' always escorted the boats for five miles, until the Isle de Groix was on the starboard beam. An hour after departure *U-175*'s lookout reported a salvo of four torpedoes approaching to port. After an emergency change of course to port they were then identified as porpoises. At about midnight the radio man detected aircraft on the Metox radar detector and sounded 'Alarm!'. *U-175* crash-dived to safety but soon resurfaced, though enemy aircraft forced repeated dives during the night and at about 0100hrs depth charges were audible. *U-175* assumed that the consort Type VIIC U-boat was under attack.

Nightly harassment by aircraft continued unabated in the Bay of Biscay. On 2 December during one forced dive the crew were kept busy tightening joints left weeping after the dry-docking. Two days later the exhaust valves were leaking badly, a frequent problem on U-boats. At 1926hrs BdU reported that *U-603* (Bertelsmann)

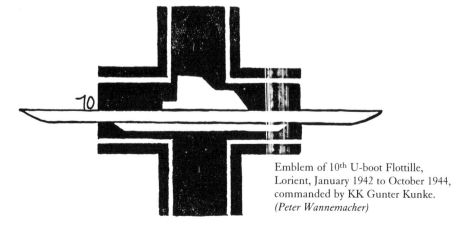

Emblem of 10th U-boot Flottille, Lorient, January 1942 to October 1944, commanded by KK Gunter Kunke. (*Peter Wannemacher*)

had sighted a convoy in Grid Square BE9826, on a southerly course. Square BE was east of Cape Finisterre. Bruns was clearing the Bay of Biscay with mechanical problems, but reported in that he would attempt to intercept the convoy, and by the following morning, 5 December, he had reached the North Atlantic. At 0520hrs a lookout reported the shadow of a destroyer, but it turned and disappeared. Bruns, unsure of his boat's seaworthiness, decided against reporting the vessel and calling attention to himself. At 0815hrs he dived so that he could attempt to repair the diesel motor and valve leaks. After no success, at 1025hrs, he had to resurface, because at high revolutions the exhaust valves were failing to close.

At 1300hrs *U-175* still had not sighted the convoy, and four hours later a seaplane at 150m forced the U-boat to crash dive. On returning to periscope depth, Bruns observed the plane circling for at least an hour. Shortly after the plane left, water streamed through the exhaust valve, forcing him to surface. At 2050hrs BdU radioed: 'Schüler [*U-720*] sighted a funnel and a Sunderland [aircraft] heading south.' The convoy was quite near, so Bruns changed course to follow, off the coast of Portugal.

Although he could now safely cruise on the surface by day at 13 knots, virtually routine night speed, until 6 December Bruns returned every half hour to periscope depth to re-tighten leaking valves. During a deep test dive on the same date, at 0812hrs, water again streamed through the exhaust valves into the bilge, as it had done during every test dive on the previous few days. Bruns judged diving to be extremely risky, believing their prolonged high speed produced high exhaust temperatures that caused materials to warp.

Since he could not safely dive, Bruns entered in the log: 'I have decided to break off and discontinue the operation against the convoy'. He radioed headquarters giving his location and notifying them of his intent to travel westward. Headquarters directed him to a new operational area, to the south with 'Details to follow'.

On reaching the latitude of the Azores, Bruns set course for the African coast and his assigned patrol area off Freetown, Sierra Leone, passing through the Canary Islands between Grand Canary and Fuerteventura. North of Madeira, on 8 December, *U-175* sighted a smoke cloud and sped in its direction, reaching the steamer just as the skies began to darken. The vessel had her lights on and Bruns ordered her to stop, but on learning she was the 4,597-ton Spanish tanker *Zorroza*, released her and continued southward, reporting to headquarters that the *Zorroza* was en route from Curaçao to Valencia, in Grid Square DH2256 on his chart.

The next few days passed without incident, and on 11 December, during a test dive, both exhaust valves finally remained properly closed, but only after repeated and lengthy regrinding at periscope level. Bruns reported the results to BdU, who next day ordered him to Cape Verde Islands, Grid Square EK4630. Until now no U-boat had been in the area so BdU had no information about minefields; they requested information about ship movements in and out of Dakar, assuming there would be traffic heading toward Morocco, the West Indies and Freetown. BdU then gave Bruns permission to fire on French naval and merchant ships.

Next day, 12 December, *U-175* arrived off the Cape Verde Islands and by 16

December lay west of Dakar, keeping an eye out for east-west traffic. An alarm, as a four-engine aircraft flew over them at 2000m, was the only interruption. On the 18th and again on 19 December BdU ordered Bruns to report his position, whether he was in fact at EK46 and how long his boat had been there. Bruns replied he had been near Dakar Harbour entrance four days, but in square EJ. On 20 December BdU ordered him immediately eastward, close to Dakar in Grid Square EK46. On 21 December Bruns found himself properly located and at 0820hrs dived in order to approach the coast unobserved. At midnight the compressor motor failed, which the machinist attempted to repair, but at 0800hrs next morning Bruns had to notify BdU that the fresh water generator had stopped functioning, as the 'anchor' (the rotating component of the compressor motor) had 'melted through'. Little of consequence ensued during the following week, only sightings of the occasional plane or coastal navigation marker. Closing the African coast U-175's crew report passing so close inshore they could see natives on the beaches. Before leaving Lorient a box marked 'Do not open until Christmas' had been embarked with their provisions. Opening it on Christmas Eve, the crew found a small artificial ornamented Christmas tree, a reminder of Christmas Eve at home, and each man received a tot of Schnapps with which to celebrate.

On 26 December BdU signalled Bruns to move farther south, to the harbour at Freetown, Sierra Leone, where west-bound convoy traffic had been discovered. Unescorted ships could also possibly be proceeding southwards. Bruns was to remain as close to the harbour as possible and be prepared to attack. Next day at 1845hrs Bruns saw a smoke plume, but the vessel turned east and U-175 proceeded south as ordered. On the 28th, off Portuguese Guinea, he again sighted smoke and two masts and dived to reconnoitre, but resurfaced when he identified the vessel as the 6,298-ton Portuguese passenger ship *Lourenço Marques* out of Lisbon.

On 29 December water was discovered in Tube III's firing chamber. On 30 December at 0920hrs Bruns reported masts in view eight miles distant, directly west of Freetown. Even though visibility was poor due to haze, at 0835hrs on 31 December, a lookout sighted the shadow of a destroyer seven miles distant and visible to her bridge. Meanwhile the destroyer, identified as a 'Forester' type, had detected the U-boat on Asdic and charged head-on, forcing the boat to crash dive. At 90m depth Asdic could no longer detect the U-boat, and no depth charges were heard. On returning to periscope depth Bruns saw the destroyer and a convoy escort on zig-zag courses at five miles distance. He dived to safety again and there he remained, reporting to BdU that a 'Forester type destroyer' and another convoy escort had forced him under for seven hours.

On New Year's Day 1943 at 0130hrs another neutral came into view, the 2,720-ton Portuguese steamer *Lobito* out of Loando, Angola. At 1137hrs the 'Alarm' was sounded. Not spotted on approach due to the poor visibility, a single-engine plane had suddenly come into view at 2,000m and Bruns crash dived. At 1853hrs, back on the surface and her position unchanged a plane was spotted at 4,000m heading straight for the U-boat; five depth charges were dropped close by, but luckily did little damage as

U-175 crash dived to a safe depth. At 2000hrs Bruns resurfaced and four minutes later a plane again appeared and again Bruns crash dived, resurfacing just 26 minutes later. After about 18 minutes of hide-and-seek the plane attacked, again without damaging the U-boat. At 2056hrs it used a searchlight, but Bruns, having dived, remained submerged, this time for over three hours.

Misfortune returned in the early hours of 2 January, this time in the form of malfunctioning equipment. Batteries and air supply were low and the compressor valves not functioning properly, but by the following day the batteries were recharged and, during a dive, the ventilators repaired. At 2000hrs Bruns reported to BdU that the seven air attacks during the previous days had forced him to spend 32 hours underwater, and that such continual air coverage seemed intended to starve them out. He proposed leaving the coastal watch, which had been unproductive in any case, especially as the boat had such restricted movement. He could not continue the present assignment with batteries at 55 per cent of their power and the compressor valve not working properly.

About sunrise on 4 January Bruns saw another U-boat surface twice. Twenty minutes later he signalled BdU: 'At Grid Square ET1699 U-boat. Question: ours or Italian?' For several minutes he kept track of the boat but lost it at 0923hrs. After two hours BdU replied: 'Not Italian, not impossible that it is our boat'. Three more days of interminable waiting followed. On 7 January BdU, having learned a surprising number of salient details about convoy traffic in another area thanks to B-Dienst intercepts, ordered Bruns to head west-northwest to Grid Square ET38: 'Convoy traffic in direction of ED99 [northeastern coast of South America and West Indies] in a 10-11 day rhythm, next run possibly 8 January. The passing points of a December convoy were ES3696, ER1515, EP1352. On 17 December another convoy was reported in 'ET38, course 295°, speed 8 knots'. This message arrived at 2320hrs. At midnight Bruns ordered both engines full speed ahead in order to reach his new position by noon, but the convoy was never sighted. Again, there was the eternal waiting. A week later, on 15 January, a lookout spotted a ship and Bruns prepared for underwater attack, until he identified her through the periscope as the 6,632-ton Spanish steamer *'Mar Negro'*, noting in the log that he intended moving in toward Freetown's main harbour for 'possible [enemy] traffic'. Next morning at 0800hrs the exhaust valve was again not closing properly and three days later it had become inoperable.

Keeping watch underwater by day and on the surface at night continued without respite, a far cry from operations in the same area a year earlier, when in the month of May U-boats sank thirty-eight ships of 176,168grt well within 600 miles of Freetown and Bathurst. Apparently, BdU was unaware that the Allies had suspended their Freetown-to-UK convoys after the disastrous convoy SL-125 ran into the 'Xanthippe' U-boat group and lost thirteen ships (85,686grt) between 26 October and 5 November 1942, with no loss to the U-boats. Another reason the Freetown convoys had stopped was because their escorts had been ordered to North Africa for the 'Operation Torch' landings. Allied ships now took greatly prolonged and more dangerous voyages alone across the southern Atlantic to join American coastal convoys to New York, then

A typical Biscay 'Speerbrecher', the M/S *Saar*, converted to a heavily
armed escort and used to accompany U-boats through the shallow,
dangerous seas between Lorient and the deep Atlantic. *(Bibliothek für
Zeitgeschichte Stuttgart)*

North Atlantic convoys to Europe, thus adding significantly to port congestion and the
size of the meagerly-protected NY-UK convoys.

Finally, at 1800hrs on 22 January, off the West African coast, Bruns sighted a
shadow in his periscope about four to five miles distant. Approaching at periscope
depth, the U-boat identified her as an American freighter that was stopped, with a
deck load of aeroplane parts, and showing a light aft near the stern gun. Bruns fired
one torpedo just as the vessel got under way, consequently missing it. The ship's
lookouts had apparently not sighted the torpedo, as she shaped a course to the
southeast. At 1815hrs a torpedo from Tube IV also missed. Fearing air patrols, Bruns
dived. On resurfacing an hour later, he saw the freighter nine miles away heading
090°. Still in pursuit after eight hours, at 0235hrs next morning Bruns finally reached
a suitable underwater attack position. According to his logbook the torpedo from
Tube I hit beneath the freighter's bridge 58 seconds after firing, but appeared to have
little effect since the vessel continued another six to eight miles. The second torpedo,
from Tube V, missed the target entirely. After 65 seconds, Tube VI scored a hit below
the mainmast and the steamer lowered her life boats and rafts into the water.

U-175 surfaced to see the freighter still under way. Approaching the boats, Bruns
learned she was the *Benjamin Smith* out of Trinidad. According to the survivors she
had a 10,000-ton cargo of cement and asphalt, destination unknown, and she had
crossed the Atlantic without escort. There is a question mark in Brun's logbook after
the declared cargo.

The ship was, in fact, the new American Liberty *Benjamin Smith* (7,100grt, built North Carolina Shipbuilding Company, Wilmington, in November 1942) on her maiden voyage to Sassandra, West Africa. According to Allied sources she was about 16 miles off Cape Palmas, Liberia, near the mouth of the Cavalla River on 23 January when *U-175*'s first torpedo hit between Number 1 and 2 holds on the starboard side. The second torpedo struck about 10ft abaft the engine room. En route from Charleston, South Carolina, *Benjamin Smith* had been sailing alone to Takoradi, Gold Coast (now Ghana) via Trinidad with a full load of war supplies. Her complement of forty-three crew and twenty-three Navy armed guard abandoned ship by order of the Master, Captain George W Johnson, after the second torpedo hit. No lives were lost.

Allied sources reported that the crew abandoned ship in three lifeboats and one raft. The submarine surfaced near the raft and, covering the survivors with a machine gun, questioned them about their ship's cargo, location of convoys and other vessels. Bruns asked for the Master and when told that he was not on the raft, he gave them a course and distance to the nearest land and released them.

At 0410hrs *U-175* noted that the vessel was not sinking, so a third torpedo was fired into the port side amidships, whereupon she sank quickly by the stern.* It had been 1hr 40mins since the first torpedo hit and 40 minutes since the crew had abandoned ship. Bruns correctly estimated her at 7,000grt, length 140m, and then prepared to dive and depart the area.

At dawn the men in the raft were taken aboard the lifeboats and, after salvaging supplies, the raft was cast adrift. The motor lifeboat then towed the other two boats to Grand Drewrin, Ivory Coast, arriving safely the following day, 24 January 1943. Survivors were transported to Accra and then flown back to the US in military aircraft via Belem, Brazil, arriving 3 March. It should be noted the *Benjamin Smith* had just departed Marshall, Liberia, near Monrovia, carrying US Army cargo but without her scheduled escort. The US Army orders for her escort had been misdirected, so that the escort arrived in Marshall the day after *Benjamin Smith*'s departure and sinking, the misdirected orders contributing directly to her loss.

Bruns meanwhile arranged with BdU for a refuelling rendezvous on 30 January, for which BdU ordered him to proceed north. Although Bruns first headed west to clear the African coast, the boat was still well within range of shore-based aircraft. On 24 January at noon a 'Consolidated' (American-built PBY-5A-Vultee amphibious Catalina aircraft) sighted the boat, but *U-175*'s lookouts barely spotted the incoming aircraft before making an emergency crash dive, taking her to safety. Depth charges missed their target but fell in her swirling wake. A plane of the same type circled twice the next day, at 0400hrs and again at 0800hrs, and Bruns crashed dived each time, avoiding attack, and *U-175* resurfaced safely at 2000hrs.

Five days later, at 1457hrs on 30 January, about 240 miles due west of Bathurst,

---

* *Kriegstagebuch des Unterseebootes 'U-175'*, entries for 23 January 1943.

U-175 was heavily bombed and sustained severe, almost fatal damage, and this on the day she was scheduled for refuelling. She was forced to dive many times during the day to escape incessant air attacks, never suspecting that British Intelligence had decoded all radio messages and knew of the planned refuelling. Bruns finally reported that the 'same aircraft', a PBY 'Consolidated', took the boat completely by surprise, approaching from the starboard bow out of the overcast sky, probably guided by radar contact. Bruns had relied solely on his lookouts and his First Watch Officer, and the GSR Metox was not in use. *U-175* crash dived but had barely submerged when a shower of depth charges fell around her, one bouncing off the afterdeck as she went down. On crash diving IWO Ehrich, as officer of the watch on deck, ordered a course change that steered the U-boat straight into the depth charges. *U-175* went straight down by the stern at an angle of 40 to 50°, completely out of control, and to an incredible depth of 310m, over 100m deeper than the boat could safely go. Falling by the stern at least meant that the propellers prevented her going deeper. One torpedo man vividly remembers looking from the bow almost straight down into the stern as she plunged. Damage was extreme, almost fatal. Everything had broken loose. Tools, dishes, gear of all sorts poured aft in a deadly shower, causing further damage and numerous injuries to the crew. Leaks developed through the stuffing box and exhaust cut-out; acid from the batteries spilled and chlorine gas formed amidships, which the crew instantly sealed off with the watertight doors, isolating themselves in the bow and stern compartments. The lighting failed and the hydrophones and rudder were damaged. Dials, gauges and instruments were smashed and Number 4 fuel tank fractured, causing an extremely serious oil leak, which was exacerbated by their remoteness from base, and left a tell-tale trail on the surface, on which the bomber continued to drop depth-charges.

Even to regain a modicum of control, the air compressor had to expel part of the 40 tons water ballast in the diving tanks. The operating handle of the air compressor, however, had blown off, striking Chief Petty Officer Keutken on the forehead and knocking him briefly unconscious. Regaining consciousness, he grabbed the air compressor wheel, replaced it and managed to open the air compressors enough to force some water out of the tanks, at which point the boat shot of its own accord to the surface, her bow now protruding at a 50° to 60° angle out of the water. In short, he saved the boat and the lives of her crew.

With no control over his boat, Bruns could only hope that the aircraft had made off, but it was still circling and, apparently out of depth charges, began to machine-gun the boat. *U-175* tried to dive but it was impossible until the whole crew had rushed into the bow compartment. She then submerged, this time without being hit and under some degree of control. Two hours later another pattern of depth charges was heard in the distance, possibly dropped in the oil slick, but they were too far away to cause further damage. Allied Naval Intelligence simply reported that a Catalina had attacked a U-boat on 30 January in position 12°08'N 20°30'W, and at the time they were probably unaware that the attack had damaged *U-175* so seriously.

With the boat still 35° to 40° down by the stern, Bruns ordered cautious blowing out once more of a diving tank and at 2200hrs the boat was able to proceed on the surface. All hands worked without respite plugging leaks and repairing damage as far as humanly possible. No one could, however, repair the most serious damage. A depth charge had deflected off the upper railing to starboard, then sunk under the boat to explode on the port quarter, shattering the base of the port diesel engine. After this the engine generated unbearable vibrations and noise without generating power and so an alternative for turning the port propeller had to be found. This was done by cutting the connection between the damaged diesel and the port electric propeller motor, then connecting the port to the starboard electric propeller motor, so that both propeller motors ran off only the starboard diesel – a serious handicap in case of a sudden need to dive.

Bruns continued on course of 300°, slow on the starboard diesel, intent on making further necessary repairs. On coming to the surface very serious warping of the hull had been observed, as well as additional leaks. Two days later the batteries were still malfunctioning, and the boat continued to leave an oil slick.

Bruns' log entry for 30 January praised the entire crew for their calmness throughout the ordeal and the careful and expeditious manner in which they had made the urgent repairs. He singled out the Chief Petty Officer in the engine room, Karl Keutken, for special praise, not only for saving the boat on this perilous occasion, but also for his very quick reactions and abilities during nine other attacks.

Prior to the attack *U-175* had about 72 tons of fuel left, adequate to reach Lorient, but with Number 4 fuel tank cracked, the situation had become critical. On 2 February, off the Cape Verde Islands, Bruns estimated his fuel loss at 30cbm and signalled BdU, again requesting a rendezvous with a supply U-boat, being desperately in need of fuel and suffering from malfunctioning equipment. BdU responded favourably, giving an approximate date and position. The fuel leak was to be Bruns' major concern for the following thirteen days, although his log indicates there were numerous other major problems with defective batteries and the port diesel. Fortunately, however, there were no more enemy attacks.

Refuelling took place on 15 February about 29°N 190°30'W after *U-175* had passed through the Cape Verde Islands between Porta Praya and Mayo. She met the 'Milchkuh' ('milk cow', an almost reverent nickname), the Type XB *U-118*, in the early hours of the morning and by noon had received 25–30 tons of fuel through a 4in diameter hose. No exchange of visits between U-boats was permitted and only essential personnel were allowed on deck due to the danger of air attack. *U-175* also received new vacuum tubes (valves) for her GSR Metox receiver, and some very welcome fresh provisions. Refuelling completed, *U-175* departed for Lorient on a course of 010° until reaching the latitude of the base, then due east for the run in, again routinely submerging by day and running on the surface at night, arriving at Lorient safely on 24 February 1943.

7

U-175's Third and Final Patrol

The U-boat, barely afloat herself, found the entire town of Lorient virtually demolished, the target of extraordinarily heavy RAF air raids only ten days earlier. *U-175* crew's previous quarters, Saltzwedel Barracks, had been destroyed and Hundius Barracks badly damaged. As no other accommodation was available they, along with other U-boat crews in port, had to be quartered in the air raid shelters of Hundius Barracks, forty-eight men to a shelter.

The boat was docked first in Scorff Shelter for several days to have her periscope unshipped, then moved briefly to Shelter III and finally dry-docked in Shelter II, Dock 8, for more extensive repairs. Most importantly, the base of the port diesel motor was rebuilt and strengthened, damaged battery cells were replaced, electric motors repaired and the Junkers compressor again removed and overhauled.

While in port *U-175* ship's company, together with all available personnel of the 2nd and 10th flotillas, were taken on an excursion to Camp Lemp, near Pont Scorff, where Admiral Dönitz received and addressed them.

On arrival in Lorient *U-175*'s former First Watch Officer, Oberleutnant zur See Heinz Ehrich, was sent to the U-boat Commanding Officers' course and afterwards placed in command of *U-334*, a Type VIIC, amid his former crew's dire predictions he would not survive the command. The prediction proved correct. *U-334* was lost on 14 June 1943 in the North Atlantic, southwest of Iceland, a victim of the frigate HMS *Jed* and the sloop HMS *Pelican*, on her first patrol with her new commander. Leutnant zur See Wolfgang Verlohr, formerly Second Watch Officer on *U-175*, age 22, was promoted to First Watch Officer. He had joined the Navy in 1939 and had served as a midshipman on the Type VIIB *U-73* under Ktlt Helmut Rosenbaum, Ritterkreuz, when that U-boat sank five ships in North Atlantic convoys off Iceland.

A slightly embarrassing personnel problem arose when 32-year-old Leutnant zur See der Reserve Paul Möller joined as Second Watch Officer just before departure. As oldest man in the crew he had more experience than Verlohr, having come from the merchant fleet after serving in the Hansa Line, Deutsche DG, reportedly as master.

Commander Kapitänleutnant Heinrich Bruns, aged 31 years, married, with two young daughters, was highly regarded by his crew as a 'humane officer' with more concern for his immediate command and men than the niceties of military protocol. His crew say he was strict but fair, dedicated to running an efficient, contented boat,

Comparison of Type VII and Type IX U-boats, with the smaller Type VII (*U-1064*) moored outside *U-861*. This photograph was taken at Trondheim in 1945. (*Imperial War Museum*)

and quietly managed to keep all his best men. He even avoided recommendations for promotions that might result in unwanted transfers, thereby treading a fine line between recognition of meritorious conduct and the morale of his crew. Certainly, Maschinenobergefreighter Walter Schroeder was one who merited a promotion, probably withheld to retain him in *U-175*.

The British evaluation of Bruns as 'too ambitious and incautious'*, contradicts *U-175* KTB entries which show him displaying caution and superior leadership at sea in frequently dangerous situations. Neither would ten sinkings, a total of 40,602grt, have been possible without a crew's unswerving loyalty and teamwork under effective leadership.

BdU, which analysed a commander's logbook, and thus his conduct of a patrol on return to port, gave Bruns two very complimentary judgements. After the first patrol of *U-175* an Oberleutnant and Adjutant to Admiral Dönitz wrote:

> The first undertaking of the commander with a new boat. Through good use of the many chances of winning against little resistance, the commander accomplished very good beginner's results.
>
> Misses were not always attributable to failures in the torpedoes. When, for instance, as on 28 September at 10.57pm a shadow comes into view and at 11pm by bright moonlight the boat dives to attack, the shooting mechanisms cannot be as accurate and the miss cannot be described as 'unexplained', or more accurately, as a 'failure'. The shooting mechanism ran purely on guesswork.
>
> A well led expedition.

On reviewing *U-175*'s KTB from her second patrol, the Chief of Operations Department wrote for Admiral Dönitz:

> This undertaking brought little comforting result on account of the lack of traffic in the area of operation. The U-boat commander took pains, sad to say without results, under difficult conditions at Dakar and Freetown. The assignment at Dakar can now be considered a poor choice [by BdU]. At Freetown he faced heavy air cover as well as no [enemy] traffic.
>
> The assignment was hampered from the outset by problems with exhaust valves, which led to the cancelling of a convoy operation on 26 December, and the aircraft attacks on 30 January made the problems more serious. Several disappointments with neutrals were a shame. The commander needs more luck next time.
>
> Results: One steamship 7,000grt sunk.
>
> (Signed: Chief of Operations Department)

When dry docking work was completed, *U-175* returned briefly to Shelter III, then finally back to Scorff Shelter again. Her scheduled date of 4 April for work to be completed was extended until 10 April, when time being of the essence, it was crucial that she should begin her third patrol. On 9 April, the day before departure, a muster revealed two midshipman absent without leave. On return they were punished with extra sea watches.

At 1800hrs on 10 April 1943, despite the fact that repairs were still incomplete, *U-175* departed Lorient armed with fourteen electric and eight air-propelled

---

* NID 03262/43 – CB 04051 (68) Interrogation of Survivors *U-175*, p 20, June 1943.

torpedoes. The space which had been occupied by a fifteenth electric torpedo on her second patrol was now filled with cases of lemons. Even more unusually, dock workers had to remain on board trying to finish repairs until *U-175* reached the 100-fathom Isobath. They then returned in the escorting vessels.

Accompanied by *U-226* (Kptlt Borchers), the usual 'Speerbrecher' and three A/S vessels, *U-175* passed between Île de Groix and Îles de Glenan, parting company with workmen, escorts and consort at 2010hrs. Then followed the routine of travelling on the surface only at night. The boat dived twice on Metox's picking-up aircraft radar impulses, and daytime speed was occasionally reduced in order to recharge batteries on the surface. By 15 April *U-175* was considered beyond the range of shore-based patrolling aircraft. Although not informed, the crew surmised they were bound for North America. On this patrol they had been ordered northwest instead of south.

Early the following day, on 16 April, BdU reported a convoy (HX-233) in Grid Square BD9345, and gave orders to attack. *U-175* proceeded to chase at full speed. Finally, after ten hours without let up, at 2331hrs on 16 April Bruns sighted HX-233 ahead in Square BE4542. Shortly after reporting this sighting, he signalled BdU again to the effect that a 'destroyer' had located him but that no attack had followed. Altering to a parallel course, *U-175* ran full speed all night, shadowing at maximum visual range to reach an attack position ahead of the convoy. In the early morning hours of 17 April Bruns submerged.

Meanwhile, *U-175*'s report to BdU had been picked up by *U-382* (OL Leopold Koch) and *U-628* (Kptlt Heinrich Hasenschar), both of which now homed in to attack HX-233.

8

The Grey Wolves Gather

Three U-boats, other than *U-175*, were involved in the attack on Convoy HX-233, and their deployments during the early months of 1943 are described in this chapter.

U-262

U-262, commanded by the experienced, Berlin-born Kptlt Heinz Franke, Ritterkreuzträger, who had previously served in the battleship *Gneisenau*, departed La Pallice U-boat base at 2300hrs on 27 March 1943 escorted by the customary Sperrbrecher for four hours. The following day the U-boat had to return to La Pallice for emergency repairs and did not get away again until 1815hrs on 6 April. While crossing the Bay of Biscay aircraft repeatedly attacked *U-262*, but alert lookouts sighted them in time to crash dive and avoid being hit.

U-262 was no stranger to the North Atlantic battlefield. She had sunk the Norwegian-manned corvette *Montbretia* (ex-*Rose*) southwest of Iceland from Convoy ONS-144 on 18 November 1942, and the 7,178grt US-built British freighter *Ocean Crusader* on her first patrol. On 6 February 1943 she sank the Polish manned *Zagloba*, 2,864grt, from Convoy SC-118 and participated in battles around convoys MKS-31 and SK-140.

Before his departure from La Pallice, Kptlt Franke had been given a sealed envelope to be opened only on receipt of a pre-arranged code word, 'Elster' ('magpie'). *U-262* would be a back-up boat to one dispatched earlier, also with 'special orders'. This boat may have been *U-376* (Marks), because Franke reports on 8 April receiving a signal from BdU ordering *U-262* along with three other boats to Grid Square AK88 (mid-Atlantic), while (*U-376*) 'Marks is to follow special orders'. Two days later, on 10 April, *U-376* was bombed and sunk in the Bay of Biscay west of Nantes.

Franke was steering west and in Grid Square BE7553 on 15 April 1943 when BdU signalled at 2315hrs: 'Sonderaufgabe Stichwort Elster durchfuhren!' ('Execute special mission Magpie.') On 10 April at 0200hrs Franke had reported hearing distant depth charges and had prudently remained submerged for three hours. The distant bombing may well have been the demise of *U-376*. Franke's orders on 15 April meant he was to replace rather than simply 'back up' Marks and *U-376* on the special mission.

On 14 April BdU had signalled U-boats at sea, including *U-262*, that it expected the German blockade runner *Silvaplana*, disguised as the Dutch *Irene* or the Norwegian *Høegh Silverstar* or *Reinholt*, in Grid Square BE9527. If sighted they were to report her immediately and operate with her. *Silvaplana* was a prize captured by the German commerce raider *Atlantis* east of Australia on 10 September 1941 and dispatched to France with a prize crew, arriving in Boulogne on 17 November 1941. A modern (built 1938) Norwegian motorship, she was engaged in blockade running thenceforth, arriving at Kobe, Japan, on 20 December 1942 and sailing for France exactly a month later on 20 January 1943.

The British minelayer HMS *Adventure*, dispatched to Gibraltar with a cargo of mines for laying in the Mediterranean, was homeward bound to the UK when she sighted *Silvaplana*, disguised as the Dutch '*Irene*', 275 miles west of Vigo, Spain, under Captain Wendt. Although still miles away *Irene* signalled *Adventure* to be careful, as a submarine had been seen that morning. At 9,000yds Captain Bowes-Lyon, flashed '*Irene*' the International Code signal, 'WBA' ('Stop. Do not lower boats. Do not radio. Do not scuttle. If you disobey I shall open fire.') Within five minutes 158 men had abandoned ship in seven boats and two floats, leaving the vessel afire with scuttling charges set.

Adventure's commander collected the survivors, many of whom, according to Brice, proved to be submariners en route home from the Far East, their capture eliminating two complete U-boat crews from the Battle of the Atlantic. According to Rohwer, however, it is difficult to account for 'two complete U-boat crews' returning from Japan as early as mid-April 1943, since the first U-boat going to Japan (to be

Kapitänleutnant Heinz Franke, just
after being awarded the Knight's Cross
(Ritterkreuz) on 8 December 1943. The
strains of command are all too evident.
(Fregattenkapitän à. D. Heinz Franke)

transferred to the Japanese Navy) was *U-511*, which arrived on 7 August 1943 in Kure and was commissioned as *Ro-500* on 16 September 1943, and the first German U-boats of group 'Monsun' arrived in Penang in October and November 1943. The loss of blockade runners *Silvaplana* and *Regensburg* (the latter intercepted by the cruiser HMS *Glasgow* about the same time) came shortly before Germany was forced to end its use of surface blockade runners about mid-1943.

U-262 was close to *Silvaplana* in Grid Square BE9253 and went full speed to intercept. However, at 1235hrs, in Grid Square BE9259, she was forced to crash dive twice by an aircraft described as a four-engined bomber. Possibly the air attack delayed her timely arrival to assist *Silvaplana*, which BdU signalled had been attacked by a cruiser and probably sunk. *U-262* arrived at the scene of the sinking at 0400hrs next day seeking survivors, but found nothing. Shortly afterwards aircraft forced her to crash dive again. On surfacing she sighted *U-176* (Dierksen) on the same mission, who reported seeing an explosion the evening before. Later that day *U-262* sighted empty lifeboats and wreckage. At 2302hrs BdU ordered the U-boats to break off the operation, and *U-262* to steer for Grid Square AK75 in mid-Atlantic. Next morning a flying boat (probably a Catalina or Sunderland) caught *U-262* on the surface and dropped nine depth charges, but the boat managed to crash dive to safety.

When Franke opened his sealed instructions on the morning of 15 April, he found himself ordered to operate off Prince Edward Island's North Cape, where he was to make contact with prisoner of war escapees and rescue them. German officers in POW Camp 70, near Fredericton, New Brunswick, Canada, had planned to break out and work their way to the coast, cross the 14km-wide Northumberland Straits and reach North Cape, or North 'Point' as described in the *U-262* KTB, where they would be picked up by a U-boat. BdU had provided Franke with relevant nautical information, possible enemy counter-measures, and granted him a free hand to act at his own discretion, but they had not supplied any charts, only a map of North America. This would have been of only very limited use.

Franke was in an additionally awkward situation, having to report and shadow convoys sighted during this outward-bound voyage, without an attack order. Therefore, at 1710hrs on the same day he requested clarification of orders to attack shipping. At 1937hrs BdU radioed permission to attack as far west as Grid Square BB9999, the Canadian coastal zone, along with a message that a meeting with the supply submarine, *U-462* (Kptlt d R Vowe), had been arranged. These transmissions, intercepted by Convoy HX-233, indicated that U-boats were in the general vicinity of the convoy on 15 April.

The following morning, only eight hours later, at 0355hrs, *U-262* was running on the surface on both diesels at economical half-speed when lookouts sighted a 'shadow in 270°', identified as a 'destroyer' steering on a northeasterly course. A few minutes later three more shadows and in another 30 minutes six shadows, as well as the destroyer, could be identified. At 0434hrs Franke sent BdU a short signal, 'Convoy BD9345 – *U-262*'. At 0515hrs BdU ordered him to attack without waiting for reinforcements and cancelled the scheduled meeting with *U-462* for fuel replenishment.

At 0540hrs Franke contacted BdU confirming that: 'The convoy is now on a clear horizon, so that its ships rise well above it. I can now clearly make out, besides three convoy escorts, at least twelve large ships, among them a number of tankers in the middle of the convoy. However, I am now ahead of the forward destroyer escort at a distance of 5,000m. He must have seen or heard me, as he is coming straight at me. He keeps following me persistently, reducing the distance.' Suddenly at a range of 3,000m, the escort came barrelling in to attack as *U-262* crash dived. After nine minutes the destroyer began dropping eight well-placed depth charges, forcing the U-boat down deeper. The hydrophones indicated that two destroyers were overhead, but no further depth charges followed. By 0730hrs asdic pings were faint, and by 0800hrs propeller sounds could no longer be heard.

When reading Franke's KTB, it is easy to imagine the excruciatingly isolating silence of waiting for, and then feeling, the impact of dangerously accurate depth charges. After two hours of diligent manoeuvring, Franke's hopes had been shattered. The U-boat had just reached a prime attack position when her luck was reversed. The escort, indubitably intercepting all signals between Franke and BdU, knew a U-boat was near, and on making a positive contact simply zeroed in.

After waiting a further half hour, Franke came to periscope depth where he sighted the stern of a 'destroyer' 4,000m distant, motionless or moving only slightly. After one minute the escort turned towards *U-262* and Franke again crash dived deep. The escort remained to port with only a slight forward motion. The sound of a second propeller, a destroyer, could be heard to starboard but no depth charges were dropped. Around 1030hrs the first destroyer's propeller noises faded and vanished, and just after 1100hrs those of the second followed suit, but Franke remained deep. At 1315hrs he risked surfacing, and seeing no more of either the escorts or the convoy, admittedly with relief, he set a course of 240° away from the convoy and, on both diesels, steamed full ahead for Canada. At 1340hrs with course changed to 260°, Franke signalled BdU: 'Since 6am forced under by destroyers. Depth charges. Contact lost. Last position of the convoy BD9356, northeast course, 9 knots, twelve large ships identified. I am resuming westerly course – 100cbm [fuel]. – Franke'. *U-262* was underway to rescue German POWs on a prearranged date at a remote site off the Canadian coast.

*　　*　　*

Anyone familiar with the circumstances of German prisoner of war camps during both World Wars will be aware of Allied prisoners' underground activities and endless escape attempts, some popularised in Hollywood films, others described more accurately in print. German prisoners of war, first in England, later in Canada and finally in the United States, also engaged in such attempts and in a few instances actually succeeded, despite the remoteness of their homeland.

Senior German officers supervised escape plans, co-ordinated the organisation and arranged skilful forging of identity documents and the tailoring of civilian clothes. Cartographic groups provided detailed maps, and tunnelling groups the means of burrowing under and out of barbed wire compounds, with U-boat officers and crew particularly prominent in these activities from early on. Admiral Dönitz, recognising fully the advantages of regular contact with his men, devised a simple code to bypass censorship of letters to and from German prisoners of war. Repatriation of wounded and disabled prisoners provided yet another link in the chain, leading ultimately to co-ordinated plans between BdU and the POWs, so that escapees could rendezvous with U-boats off the Canadian coast for rescue.

Dönitz had also foreseen that the return of escaped prisoners from Canadian camps would force the Allies to divert considerable resources, while offering his men on both sides of the barbed wire tremendous encouragement by extricating invaluable, trained personnel at a time of increasing losses. Always a propaganda triumph of unprecedented proportions, an escape could also become a potential source of vital intelligence.

KKpt Peter 'Ali' Cramer, commanding officer of *U-333* temporarily assigned to BdU whilst recovering from severe wounds received at sea, supervised the development of these plans and by 27 March 1943 arranged that *U-262* would depart from La Pallice, France, with the secret envelope. The boat was actually en route to the Gulf of St. Lawrence for a rendezvous with escaped German POW's when she encountered Convoy HX-233.

U-262's KTB for 16 February to 25 May 1943, including the six attached track charts and extracts of radio traffic, show that *U-262* operated off 'North Point' (North Cape), Prince Edward Island, Canada, for some time. Because the spring ice in the St Lawrence River and Gulf tends to accumulate at the narrow, congested, 56-mile wide Cabot Straits, Franke faced a formidable barrier in his only access to the proposed rendezvous site. There followed a little-known, successful epic of under-ice navigation, perhaps the first for a submarine. Despite substantial inadvertent damage, including the jamming shut of three torpedo tube doors, which left the U-boat virtually defenceless, *U-262* reached and operated for several days within sight of North Cape, but to no avail. Despite favourable weather conditions, no escaped prisoners appeared, and at noon on 6 May *U-262* finally withdrew. Franke wrote in his KTB: 'It is such a shame that I must return without success'. As Professor Hadley agreed: 'It is one of the finest failed operations on record.' The reason for the 'failure', as described by KKpt Peter Cramer, was that following a previously unsuccessful breakout attempt, the Royal Canadian Mounted Police suspected something still in the wind at Camp 70 and tightened security. The planned escape never took place.

After refuelling and receiving fresh stores on 18 May from 'Milch Kuh' *U-459* (KKpt z u v Wilomowitz-Moellendorf) in Grid Square BD9739, *U-262* returned safely to La Pallice, France, arriving on 25 May.* BdU's evaluation of Franke's logbook from 16 February to 25 May does not mention his encounter with Convoy HX-233 but commends him as follows:

---

* Franke went on to command one of the new Type XXI boats, *U-2502*, built in Hamburg by Blohm & Voss, which he had to surrender at Horten, Norway on 29 May 1945. She was taken to England and sunk at sea in Operation Deadlight.

The special assignment was well considered and correctly understood by the commander. The difficulties encountered on account of ice were extreme but energetically overcome through well-thought out countermeasures (including diving under ice!). The expected outcome, without any blame falling on the commander, was not reached.

. . . Otherwise, no further comments.

(signed by) Chief of Operations for BdU

U-628

U-628, the only U-boat to launch a successful attack on Convoy HX-233, departed Brest at 0435hrs on 8 April 1943 under escort, proceeding independently from 2018hrs on course 270° with both diesels running at economical speed. *U-628*, under her experienced commander, Kptlt Hasenschar, was also no stranger to the Atlantic battle having already operated against Convoys ONS-154 and ON-166.

Shortly after her escort left, *U-628*'s deadly game of hide and seek with enemy aircraft began. She had to crash dive repeatedly, but with the help of a new radar detector and alert lookouts she avoided being hit. At noon on 15 April BdU signalled a new course, and *U-628* cleared the Bay of Biscay for mid-Atlantic.

At 0520hrs next day BdU transmitted Franke's sighting of a convoy in Grid Square BD9345, heading northeast at 9 knots, and ordered Hasenschar (*U-628*), Bruns (*U-175*), Borchers, (*U-226*), Koch (*U-382*), and Looks (*U-264*) to proceed at full speed to intercept the convoy while ordering Franke (*U-262*) to attack.

U-628, proceeding on the surface, reached the designated rendezvous without sighting the convoy or receiving any further information about Franke. Then, just

Kapitänleutnant Heinrich Hasenschar, commanding officer of *U-628,* torpedoed S/S *Fort Rampart. (Gustav Brückmann)*

before midnight, Hasenschar heard Bruns (*U-175*) report a destroyer in (BE?)4542 and the following entries appear in Kptlt Hasenschar's logbook for 17 April:

0307hrs BE4288:	Dived to listen. Weak sounds in 130°–160°.
0714hrs—4614:	2 loud detonations (torpedoes or depth charges) heard, so must be near the convoy.
0724hrs	At 190° a destroyer sighted. A short time later *to the south* several large shadows. *U-628* sights the convoy, which steers 50–60° astern of the destroyer.
0753hrs	Short Signal to BdU: 'Holding convoy contact – *U-628*.'

With little time left till dawn, immediate attack is begun. I have managed, close to the forward flank escort, to penetrate unnoticed between the two flank destroyers, which zigzag sharply about 5000m from the flank of the convoy. The convoy itself travels in a wide formation of columns 2 or 3 ships deep. At least 15 very large, heavily laden ships could be made out. Presumably there are more. Between the ships or at a slight distance to the side, 2 further escorts visible. I had intended making a double torpedo spread at each of 2 overlapping freighters out of Tubes I and III, but due to a BÜ-failure must release manually without proper aim. Released. Miss.

Round from Tubes II and IV at 2 deep-lying, middle-sized freighters. Turned about for a stern shot out of Tube V at the next following freighter – after 2min 55sec a hit on forward freighter, 2secs later the explosion is heard perfectly within the boat. After about 3min., which means a running time of 4½ mins, the last shot hit on the last freighter torpedoed. Forward edge of the bridge. Bright flash, otherwise no direct effect to be seen. [NB. a puzzling entry, possibly a premature explosion in the water, as no other ship in the convoy was hit, and *Fort Rampart* was torpedoed only once, aft, at this point. See also BdU's evaluation at end of this section regarding other questionable entries by Hasenschar]. The first ship hit [*Fort Rampart*] set out a white topmast light.

0815hrs Sq 4617:	It has meanwhile got very light, in spite of which it has been possible for me to travel unseen, on the surface, to get back outside the escort screen again. It is impossible for me to understand that the 5–6000m distant destroyers, [cutters *Spencer* and *Duane*] which can be made out with the naked eye, do not see me. I travel away in SW direction. It is so light now I have decided to dive so as to not further risk being seen. Dived. In the periscope I observe a ship sinking by the stern. I order 2 torpedoes loaded, and travel submerged to the ship, lying

motionless in the water [*Fort Rampart*]. During the run along to this point, the hydrophones record from 3 different directions the sounds of destroyers. Nothing to be seen in the periscope.

1130hrs Sq 4615: A shot out of Tube II, depth 7m – after 20secs a hit midships, followed by a high, wide plume. Ship rears up in the middle and breaks through. Stern flooded quickly. Freighter estimated 5000grt, British, 2 stump masts, heavily laden, 5 hatches. Also a signal mast on the bridge with 'NSA'. Armament astern and midships, one deck gun each 7.5cm. On the stern, elevated, quadruple anti-aircraft guns. On the bridge one 3.7cm. gun each, the same on the bridge decks. Deck load lumber, ca. 8m long spars, probably for cellulose. Crew had already left the ship.

HMS *Offa*, an 'O' class destroyer, commissioned 1941, which carried a complement of 175. (*Imperial War Museum*)

Shortly after the shot: 'a destroyer comes into view, approaching the wreck at high speed. A few minutes later two more destroyers approach from different directions, apparently a search group that waited just out of sight till the ship had been hit. Possibly the same group reported by Looks (*U-264*).' Anticipating an attack to be hopeless with only one torpedo in a tube, Hasenschar dived deep. He had correctly deduced the ships to be destroyers. They were a search group, from the 3rd Support Group of British destroyers, consisting of HM Ships *Offa*, *Penn*, *Panther* and *Impulsive*, which had just arrived to reinforce HX-233's Escort Group. *Offa* had detected the U-boat on asdic.

Two destroyers came gradually nearer, taking sonar bearings. After some poorly aimed depth charges, at 1249hrs and again 1309hrs two very accurate patterns, each of about fifteen almost simultaneously exploding depth charges, badly damaged the U-boat, which remained deeply submerged and silent. After the destroyers finally left, *U-628* proceeded underwater southwards, away from the area of the convoy.

Once under way, Hasenschar sighted through the periscope the fore part of a wreck, surrounded by empty lifeboats and wreckage in a huge field of driftwood. He announced that 'We are going to shell her with the deck gun', surfaced. The gun crew fired 130 rounds from the 3.4in (8.8mm) deck gun into *Fort Rampart*'s battered remains, setting fire to her bridge area and wood deck cargo, but the ship's bow remained on an even keel and stubbornly afloat. At noon, after submitting the routine daily report, Hasenschar departed on his prescribed westerly course.

U-628 later joined the new wolf pack 'Specht' which comprised seventeen U-boats and which attacked Convoy ONS-5 with considerable success; during this spell *U-628* sank one ship and damaged another. She arrived back in Brest and was safely moored in her bunker at 1946hrs on 19 May 1943 after a patrol of five weeks and 6993.5 nautical miles, 522.7 of them under water.

BdU's evaluation of Hasenschar's logbook during his mission 8 April to 19 May 1943 contains the following passages:

> The patrol brought the boat onto three convoys. From 16.–17. 04. the boat operated exceptionally well against the 'Franke Convoy', made contact quickly and immediately decided that a night attack was the only chance . . .
> The observation of a hit on 5 May after a 7–9min run is very questionable, because the steering mechanism [of a torpedo] normally functions at most for seven minutes . . . The reported sinkings are therefore regarded as questionable.

Chief of Operations for BdU

Of his six reported sinkings, Hasenschar is credited with only three: a freighter (considering its designation and place on the list, *Fort Rampart*), a steamer and a corvette.

*   *   *

Fort Rampart, photographed here in New York with a deck load of lumber, just prior to joining Convoy HX-233. *(The Steamship Historical Society of America)*

U-226

U-226 was a Type VIIC, 750-ton U-boat built at Germania Werft, Kiel, and commissioned on 1 August 1942. She sailed her second patrol under the command of Kptlt Rolf Borchers, departing from Lorient at 1755hrs on 10 April 1943 in company with *U-175* (Kptlt Bruns). After their usual 'Sperrbrecher' escort departed, the boats separated to proceed westward alone.

U-226 cleared the Bay of Biscay on 15 April, arriving in Grid Square BE2648 by midnight. At 0624hrs on 16 April Borchers received BdU's message that Franke had sighted a convoy (HX-233) at 0434hrs, steering a northeasterly course, in Grid Square BD9345, southwest of *U-226*'s position. BdU ordered Borchers to join Franke against the convoy 'with the utmost speed'. At 0350hrs *U-226* received Franke's message, sent to BdU at 1340hrs, that he had been attacked by a 'destroyer' and lost contact, giving the convoy's last known position as Square BD9356, course 090°.

At 0650hrs on 17 April BdU sent a short signal that *U-382* (Koch) had sighted the convoy in Square BE4537, and since Franke had been driven away, it had become 'Koch's Convoy'. Borchers was in Square BE1999, en route to join. At 0737hrs *U-226* sighted HX-233 at 230° in wide formation in Square BE4585. Borchers noted a puzzling 30 miles' difference between his reckoning of the position and *U-382*'s. More importantly, as it was rapidly becoming daylight, Borchers planned an immediate submerged attack and realised that there was no time to inform BdU he had found the convoy. *U-226* dived to 30m seeking an attack position close to the convoy. On returning to periscope depth to attack, the boat lost her trim momentarily and came to the surface.* As Borchers crash dived deep, he fully expected an immediate barrage of depth charges, which failed to materialise, but he had lost an excellent attack opportunity. To foil an anticipated heavy counter attack *U-226* released three 'Bolde' – hydrogen bubbles – which effectively misled the escorts into depth charging the decoys. The U-boat counted nine patterns between 0856hrs and 0900hrs, fortunately at some distance off toward the convoy. This would have been the initial attack on *U-175* which led to her loss.

U-226 was certainly detected about 0900hrs on 17 April by asdic from the corvette HMS *Bergamot*, one of the 'two destroyers' overhead which stopped, listened, and then began to attack. By 1330hrs *U-226* had recorded fifty-three depth charges, some close enough to cause significant damage to the boat, particularly to diving tank III and the magnetic compass, as well as doing considerable minor damage. The boat began sinking by the stern, and Borchers ordered diving tank III blown out in order to right her; this the escorts' sounding apparatus immediately picked up, and depth charging began anew. The boat remained perfectly silent and by 1400hrs the sounds of listening devices were fading while depth charges could be heard at an ever increasing distance, but even at 2318hrs a series of depth charges at 6-minute intervals could still be heard making it unsafe to surface.‡

By shortly before midnight more than ninety depth charges had been counted, possibly some of them echoes, and Borchers began repairs to the damage that *U-226* had sustained. The magnetic compass was malfunctioning due to water penetration; some of the air valves were not working and a few others had minor damage, and available air was down to 75kg. (Could *U-226* have suffered concomitant damage during *U-175*'s sinking? There are indications she could have been close enough.) At midnight Borchers surfaced to find his topside torpedo supply and protective coverings in good order – a comforting discovery. Just four minutes later lookouts spotted a shadow astern and since the vessel did not pursue him, and in spite of bright moonlight, Borchers risked heading toward it, and determined at close range that it was 'quite a large, damaged steamer, whose crew have not left'. The U-boat, still replenishing her air supply and charging the batteries, slowly passed by first without attempting to sink her.

---

* This was the 'wreck' sighted and reported by the Chief Officer and lookout on the Norwegian tanker *Stiklestad*, position 92 in the convoy.

‡ This is difficult to explain, as it is not supported in the Allied records.

A few minutes later Borchers signalled BdU he had been depth charged but would resume pursuit. At 0115hrs BdU signalled that *U-614* (Sträter) had reported aircraft and that 'destroyers' had forced him to dive at 0027hrs; they also relayed that the last convoy sighting had been at 2220hrs in Grid Square BE2795 steering 20°, and that a signal from *U-382* (Koch) suggested night attack might be possible.

At 0225hrs *U-226* received BdU's message, released 1301hrs the previous day, 17 April, informing the 'boats in Koch's Convoy' that:

1) Because of the long days by all means make use of daylight for underwater attacks. 2) For the night arrange it so that at the beginning of darkness the boats are ahead of the convoy in order to attack in a pack, as simultaneous, surprise attacks from a number of boats offer the best chance of success. Beginning tomorrow strong resistance is to be expected, therefore operate with all energy and at every chance today and in the coming night.

At last, Borchers was able to direct his attention to the still floating wreck of *Fort Rampart*. At 0333hrs he fired a torpedo, recording a hit; 18 minutes later a second torpedo hit, and a few minutes later a third. Shortly afterwards BdU ordered: 'Break off the operation on 18.04. before noon', with Borchers to steer for Grid Square BD51, the same as Hasenschar. Borchers reported the sinking of a '7,000 tonner' and confirmed that he had 95cbm of fuel remaining. *U-226* continued operations, arriving back in St Nazaire at 1845hrs on 17 May 1943, only to be lost on her following patrol in the North Atlantic off Newfoundland to the Royal Navy sloops *Starling, Woodcock* and *Kite*. BdU awarded *U-226* credit for sinking one 'damaged, 1/2 ship, 3,500grt,' and gave Borchers' patrol the following assessment on 17 May:

An unusually advantageous occasion to attack was lost [17 April] due to a mechanical failure in the steering mechanism of the diving equipment. The commander should have tried *sooner* after the sound detection and depth charging [ceased] to come to periscope depth to investigate. The sinking of the damaged ship was a consolation.

From 05.05. till 06.05 the boat operated in the Group 'Fink' on the 'Hasenschar's Convoy' and made contact quickly. An attack opportunity could not be reached, however, as the boat was forced by destroyers and depth charge attacks to dive deep. The failure and damage to [vital equipment] along with a low fuel supply plagued the commander, who had to break off the operation.

The commander conducted his boat properly under the circumstances and, through valuable experiences against strong air and destroyer offensives as well as the sinking of a damaged ship, has completed a satisfactory mission.

Chief of Operations Department

9

The Battle of Convoy HX-233 and the Loss of U-175

As far as anyone from the Allied side knew until recently, there were two or three, perhaps four, U-boats deployed against Convoy HX-233 between 16 and 18 April 1943. BdU's Kriegstagebuch and signal files reveal, however, that there were an astonishing eight U-boats swirling around the convoy. All outbound, they included *U-175, U-226, U-262, U-264, U-358, U-382, U-614* and *U-628*. The Allies lost only one vessel, *Fort Rampart*, at dawn on 17 April. Later the same morning the Allies sank *U-175*.

HF/DF bearings and Submarine Reports on 15 April, ignored as too distant, should have alerted the escort commander in US Coast Guard cutter *Spencer* that at least one U-boat (*U-262*) could be steering to intercept the convoy. At 0340hrs the following day, while maintaining escort position ahead of the convoy, *Spencer* received a radar response on an unidentified object bearing 150° at 7,100yds, and proceeded full speed to investigate but then lost contact at 3,200yds, as the submarine dived. A few minutes later she delivered an attack of six Mark VI and five Mark VII depth charges on the suspect. A box search followed, and with contact regained at 1,500yds she fired eight rounds of mousetrap without effect.* A second mousetrap barrage again brought no result and, although a dubious oil slick was noted, all three attacks were classed negative.

Franke (*U-262*) reported a similar attack commencing at 0545hrs German time, with repeated depth charges forcing him to stay submerged until after noon and making him lose touch with the convoy. HMCS *Wetaskiwin*, which joined *Spencer* in the search for *U-262*, would have been the 'second destroyer' in Franke's report, in an attack which was much more effective than the escorts realised. Lacking further contact, by 0234pm, both escorts left the scene on evasive courses, rejoining the convoy at 1530hrs, in position 45°49'N 24°15'W, as the U-boat departed, on a course that would take her to Canada.

Next morning, on 17 April, at 0412hrs *Spencer*, on station 'Able' in the convoy

---

* An American innovation similar to the hedgehog battery of twenty-four 65lb spigotted bombs, but firing four to eight rocket-propelled bombs from a fore deck projector.

The tanker *G Harrison Smith*. She delivered 125,392 barrels of pool gas to Bowling on the Clyde after occupying convoy position 031 and being the target of the aborted attack by *U-175*. (*The Steamship Historical Society of America*)

The US Coast Guard cutters *Spencer* (foreground) and *Duane* searching and listening astern of Convoy HX-233 after the second depth charge attack. (*US National Archives*)

van, obtained a radar contact bearing 092° at 13,200yds, in position 47°04N 22°06'W. Thirty-six minutes later she sighted a 'dark object dead ahead', then obtained a sound echo bearing 089°, but lost radar and visual contact five minutes later at 2,100yds when the U-boat submerged. Joined by HMS *Dianthus*, *Spencer* dropped two Mark 7 depth charges in position 47°10'N 22°12'W, one of which failed to explode.

The contact could not have been *U-175*, which was then only just in sight, and Borchers did not arrive until an hour later. Possibly it was Koch, whose sighting Borchers received without details at 0650hrs German time. Hasenschar was certainly not under attack, but he did report hearing 'two loud detonations over water' shortly before he torpedoed *Fort Rampart*, from inside the convoy screen at about 05553hrs Greenwich time.

The explosion aboard *Fort Rampart* woke the author, off watch and asleep in his bunk in *G Harrison Smith*. Rushing on deck, he saw *Fort Rampart* showing a red light ('I have been torpedoed') and drifting rapidly astern of the convoy. The *G Harrison Smith* was by then the largest tanker in the US merchant fleet, having survived the slaughters in the Caribbean and off the North American coast a year earlier, and her luck seemed to be holding. The torpedo had narrowly missed her, hitting the *Fort Rampart* in the next column, which, having been astern out of position, had become an exposed target. A search in *U-628*'s logbook reveals, interestingly, that Hasenschar identified none of the tankers in the convoy, and it is inconceivable he would have targeted a 7,000grt freighter if he had seen a 12,000grt oil tanker abeam of her.

Although virtually impossible to deduce exactly which ship besides *Fort Rampart* Hasenschar saw on the surface in the uncertain light of the dawn, it is clear from her logbook data that *U-628* was well inside the escort screen when her torpedo struck the freighter in the starboard after peak. The Master reported *Fort Rampart* in position 47°28'N 22°00'W and no one saw the torpedo's track in the grey, overcast, dawn. She was lead ship in the first column, and *G Harrison Smith* the lead ship in the second column at that point.

When the corvette *Arvida* reported that a vessel (*Fort Rampart*) had been torpedoed, *Spencer* went to screen the corvette while she carried out rescue operations in position 47°20'N 22°11'W. At 0754hrs, after screening *Arvida* but meanwhile never sighting *U-628* on the surface, *Spencer* went full speed to rejoin the convoy. As she caught up, then passed ahead of the convoy to take up her station, she surprised *U-175* preparing to attack.

Unknowingly, *U-175* was carrying out, exactly, BdU's orders issued later that day to all U-boats operating against Convoy HX-233. The message, dated 1301hrs 17 April 1943, urged the full use of the long daylight hours for submerged attacks. It was sent just after *U-175* was sunk and received by the U-boats at 0225hrs the following morning.

*   *   *

In the early hours of 17 April *U-175* submerged well ahead of the convoy. At 0830hrs Bruns gave the order to man battle stations. He had observed a 'destroyer' (probably *Bergamot*) astern of his position, but through his periscope had also spotted a larger tanker as lead ship in the second port column. The *G Harrison Smith*, 11,752grt, was to pass down his starboard beam, but was then about 4,000yds distant. He announced 'That is the ship I want!' and gave the order to prepare to fire a spread of three torpedoes.

U-175 remained at periscope depth, awaiting the convoy. Torpedo man Mechanikergefreiter Peter Wannemacher, after entering the firing data into the Torpedo

A depth charge in flight from K-gun on *Spencer*. The convoy can be seen in the background. (*US National Archives*)

Schuss Empfänger (computer) as ordered, was waiting for the expected final order to fire manually, when, suddenly, the soundman announced: 'Propeller noises in 120°!'

The noises came closer, ever closer, and finally, as *Spencer* approached, so loud that their 'swish, swish, swish' was audible to all hands, directly over the U-boat. Only Bruns continued to ignore them, to his peril, so intent was he on attack. The First Watch Officer's recommendation they wait for darkness went unheeded.

Spencer, coming up to her position ahead of the convoy, established a sound contact on *U-175*, bearing 040°, 1,500yds, then bearing 245°, 500yds distant in position 47°58'N 21°12'W. The hammering pings of her Asdic, along the entire length of the boat's hull, finally woke Bruns to his danger. Within seconds of his order to fire,

Depth charge detonation and a water spout rise from the depths astern of *Spencer*. The depth charge racks are shown clearly in this photograph. *(US National Archives)*

Bruns broke off the attack and ordered: 'Absolute silence and dive!'

It was too late. At that moment, 0950hrs, *Spencer* obtained a firm contact and attacked with eleven depth charges set between 50ft and 100ft (mean depth 85ft). They detonated above and below *U-175* sending the boat even deeper, by the bow, to 260m, already off the scale. To right *U-175* and prevent further diving Bruns' command was repeated through the boat, 'All men to stern!' But this was not so easy to achieve at 40° down by the bow. The men helped pull each other up into the stern compartment, until finally the boat lay horizontally, but at a calculated depth of 350m, possibly, as one survivor, Bickel, surmises, a record. The resultant damage was massive, devastating, decisive, and at least partially as follows:

- fractures to the air trunking;
- fracture of the pressure hull between forward torpedo tubes, causing water leaks;
- bilge pumps rendered inoperable;
- hydroplanes damaged;
- bolts of the diesel engines sheered;
- entire pressure hull strained;
- watertight bulkhead doors damaged;
- partial lighting failure;
- pressure, depth and other gauges smashed;
- wireless telegraphy equipment torn from bulkhead, held only by wiring.

As soon as control was partially regained, the crew began working frantically to halt the leaks. When leaks in the battery room were noted, and an attempt to pump the water out failed, a final attempt to blow out the diving tanks to surface was made. The boat rose as rapidly as she had plunged, just as *Spencer* delivered a second, devastating attack, almost directly under the bows of the approaching merchant ships.

Normally the convoy commodore would have ordered a 45° course alteration so the convoy would avoid the battle area, but there was no time as the merchant ships were too close, plodding stolidly forward at 9 knots, course 043°, directly over the disabled U-boat.

Meanwhile *Duane*, with medical facilities, had taken three injured crewman off *Fort Rampart*, via *Arvida* off the convoy's port quarter, and been ordered to replace *Spencer* at station 'Able' in the van. Five minutes later she was ordered to support *Spencer* and take over sound contact on *U-175*, astern of the last ship of the convoy as it passed over the stricken U-boat.

As the convoy proceeded overhead, *U-175* found herself in the gravest distress. The second attack had caused another pressure hull fracture, resulting in more leaks, and putting an electric motor out of action; in addition, the propeller driving wheel for the revolution-indicator was slipping, and several broken battery cells were generating poisonous chlorine gas.

Spencer again obtained a firm sound contact, bearing 042°, 1,700yds and fired a mousetrap pattern, without effect, then briefly lost contact as she coached *Duane* in to assist. No periscope was observed until the fatally damaged *U-175* broke the surface,

bearing 270°, 2,500yds from *Spencer* and about 2,500yds astern of the last ship in Column 8, the tanker *Santos*. *Spencer* immediately opened fire with every weapon that would bear. As she began to close, intending to ram, the crew of *U-175* could be seen rapidly abandoning ship, and Cdr Berdine altered course, exclaiming, 'I don't have to ram the damn thing'.*

Conditions on *U-175* had deteriorated to a critical point, leaving no alternative but to abandon ship. The commander, fully aware of the situation, ordered: 'All hands to the control room!' With all means of communication destroyed, only part of the crew heard Bruns' order, but Maschinenobergefreiter Werner Bickel, on duty in the control room, remembers also hearing Bruns' orders to 'Surface!' and 'Abandon'.

Immediately after giving the orders, Bruns himself proceeded up the conning tower as first man out to face the deadly onslaught of gunfire, his appearance on deck being his only means of letting the enemy know that his crew was going to abandon. The crew on board *Spencer*, however, was not quick enough to interpret his actions and Kptlt Heinrich Bruns was shot through the head and stomach, killed instantly, and subsequently so terribly mangled by large-calibre shells striking the tower where he fell that one of the last survivors out, sheltering on deck from the hail of gunfire, found himself on the captain's body and only able to recognise it by a distinctive ring on his finger. The first men to follow Bruns also faced heavy fire and a number were killed. Those who managed to abandon ship safely exchanged, with extreme reluctance, the illusionary safety of the wrecked and sinking U-boat for the trackless waste of the bitter-cold, forbidding, grey Atlantic.

Meanwhile, seven men were isolated in the bow torpedo compartment, forgotten. With communications destroyed, they had continued repairing damage, unaware that *U-175* had surfaced until they felt the typical motion of the boat in the gentle northeasterly swell and heard the surface waves against the hull. One of them went midships to determine what was happening but never returned. The others, hearing shooting, ran midships as well. The first man to leave was gone; seeing the hatch open and forgetting all else, he had jumped overboard. The remaining six reached the control room but were afraid to follow up the ladder due to the intensity of shell fire

Page opposite top: *U-175* surfaced and bracketed by shell fire, with the bows of *Spencer* in the foreground. Middle: *Spencer* approaching *U-175*. Bottom: *U-175* with the convoy in the background. *(US National Archives)*

* The seemingly irresistible impulse to ram defies logic, when gunfire and/or depth charges would effectively destroy a surfaced U-boat. Yet it often seems to have been the reaction of escort commanders, despite the obvious concomitant result that the ramming vessel will be heavily damaged, or, as in at least one case, eventually lost. Even the expert U-boat hunter, Captain F J Walker, RN, could not resist, as late as 24 June 1943, ordering the sloop *Starling* to ram the badly damaged and already sinking 'Milch Kuh' *U-119* in mid-Atlantic, badly damaging *Starling* in the process. Cdr Berdine doubtless recalled the earlier ramming of the *U-606*, brought to the surface by the Polish destroyer *Burza*, protecting Convoy ON-166. *Spencer's* sister ship *Campbell*, under Cdr James A Hirschfield, USCG, rammed the U-boat, whose hydroplanes sliced open *Campbell's* hull, flooding the engine-room (Price, p 9, et al), and she had to be towed to Newfoundland. Despite temporary repairs *Campbell* was out of service for a long period, thereby removing an urgently needed, superior class escort from the North Atlantic at a crucial juncture.

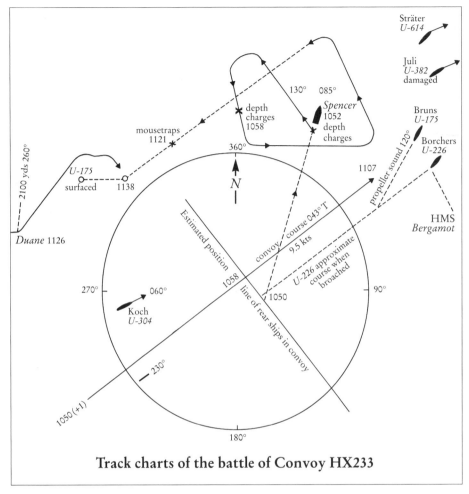

Track charts of the battle of Convoy HX233

and the audible hits on the conning tower. Five agreed that they could not dare expose themselves to the fire: Mechanikergefreiter Wannemacher countered that, 'Either we drown here or risk getting shot up there!' Of the next four men up, one was literally torn apart by the hail of 20mm gunfire; Matrosengefreiter Wilhelm Kistler was badly wounded in the left arm and cheek but survived. Matrosenobergefreiter Dieter Wolf fell back saying, 'They are still shooting up there', as Fähnrich zur See Hans Lohmeier above, aged 20 years, had his head blown away and his left side torn open, and two others above them were killed instantly by exploding 20mm shells. As the firing let up, the last two men, Wannemacher and Wolf, reached the shattered and wrecked conning tower and leaped into the sea on the port side away from *Spencer* and the source of gunfire, following Winkler, Schroeder and Bamberg into the cold North Atlantic.

On passing the control room, the torpedo man, last man out and overboard, noticed that all control valves had been fully opened to flood except for the bow, indicating a

The *Spencer* boarding party is lowered away. *(US National Archives)*

concern for any fellow crew members who might still have been in the forward compartment. The flooding also served as evidence that there was no thought of fighting back, and the firing from the convoy and escorts ceased shortly thereafter.

The weather, a vital aspect of all U-boat attacks but particularly against a strongly defended convoy, was particularly unfavourable for *U-175* and hardly conducive to a successful daylight U-boat attack, though the sea state was favourable for a successful rescue, with temperatures, although extremely low, significantly higher than along the usual convoy routes farther north, or in the Arctic. In addition, the sea was calm, almost oily.

Matrosenobergefreiter Herbert Schwarze reported that the men around him in the water were in despair, feeling that they were not likely to be picked up. Walter Schroeder heard the senior surviving officer, Leutnant zur See Paul Möller, saying the Lord's Prayer. A few seemed to smile, others prayed along, amid fading cries for help. Maschinenobergefreiter Wilhelm Flickinger, aged 21, badly wounded and bleeding profusely, quietly slipped under the water. Bootsmannsmaat Kurt Schlüter, aged 27, drowned with his wife's name on his lips. The day before departing Lorient he had received a telegram saying he was the father of a baby girl.

Schwarze had completely given up hope of rescue, when strong hands seized his

U-175 survivors in the sea between *Duane* and *Spencer*. A 20mm AA
gun is visible in the foreground. *(US National Archives)*

collar from behind and dragged him into *Spencer*'s boat along with five other men, all
officers. Also mistaken for an officer, Schwarze was taken aboard the cutter, where he,
Leutnant zur See Möller, Obersteuermann Helmut Klotzch and three others, had
their clothes removed before being given hot showers and then confined in the
officer's quarters. Before abandonment Senior Petty Officer Klotzsch, regarded by the
crew as arrogant, had ordered them not to cry for help or plead for assistance from
rescuers, but apparently he himself did, and several Allied reports, including
Heinemann's, speak of hysteria among the survivors.

Unaware that the crew had begun to abandon ship as soon as the U-boat surfaced,
both Coast Guard cutters and several convoy merchant ships opened fire with all
guns. Firing from both cutters was rapid, continuous and devastating, though despite
at least one or two 5in hits on the conning tower, the U-boat herself withstood the
battering very well indeed.

U-175's guns consisted of one 105mm (4.1in) deck gun forward, with a maximum elevation 50°, one 37mm AA deck gun aft, one 20mm anti-aircraft machine gun mounted on the 'Wintergarten' abaft the conning tower, and two portable 7.9mm machine guns. The bridge 20mm AA gun is cock-billed in the photograph and although the barrel was shipped, as was customary, no magazine or ammunition was present, making it impossible for *U-175* to have fired back; casualties on the cutter were caused by 'friendly fire' from gunners on the merchant ships.

Of the thirteen German lives lost, at least two were killed and fell back inside on following their commander out of the conning tower, while others were shot jumping overboard or after abandonment. Three dead were seen in the conning tower and went down with the boat. *Duane* personnel observed a further three bodies in the water during rescue operations. Others, possibly with injuries, simply gave up the struggle for life in the cold water and quietly drifted away.

A pulling boat was launched from *Spencer* with a trained boarding party to attempt salvage of the U-boat. The pulling boat was used because the motor boat had been damaged by shell fire and this substantially slowed the whole operation; it is possible that had the boarding party arrived earlier it might have gone below and been lost along with the sinking U-boat. On return from its aborted operation, the pulling boat was ordered to pick up the survivors and seven were found, some in the water and some on a raft dropped by *Duane*. One survivor remembers vividly the raft capsizing as he tried to clamber on and dragging him under until his lifejacket forced him to the surface and a comrade pulled him to safety. All men on the raft were put aboard *Spencer*. Meantime, screened by the corvette HMS *Dianthus*, other survivors were

Mastrosenobergefreiter Dieter Wolf supported by two young US Coast Guardsmen on the deck of *Duane*. Note the U-boat escape apparatus which doubled up as a life jacket on reaching the surface. *(US National Archives)*

hauled aboard the cutters by scrambling nets and bowline, including the wounded. Though one survivor complained that he was left in the water several hours, which at the time may well have seemed the case, the cutter log books show that the entire rescue took just under an hour. *Spencer*'s pulling-boat was lowered at 1215hrs and she was underway again at 1307hrs to catch up the convoy.

Once aboard the cutters, the cold and exhausted survivors, now prisoners of war, needed help to walk to an area of the deck where they could lie down. Next, wet clothing was removed with knives, which caused them a little apprehension, and then they were wrapped in soft, warm navy blankets, given coffee and freshly lit cigarettes. As soon as the prisoners were able, they were taken to a small room next to the crew's mess from where they watched the off-duty crew dine. The table was then cleared, spread with a clean, white tablecloth, replenished with food and the prisoners were invited to a feast. During the meal, however, a loud detonation shook the ship, and they found themselves reliving all their recent horrors, and with it, a loss of appetite. They imagined another U-boat attack, well aware of the presence of other U-boats around the convoy.

The wounded and injured aboard *Duane* were treated by the ship's doctor, and there are still vivid memories among the survivors of the attention and concern exhibited by the solicitous crews of both the cutters. Though they found it ludicrous that visits to the heads were made under armed guard, in their helpless state, they did not feel threatened. Articles of clothing and equipment were listed, and usable clothing returned, dried, to their owners. Some prisoners received no clothing back at all, but instead were handed a cellophane-wrapped packet containing underwear, trousers, socks, slippers and a toothbrush. Werner Bickel, prisoner on *Spencer* and the naked recipient of such a packet, found himself waiting in the heads one day while his guard left on an errand. He came back with a brand new pair of black leather shoes that fitted perfectly.

On *Spencer* only, during the six days en route to Scotland, the men were manacled in pairs when allowed on deck for fresh air and exercise; Matrosenobergefreiter Herbert Schwarze remembers being shackled in irons before being taken on deck of the *Spencer* for the first time on the second day aboard and counting 'seventy-two' ships in the convoy, an understandable miscount of vessels, given that the convoy and escorts were spread over several miles of ocean. Other survivors also recall the practice clearly, and the officers on *Spencer*, on arrival in Scotland, handcuffed the prisoners before turning them over to the British. Once ashore the shackles were promptly removed, in line with POW regulations.

As the US Coast Guard had no experience of coping with POWs, and in its entire history only one member of this service had ever been held as a POW, the precaution of using handcuffs may be understandable, but it was nonetheless in violation of an international agreement to which the United States had been a leading signatory.

On both cutters the officers were confined in the ship's brig and the enlisted men in the crew's recreation space, and both were fed in the appropriate mess areas. On arrival at Western Approaches base in Greenock, Scotland, all the POWs were turned

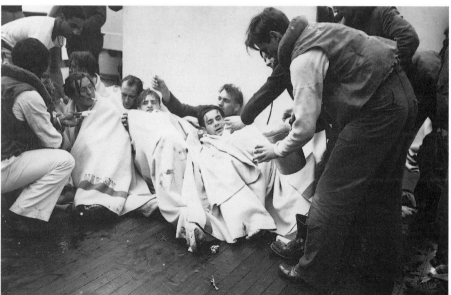

Top: The *Spencer* boat standing by *U-175* as she sinks by the stern.
The emblem is clearly visible just below the wind deflector on the
conning tower. *(US National Archives)* Above: Shivering survivors of
U-175 are given hot coffee and cigarettes on the deck of *Spencer*. *(US
National Archives)*

over to the British military authorities and they all invariably emphasise they were treated with 'absolute fairness' in British custody. British guards searched them shortly after accepting custody, and survivors relate that though they were laden with a bounty of cigarettes bestowed on them by the sympathetic American crews the British guards scrupulously returned them all.

Relinquishing the POWs to British authority came as a result of an agreement with the US Navy, but the prisoners were later returned to US custody and shipped to the USA. Under British authority the prisoners were taken by train to the London U-boat interrogation centre to be questioned in the minutest detail. There they were retained for four weeks in the intelligence detention barracks in individual cells.

According to British Intelligence *U-175*'s crew seemed to consider her an unlucky boat and there was a general air of foreboding when she departed on her final patrol, but the former crew members disagree with that assessment. Bruns, rightly security-conscious, routinely lectured his crew that if captured they were not to give any information beyond name, rank or rating, service number and home address or they would be subject to trial for treason on their eventual return home.

His British captors found First Watch Officer Wolfgang Verlohr inclined to be talkative and described him as 'conceited', seeming to feel his 195 days at sea in U-boats entitled him to criticise his late commander and other members of the crew. He was perhaps justifiably critical of Bruns for making the last daylight attack instead of waiting for cover of darkness, but, in fact, *U-175* was never sighted during her attempt to attack Convoy HX-233. She was located by sound contact only, leaving the point of daylight a moot one. But given sea and weather conditions at the time, the final fatal attack seems to have been incautious to say the least and not in keeping with Bruns' usual prudence.

Second Watch Officer, Leutnant zur See der Reserve Paul Möller evidenced little enthusiasm for his short life in a U-boat, understandable in an officer from the Merchant Marine. He was keenest on security, allegedly a fervent Nazi, and later described by his American captors as 'arrogant' and reportedly uncooperative. Perhaps this caused unusual hardship on his shipmates. Later, in the POW camp at Trinidad, Colorado, however, the former crew remembers a speech he made before assembled German officers, declaring that the War was irretrievably lost, hardly the act of an ardent Nazi.

Obersteurmann (Chief Quartermaster) Helmut Klotzsch, aged 29, had served earlier in the 36th M/S Flotilla at Ostend and Dunkirk, B-Group Ostend. A professional navy man, he was also posted to *U-175* just before departure on her final patrol. Vehemently anti-Nazi, he vanished from the London British POW interrogation centre, and was believed to have been retained by his captors for an anti-Nazi role. He died in Bremen in 1971.

His captors described surviving Midshipman Walter Weppelmann as 'insignificant' with 'little to say', and Engineer Midshipman Karl Voelker as an 'ardent Nazi', even rarer in U-boats than in the German Navy generally. His former fellow crew members thought this judgment incredible when they heard of it some years after the end of the War.

During the POWs' confinement in London, the British made a practice of placing two or three men together, of the same rate or rank but captured from different units, in a room with concealed listening devices to record conversations. These were then translated and the information added to the accumulating intelligence picture, which ultimately proved substantial. The Boatswain's mate from *U-659* (Type VIIC, Kptlt Hans Stock), sunk in collision with *U-439* (also a Type VIIC, Oblt von Tippelskirch) in the North Atlantic west of Cape Ortegal on 4 May 1943 and rescued by the convoy escort, was isolated with Chief Quartermaster Helmut Klotzsch from *U-175*. Officers were also placed together. Oberleutnant (Ing) Leopold Nowroth from *U-175* was confined with a Leutnant zur See from *U-752* (Type VIIC, Kptlt Karl Ernest Schroter), sunk in mid-Atlantic on 23 May 1943 by aircraft from *Archer*. As an example of intelligence gleaned from these encounters was the revelation of a mass breakout of English POWs, near Bonn, which promoted a hunt for the escapees.

Following their interrogation the prisoners were transported to Oxford and returned to American custody before being forwarded to Liverpool, where they boarded a large trooper and were shipped to Norfolk, Virginia. On arrival in Norfolk they, along with two hundred other German prisoners, were stripped and sprayed with insecticides and then subjected to having their heads roughly shaved until an American colonel, coming on the scene, intervened and ordered normal hair cuts. With a new issue of clothes, the prisoners boarded a train for Denver, Colorado, via Chicago, and were then transported to the huge POW camp at Trinidad, Colorado, where they were confined. Later they were transferred to Papago Park, Arizona, where some participated in the 'Great Escape' of twenty-five German POWs who tunnelled their way out of the camp on 23 December 1944, only to be returned to prison camp a short time later.

*   *   *

On the Allied side the sinking of *U-175* was the cause of a certain amount of bitterness between the crew of the Royal Navy corvette *Bergamot* and *Spencer* and this had been bubbling for some time. The British and Canadian escorts, all hardened, seasoned veterans of countless North Atlantic and Arctic Russian convoys, viewed mixed escorts with inexperienced US Navy warships with scepticism. This was particularly true of HMS *Bergamot*, whose crew were curious to see how the Senior Officer in *Spencer* would organise the group. Sharply critical of some aspects, they were bewildered in particular by the US Senior Officer's determination to keep the escorts topped up with fuel at all times, far in excess of the norm. One of the escorts commented: 'We spent more time *surrounded by* merchant ships than protecting them ourselves, as escorts.' Also irritating was the steady stream of 'petty and fussy orders and instructions' emanating from the Senior Officer. The escorts were further frustrated by having to close up at action stations, frequently for long hours, doing nothing, though when *Spencer* detected *U-175*, she herself was not, in fact, at action stations and nor in the heat of battle, did she hoist the Black Flag to announce: 'I am attacking a U-boat'.

Every British escort commander's policy for his well-trained, experienced crew was to give all hands as much rest as possible, in order to be as bright and sharp when required and were able to close up in a very short time with maximum efficiency. On the small, lively corvettes, rest was of paramount importance.

Although it was *Spencer* which attacked, damaged, and brought *U-175* to the surface on the morning of 17 April 1943, and reaped the subsequent harvest of publicity and propaganda for the US Coast Guard, it was the corvette HMS *Bergamot*, on station ahead of the convoy, who first detected and was actually beginning to attack a U-boat, not yet identified, before *Spencer* arrived. A firm, clear asdic echo had come over *Bergamot*'s bridge repeater, and the asdic operator and signalman on the bridge that morning both remember Lieutnant R T Horan saying 'This is it', as he ordered the Black Flag to be hoisted and went on an attacking course to depth charge the contact.

At this point, *Spencer*, emerging from the convoy, ordered *Bergamot* to break off the attack and elbowed her out of the way. Normally, the escort making the initial contact continued to attack, with other escorts supporting in a team effort. Either, in relishing the 'kill', he reckoned *Bergamot* as a rival, or he considered her too close for their mutual safety and effectiveness during attack. Due to the proximity of the two contacts, the possibility of their being from two different U-boats seems not to have been considered. What neither ship realised was that *Bergamot* was actually in contact with a second U-boat, *U-226* (Borchers) which had approached the convoy from ahead after a high speed run to intercept, coming in on a nearly reciprocal course to *Bergamot*'s 225°, submerging ahead in the growing daylight and lining up for a submerged attack (as *U-175* in approaching the convoy had done).

By ordering *Bergamot* to desist, *Spencer* imperiled the convoy and permitted the second U-boat to escape later with minor damage. It was sheer good luck for the convoy that *U-226* lost trim control, causing her to broach at the critical moment of attack at periscope depth between Columns 9 and 10, as sighted by the Chief Officer and lookout on the Norwegian tanker *Stiklestad*, No 92. Had *U-226* been able to launch an attack from that position, she would have been unlikely to have missed the massed ships around her, and the convoy would have unquestionably suffered additional losses or damage.

Although *Spencer* received the credit for the successful attack, in fact her overall performance left much to be desired for a Senior Officer escort by failing to follow-up on HF/DF bearings, then ignoring U-boat transmissions around the convoy, and failing to detect U-boats operating on the surface within visual distance, in one case within the convoy itself resulting in the loss of a new and invaluable ship and cargo, with six dead and three wounded. Finally, forcing a highly experienced veteran escort to abort her attack at the last moment was a very risky action that could easily have resulted in failure of her own attack. It did, indeed, allow one U-boat to escape, and only bad luck on the German side avoided additional losses to the convoy.

The fact that both US Coast Guard cutters with the latest electronic equipment failed to detect at least four shadowing U-boats in visual contact, leaves another open question as to the cutters' overall performances. A year earlier the corvette HMS *Vetch*

HMS *Bergamot,* the Flower class corvette which made contact with
U-226 ahead of the convoy *(Imperial War Museum)*

of 36th Escort Group, Cdr Walker, using 9cm 271m radar in Convoy OG-82 located
U-252 at 7,600yds.

The signalman and asdic operator on *Bergamot*'s bridge reported that their commander was visibly disappointed and annoyed. The author, from his vantage point as
watch on the bridge of *G Harrison Smith* with an overall view of the battle, vividly
recalls a corvette flying the Black Flag, going in to the attack out ahead of the convoy,
then *Spencer* starting to drop her first pattern of depth charges. Wrongly assuming it
was a team effort between cutter and corvette, it meant nothing to him at the time.

10

The Role of US Coast Guard Cutter Spencer

The presence of U-boats was first noticed by *Spencer* on 15 April, when four inter-cepted radio transmissions, deemed by the escort commander not sufficiently close to require action, were ignored. Dispatches found in three U-boat logbooks may have been among those heard. At 1047hrs German time on 15 April, the KTBs of Borchers (*U-226*) and Hasenschar (*U-628*) show that BdU radioed ten outbound U-boats* just departing the Bay of Biscay on passage to the North Atlantic west of Ireland, crossing the route of HX-233 to Scotland. Unknown to the Allies, following the harrowing spring campaigns in the Atlantic, many U-boats had been forced to return to base for repairs, with fuel and torpedo supplies depleted, and some of the next wave of boats would be sailing almost directly into the path of HX-233.

On 15 April at 2337hrs *U-226* signalled BdU her position, which theoretically might have eliminated her as a threat to HX-233, but she was close enough to reach the battle that began only six hours later. *U-628*'s position report is not in her KTB for that date, but Hasenschar was in the same general area as Borchers and daily position reports were routine.

The third logbook contains more illuminating entries. At 1045hrs on 15 April BdU ordered Franke (*U-262*) to carry out his 'special mission'. Taken in context with the next radio traffic between Franke and BdU, the first brief signal told a significant story. At 1631hrs Franke requested clarification of whether he need attack convoys encountered en route, and BdU ordered him to do so as far as Nova Scotia, thus revealing his track. This should have identified *U-262* as an acute source of danger to the convoy and allowed adequate time for a considered course change. Franke was literally on a collision course with HX-233, and twelve hours later sighted it. *Spencer* recorded her first radar contact in the early hours of 16 April, indubitably *U-262*.

Although escorts *Spencer* and *Wetaskiwin* held *U-262* under for several hours, causing her to lose contact, U-boat reinforcements were already on their way. Franke had radioed BdU the convoy's position at 0434hrs. *U-175* sighted the convoy next, *during the night of 16–17 April, homing in U-382 and U-628.*

On Saturday 17 April 1943, at 0412hrs, *Spencer* obtained a radar contact and dropped two depth charges on an unidentified U-boat's estimated position. Meanwhile, *U-628* had entered the convoy unseen on the surface and, all the while undetected, fired five torpedoes, one of which hit the *Fort Rampart* at dawn.

At 1050hrs *Spencer* made an underwater sound contact at 5,000yds. It was *U-175*, and although no periscope had been sighted, *Spencer* went directly in to the attack, stopping *U-175*'s own attack within seconds of launch. The sequence of events on *Spencer* began when sound man Harold V Anderson, SOM 2/c, obtained an echo ranging contact bearing 039° at 1,500yds. OD Lt jg Wm F Andersen, USCGR, brought the ship onto the bearing and reported to Cdr Berdine, who ordered the firing of an urgent (immediate) barrage of five Mark VII and six Mark VI depth charges set to 50ft and 100ft, 500yds ahead of convoy.

Because of the proximity of the following convoy which he had just cleared, the commanding officer of the *Spencer* observed there was no time to fire a deliberate barrage before the convoy would be over the position. The convoy Commodore aboard *Devis* noted in his report that if an emergency turn had been ordered, *Spencer* would not have been able to follow the contact through beneath the convoy, but furthermore it is extremely doubtful that if such a turn had been ordered, it could have been executed in time to avoid the scene of action in any case and immense confusion may have resulted. Therefore, CO *Spencer* ordered a second 'urgent' barrage of eleven charges set at 200ft and 250ft, as his vessel closed the U-boat. In fact, the second attack was so close to the oncoming merchant vessels that even at a depth of 200ft–250ft the depth-charge concussions shook them all severely.

Curiously, SOM 2/c Anderson was relieved by Robert O Sondrol, SOM 3/c, a less experienced rating, and the hunt continued. As *Spencer* virtually stopped, she passed down between convoy columns 6 and 7. Despite the noises from the convoy she reported maintaining sound contact, so a pattern of mousetraps was fired once clear of the rear of the convoy, again to no visible effect. Then sound contact was lost, and *Spencer* began a search astern of the convoy in an effort to regain it.

Ten minutes later a submarine was sighted surfacing, bearing 270° at 2,500yds from *Spencer* and at 260° and 2,100yds from *Duane*. Both escorts went in to attack, *Spencer* with the intention to ram, while both cutters opened fire with every weapon that would bear. *Spencer* fired two rounds of 5in and fifty-seven rounds of 3in, recording 'numerous' hits and severe damage. *Duane* fired twenty-eight rounds from her main battery and observed a hit at the base of the conning tower. *Spencer*'s log book reported the U-boat as returning fire, as do numerous other copied sources, but this is refuted by documented facts cited elsewhere. Immediately, a number of merchant vessels had also opened fire with deck guns, and Liberty ship *James Jackson* also claimed a hit at the base of the U-boat's conning tower.

It remains unclear which or whether any merchant ships' fire actually hit the surfaced U-boat, and impossible to determine which vessel hit *Spencer*, which, according to paragraph 7 of the CO's report, 'Enclosure V', dated 21 April 1943, lay between

The US Liberty ship *James Jackson* which claimed to be the first to spot
U-175 and the first to open fire with her 4in deck gun.
(*US Navy Photograph*)

the convoy and the surfacing U-boat. It is certain that *Spencer*'s damage and injuries
came from shell fire, with one man fatally wounded, and equally certain that the fire
was 'friendly', since no gunfire originated from *U-175* at any time during the battle.

Spencer's log relates shells passing or landing close aboard her, with one striking on
the starboard side and nearly severing a boat davit for the No 1 boat, holing the boat
and spattering the superstructure with shrapnel, killing one man, Julius T Petrella
(224–430), USCG RM 3/c, and wounding twelve crewmen. The large number of
wounded on *Spencer*, especially among odd ratings, demonstrates a serious lack of

The crew of *Spencer* racing to action stations. Note the depth charges at right and the rafts lashed to left. *(US National Archives)*

discipline, confirmed by contemporary photographs showing idlers, not on battle stations where they belonged, but lounging on deck. A further confirmation of the cause of such a large number of casualties is found in the gunnery officer's statement: 'There were too many persons watching the submarine instead of going to their assigned stations below decks. In one instance the gun captain had to push personnel out of the way so that his gun might be fired on the target.' That there were apparently disciplinary problems on *Spencer* at this time is supported by the large number of defaulters noted in her log book as compared to that of *Duane* over the same period.

Spencer ordered a cease-fire as soon as *U-175* was seen abandoning, but clearly

Spencer passing over the stern of *U-175*. The damage to the
'wintergarten' is clearly visible and the deck guns are trained fore and
aft. *(US National Archives)*

could not check it as quickly as circumstances warranted. Once fire is opened, it is
difficult to restrain gunners regardless of the degree of discipline, and *Spencer*'s
gunnery officer confirms this problem in paragraph five of his report that '. . . there
was too much talking at the guns, too little attention paid to the cease-fire signals, and
certain members of the ready gun failed to report to their regular stations for General
Quarters but remained at the ready gun.' As a result, firing on the *U-175* continued
even as the last man went overboard.

Ensign Chester O Kasiea, Armed Guard Commander on *U-175*'s target ship, US tanker *G Harrison Smith*, noted that 'Gunfire was observed . . . from three four or five ships . . . as well as from two destroyers'.

Armed Guard Commander, Lt (jg) J J Stevenson on S/S *Lena Luckenbach* maintained that 'fire was held because of the position of two destroyers [*Spencer* and *Duane*] between the ship and the target'. It is clear, then, *Luckenbach* (probably the closest ship, except *James Jackson*, to the surfacing *U-175*), was not responsible for hitting *Spencer*. The Commodore hoisted the cease-fire signal as soon as it was obvious that fire from the merchant ships was endangering the escorts, particularly *Spencer*, although according to her CO at least two shots also fell near *Duane*.

Heavy and rapid 20mm AA fire from both cutters was mainly responsible for the casualties on the U-boat. It swept her decks and killed her commander as well as those who immediately followed him up the conning tower hatch, and subsequently several men in the water after they had abandoned; some survivors felt at the time this was deliberate. Reports that men were in the water *before* she surfaced, suggesting abandonment from another hatch, is not supported by the facts, but abandonment began immediately upon surfacing on orders of her commanding officer.

The 20mm fire apparently penetrated the outer conning tower structure and outside 'skin' (0.5cm or 0.2in) but ricocheted off the 2cm (0.79in) thick pressure hull. The close-up photo of *U-175* shows extensive damage at the base of the conning tower (aft beneath the 'Wintergarten' AA mounting, obviously created by 5in and 3in shell fire), as well as wreckage on the deck above, with smoke rising from the conning tower itself.

With *Spencer* on a course to ram, the U-boat was seen to be heavily damaged and abandoning and so she then slowed and launched a boat at 1215hrs. *Duane* noted twelve men abandoning the U-boat, presumably the last of the crew aboard. At least one electric motor had been left running in the U-boat, which, giving about two knots, was audible to the escort sound men. With some right rudder, the U-boat was circling slowly ahead as water entered and she sank lower. No scuttling charges were necessary to hasten the boat's sinking, as all but one flood valve had been opened by the engineering officer on leaving the control room. No signal to BdU had been made or was possible, since all wireless telegraph equipment had been wrecked.

The *Spencer* boarding party, mustering at No 1 motor monomoy boat, found it holed by the shrapnel of the shell hit, so No 2 monomoy propelled by oars was launched. The trained boarding party of ten – five officers and five enlisted men – with a boat crew of six according to the report from *Spencer*, though the photograph shows thirteen, was under the command of Lt Cdr J B Oren, USCG. The boat approached the U-boat, but boarding was difficult due to the rounded hull, so a second attempt had to be made midships. All ten members of the party commanded by Lt Ross Bullard managed to get aboard, although the U-boat was clearly sinking by the stern. *Spencer* signalled 'Do not board', but noting the party already on the wreck, ordered them to make a topside survey. Three dead were observed in the upper conning tower and another body on the deck. The enlisted men were ordered to return to the boat as *U-175*'s stern settled rapidly, while Bullard was instructed to investigate the sights of the forward gun. The same literature indicates the wreck was boarded only by Lt Bullard but it was in fact boarded by all ten. Clarence S Hall Jr, BM 2/c, according to his own version, was the 'lead man' whose task was to open the conning tower hatch and drop a hand grenade below to 'eliminate' any resistance, then go down and collect 'classified material'. When Hall 'lifted the scuttle, seawater started to pour through the hatch about six inches deep' and Bullard, who was with him, said they would not enter. Both were swimming moments later, with Hall wondering why opening the hatch had caused flooding. The report by Lt Cdr Oren stating Lieutenants Bullard and Lumpkin had to jump off the sinking U-boat and swim back to the boat is evidently somewhat in error.

The *Duane* had meanwhile dropped a liferaft, and the boat from *Spencer* began picking up German survivors. Prisoners were ordered to sit in the bottom of the boat and keep quiet. *Spencer*'s boat picked up single prisoners until they had collected seven, when they were ordered to return to the ship, arriving at 1255hrs. The boat was hoisted aboard. The last to leave *U-175* and the last to climb the scramble net onto *Duane* were swimmers Matrosenobergefreiter Dieter Wolf and Mechanikergefreiter Peter Wannemacher.

Reports mention that the prisoners used their escape lungs as life preservers, that they were all warmly dressed in cloth trousers, woollen sweaters or grey leather suits. The reports also mention the good quality of the German equipment.

The German survivors were extremely lucky to have been picked up at all when it was known that several other U-boats were in the immediate area of the convoy, posing a real threat to the escorts themselves despite escort screening.

Duane's and *Spencer*'s logbooks describe the weather as: northeast to northeast-by-east wind at Force 4–5, barometer 30.38–30.48, air temperature 6 °C, water temperature at surface 7°C, sky cloudy to overcast, clouds moving from the northeast 9–10 tenths overcast, visibility 8 miles. Sea was slight with a northeast swell. *Spencer* gave her noon position as 47°59'N 21°10'W.

In describing the sinking, Captain Heineman stated that *U-175* settled slowly by the stern, with the bow of *Spencer* actually passing over it, but with sufficient clearance to avoid striking. Buoyancy was gradually lost until, by 1320hrs, water had reached the conning tower hatch, flooding into the control room, and seven minutes later *U-175* sank, in position 47°59'N 21°12'W.

Captain Heinemann's report states incorrectly that several of the *Spencer*'s and *Duane*'s crew noted 'firing by the U-boat's bridge machine gun'. However, a questionnaire distributed on *Spencer* to fifty-nine officers and men, who were in a position to have observed firing from the *U-175* confirmed that there was no return fire. Even if it would have been expedient to let the record show Allied casualties came from the U-boat, all evidence indicates otherwise, and the official report concedes that the damage to the starboard side of *Spencer*, including holing of a boat and a nearly severed boat davit, came from inaccurate firing by ships of the convoy shortly after the sighting of the conning tower.

On *Duane*, with two officer POWs (chief engineer and first watch officer) and

Mastrosenobergefreiter Dieter Wolf reaches the safety of *Duane*'s scramble net. *(US National Archives)*

nineteen seamen, four of the injured were treated in sick bay: the chief engineer and one seaman for shrapnel wounds, one seaman for a broken arm and one for shock. Oberleutenant Leopold Nowroth had shrapnel wounds in the face and head and a broken jaw; Seaman Wilhelm Kistler in the left chest, arm and cheek; Seaman Josef Butscheidt had a broken arm, and Alois Saurbach was suffering from shock. First WO Wolfgang Verlohr was confined in the junior officers' quarters on *Duane* and talked rather freely to two officers, expressing considerable concern for the other members of the crew, perhaps partly due to the shock of finding himself in such a situation. The conversations were, of course, duly recorded and reported in writing for any limited intelligence value they might contain. As British interrogators dryly observed later, he seemed to have, 'no undue qualms about security'.

The following incident on *Spencer* was apparently no problem on *Duane*. According to one report, after removing the prisoners' clothes, *Spencer* personnel could no longer identify the officers, and lack of cooperation presented a problem of segregation. The *Spencer* logbook records that 'officers . . . would not give their rank or home address: Karl Foalker, Albert Sirchler, Peter Paul Moeller, Helmut Klotsch, Herbert Schwarze, Max Klinger'. (Sichler, Klotsch, Schwarze and Klinger were not officers.)

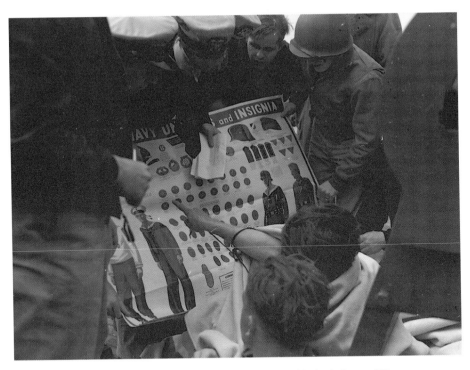

Prisoners onboard *Spencer* identify German naval insignia from a US
Navy intelligence identity chart. *(US National Archives)*

However, the photograph on this page shows the prisoners identifying insignia from
an over-sized US Navy intelligence chart of German Navy insignia and uniforms,
apparently co-operating. That the photograph was taken aboard *Spencer* is beyond
doubt, since two officers are wearing US Navy insignia, and there were no US Naval
officers on *Duane*, only on *Spencer* as Senior Officer US Navy staff.

   Spencer reported a total of six separate U-boat contacts and attacks during transit of
HX-233, out of eight U-boats now known to have been present. HMS *Bryony* made
the final attack, in accordance with her Report of Proceedings by Commanding
Officer, Lt T Hand RNR on 20 April 1943.

   On 18 April at 1630hrs at 51°22'N 15°55'W, *Bryony* made a firm U-boat sound
contact while on the port wing of the convoy. She went immediately in to the attack,
eight minutes later firing a pattern of seven depth charges without result, but regaining contact at once following their detonation. A prolonged hunt followed, supported
by *Spencer*, with repeated attacks made on contact. There were no tangible results,
however, so it was deemed prudent to rejoin the convoy, by now 14 miles distant and
short of escorts. It is by no means clear whether any U-boat was involved in this
particular attack.

   Observers from HMS *Bryony*, including former gunner Harry K Rawlings and
CPO Stanley James Haskell DSM, remember 'on the previous day the men coming

The crew of *Spencer* celebrate their triumph over *U-175* with a Popeye cartoon on the ship's funnel. *(US National Archives)*

out of the conning tower and jumping into the sea when the USCGC *Spencer* was firing at it'. Mr Rawlings also recalls the following day, 'when we carried out a heavy depth charge attack and recorded nine explosions', while Mr Haskell admits he 'was too busy watching gauge glasses bend to count the bangs, but *Bryony* couldn't claim a kill as nothing came up and we didn't hang around' during the attack on 18 April.

Meanwhile, according to the BdU war diary, *U-614* was the last boat to lose contact with the convoy, on 18 April, leaving the U-boat attacked by HMS *Bryony* undetermined. It is noteworthy that BdU reported *U-264, U-226* and *U-382* had all been forced under the previous day by 3rd Support Group attacks, thereby emphasising the vital role the British ships played in the battle.

* According to Hasenschar's logbook (*U-628*) they were: 'Hasenschar, Looks, Koch, Bruns, Borchers, Ölrich, Manke, Gretschel, Sträter and Folkers'.

11

The Loss of Fort Rampart

Fort Rampart (7,130grt), was the thirteenth of 354 *Fort* ships of the 'North Sands type'* dry cargo emergency vessels built by West Coast Shipbuilders Ltd of Vancouver, British Columbia, and engined by the John Inglis Co Ltd of Toronto, Ontario, Canada. The first, *Fort St James*, was delivered on 29 January 1942. Launched on 23 January 1943, *Fort Rampart* was on her maiden voyage with convoy HX-233. She was partially loaded with lumber on departure from British Columbia and at either Balboa or Colon, on transit through the Panama Canal, topped up with balsa wood, much in demand by the British aircraft industry for its De Havilland Mosquito twin-engined light bombers.

Her final cargo included 1,400grt of 'metal' in the lower holds and 7,300grt of lumber, including her huge deck load. Her armament consisted of one 12-pounder, two 20mm AA Oerlikons, two Colt machine guns, and two PAC (parachute and cable) rockets. Her crew of fifty-two included six naval gunners, and she carried three DBS (Distressed British Seamen) for repatriation. After the vessel was torpedoed, three of the crew were injured and six missing, probably killed in the explosion beneath the crew's quarters.

The freighter departed New York 6 April 1943 to join Convoy HX-233. Her Master, Captain Stein,‡ reported that he had no idea there were submarines in the area or that an attack was imminent, a reflection of the general ignorance shared, in retrospect perhaps just as well, by merchant navy men throughout the convoys.

---

* So named to distinguish them from the US-constructed 'Ocean type' vessels. The Canadian hulls conformed to British working drawings supplied by North Sands Shipyard of J L Thompson & Son, Sunderland, UK, with specifications based on the parent ship, *Empire Liberty*, 7,157 tons x 439ft x 60ft, built 1941.

‡Captain W H Stein OBE, was awarded Lloyd's War Medal for Bravery when in command of *Empire Starlight*, abandoned as war loss 1.6.42, but salvaged by the Russians, now renamed *Murmansk*. His citation reads: 'The ship which was in convoy reached a North Russian port undamaged in spite of heavy enemy air attacks. While in port she was again subjected to persistent attacks and sank. Throughout these fierce onslaughts, Captain Stein showed high courage and outstanding leadership. He did all that was possible to save his ship and obtained the discharge of a large part of her valuable cargo before she sank.'

At 0505hrs on 17 April, in position 47°20′N 22°00′W, as reported by the Master, the vessel was struck by a single torpedo while steering a course of 043°, at 9 knots. Sea was moderate with heavy swell, wind southwest, force 2/3, and the visibility good with about half light at dawn.

The torpedo was not seen before it hit the starboard quarter in the after peak, creating a loud explosion followed by a bright flash. A column of water shot upwards, though none fell on deck, and the lights went out aft and on the bridge, but not amidships. The propeller and rudder were blown away, causing the engines to race, and the vessel began settling by the stern. The Master judged by her settling aft so quickly that both the after peak and double bottom tank had filled.

Deck damage to the part welded, part riveted ship was extensive. A huge crack extended right across the after deck between No 5 Hatch and the break of the poop,

HMS *Penn,* a 'P' class destroyer, one of the Home Fleet destroyers which rendezvoued with Convoy HX-233 on 17 April. *(Imperial War Museum)*

and reached to the waterline; another extended across the hull between No 3 Hatch-coaming and the bridge, while a third crack was noted abaft the funnel on the port side, which also reached the waterline.

The compass had been blown out of the binnacle, telegraph leads broken, and all communications severed. Rockets could not be fired as they had been blown out of their launchers, but a red light ('I have been torpedoed') was hoisted, though it was not spotted by several escorts. The Master threw the confidential books and wireless codes over the side in their weighted boxes according to regulations and went aft to determine the damage. The entire crew's accommodation had been destroyed and water was pouring in. Surviving crew, having been asleep, were dazed, and it took the Master and two men to get them out and forward over the after deck cargo of lumber, which was in complete disarray. The vessel suddenly settled aft and forced immediate abandonment in the four lifeboats.

One man with internal injuries was in great pain, and as the ship was still partially afloat after about an hour, the Master decided to try to return to get morphine. The convoy, continuing on its course, was by then well out of sight, but when the boat was nearly alongside the wreck, the corvette HMS *Arvida* arrived on the scene.

Apparently, this escort and HMS *Bergamot* were the only two to see *Fort Rampart*'s signal. *Arvida*'s log recorded that at 0600hrs the watch officer observed, 'Position 21 falling out of line,' and at 0630hrs, 'Pt 21 displaying one red light'. HMS *Arvida* closed at best speed to begin rescue, while *Spencer* screened her operations. She first circled the wreck two or three times and dropped three depth charges set at 300ft, to discourage any lurking U-boat. By 0714hrs all fifty-two survivors were aboard HMS *Arvida* and she rejoined the convoy, resuming her station by 1040hrs. *Spencer* had meanwhile resumed her screen position ahead of the convoy and made the sound contact that prompted her attacks on *U-175*.

With three badly injured survivors from *Fort Rampart* aboard and lacking adequate medical facilities to cope, *Arvida* was instructed to close with the US Coast Guard cutter *Duane* (which carried a doctor) for their transfer, which was carried out between 1138hrs and 1152hrs. Meanwhile, 3rd Support Group, consisting of HM destroyers *Offa, Penn, Panther* and *Impulsive*, had come up in support of the other escorts.

Since *Fort Rampart* still remained afloat, her Master reckoned the wreck salvageable if she could be towed, so at 1120hrs *Penn* and *Panther* were ordered to investigate the derelict ship, by now some 20 miles behind the convoy. On approach *Panther* carried out a search to screen and *Penn*, obtaining a dubious contact, dropped five depth charges. These fell on *U-628*, who reported torpedoing the wreck of *Fort Rampart*, taking her for a straggler, at 1120hrs. Hasenschar's KTB also records the attacks by three destroyers.

U-628 and *U-226* had separately begun searching for stragglers astern of the convoy, and each, without the knowledge of the other, encountered *Fort Rampart*, abandoned but still afloat, well down by the stern, apparently sustained by her load of lumber.

As *Penn* approached, still about seven miles away, a torpedo hit the wreck. Rohwer accurately credits both *U-628* and *U-226* with the sinking, fairly enough from KTB evidence, but *Penn* also played a part. The lumber-loaded *Fort Rampart*, repeatedly torpedoed and strafed, steadfastly refused to sink. Hasenschar recorded the first hit, which *Penn* would have observed, and *U-226* was later to deliver the *coup de grâce*, but neither U-boat knew about the help they received from *Penn*.

Taking immediate action against the torpedoing *U-628*, *Penn* approached the area at 27 knots then reduced to 20 knots to make a sound-sweep at one mile from *Fort Rampart*'s port beam, the side on which she had just been hit. Although *Penn*'s asdic was temporarily out of action, she ran down the probable torpedo track for three miles, without result, then returned to the wreck, requesting *Panther*, also on the scene, to sweep whilst she approached the wreck. As *Penn* came close, *Fort Rampart* broke in two and the after part sank at once. *Penn*, knowing that the derelict was abandoned, fired three depth charges under the fore part just as *Panther* made a weak contact, probably on *U-628*, and depth charged the suspected U-boat. As the destroyers were short of oil and the convoy now well ahead of them, *Penn* left *Panther* on the contact and confirmed her attack on the wreck, firing several rounds of 4.7in into the remains before both leaving her to rejoin the convoy, arriving 0630hrs. Early morning 18 April, they both refuelled from tanker *Fjordaas*, No 34. Meanwhile, *U-628* had been badly shaken and was unable to catch up with the convoy which was by then 50 miles away, still plodding along at 9 knots.

Fort Rampart was a costly casualty for both the Allies and the Germans, requiring three torpedoes and 130 rounds of 8.8mm shells from *U-628*, three depth charges plus 'several' rounds of 4.7in shelling from *Penn*, and, on the following day, three more torpedoes from *U-226*, who reported that the wreck finally sank on 18 April 1943.

Commodore O H Dawson RNR, in *Devis* No 71, reported that the attack on *Fort Rampart* occurred at 0455hrs, forty minutes before sunrise, while the convoy was steering 043°, in eleven columns, in 47°17'N 22°06'W, weather 'light airs, visibility 10 miles'. Significantly, he stated in his report he knew nothing about the torpedoing until he *saw* the *Fort Rampart* some twenty minutes later, by then well astern of the convoy. He had mistaken the noise of the explosion for depth charges, suggesting there may actually have been more than one explosion, as Hasenschar reported. Vice Commodore, E R Smith, Master of *Empire Pakeha*, No 41, reported that *Fort Rampart* had made two sets of shorts on her siren and displayed and prescribed one red light ('I have been torpedoed'). There has been no record found of a report from the Master of the *G Harrison Smith*, No 31, or any other nearby ships. It is odd too that the Vice Commodore, clearly aware of the attack from the outset, never alerted his Senior Officer.

HMS *Bergamot*, from Position L in the convoy escort (ie, port bow) reported observing the leader of the port column (*Fort Rampart*, No 21) haul out of station. But hearing no explosion nor seeing any signal, she assumed the vessel had an engine breakdown so continued to observe at approximately 4,500yds distance. It was not until she later received a general signal that she became aware of the attack. Since

The US Liberty ship *Jonathan Worth*, one of the vessels following *Fort Rampart* in the same column which failed to report the attack on *Fort Rampart*. *(US Navy Photograph)*

Bergamot observed what happened, it is a puzzle why none of the three ships follow-ing *Fort Rampart* astern in the same column, US Liberty *William D Pender* (No 22), Norwegian *John Bakke* (No 23), and US Liberty *Jonathan Worth* (No 24), whom she had to pass close aboard, failed to inform the escorts or Commodore of *Fort Rampart*'s distress. No one seems to have sighted the torpedoes crossing through the convoy in the dim light of dawn, but it seems probable that the *William D Pender*, about 800yds astern would have heard, seen and felt the explosion and observed the red light at the time. The explosion was clearly heard and felt on the US tanker *G Harrison Smith* (No 31), 1,000yds to starboard, but from her too apparently no report was made, although the red light was clearly visible.

HMS *Dianthus* was unaware of the attack until a general message was received and she was ordered, along with *Spencer*, to screen *Arvida* while the latter acted as rescue ship and picked up survivors from the wreck, by now some 9 miles astern. Third Escort Group could be seen arriving on the horizon. *Dianthus* suggests the U-boat may have entered the convoy from ahead submerged and passed between columns 2 and 3, likely firing from the starboard quarter of the convoy, inside the screen. Evidence from the *U-628* KTB shows she entered the convoy from the north on the surface and fired five torpedoes before prudently submerging in the growing dawn light, unseen and undetected. All other supporting escorts had neither seen nor heard the attack on the convoy and remained on station until ordered otherwise.

Dianthus also acted as screen for *Spencer* and *Duane* when their rescue work was in progress for *U-175* survivors. Approaching to within 600yds, she made a good report of the U-boat during the final battle, as observed and recounted in her 'Report of Proceedings'.

A priority signal from CO, CTU 24.1.3 (Heinemann), to CINCWA, 18 April 1943, with information to CTF 24, Admiralty, Ottawa, Iceland and others, reported: '*Spencer* captured [sic] 750grt U-boat number 175 which subsequently sank as a result of three depth charge attacks and gunfire . . . forty-four prisoners . . . three killed [sic] by gunfire including U-boat Captain Gerhardt Muntz from Berndt [sic] . . . ship in company *Fort Rampart* sunk by escort [sic]'.

Third Support Group Operations

The destroyer HMS *Offa*, with senior officer Captain J W McCoy RN left Liverpool on 13 April to join *Penn, Panther*, and *Impulsive* at Londonderry, sailing on 14 April to rendezvous with Convoy HX-233 on 17 April, at 47°N 24°W, in support. *Penn* reported weather damage to the starboard side and a persistent leak but still sailed. Due to the short-leggedness of Home Fleet destroyers, fuel was a constant concern and refuelling was necessary from designated tankers in each convoy they supported. Third Support Group arrived in the early hours of 17 April in the vicinity of Convoy HX-233, deliberately approaching from windward and down moon, in accordance with the U-boat practice whereby submarines also approached from that quarter.

The Support Group sighted the convoy at 0840hrs while *Spencer* was searching astern. As they approached, an alert lookout on *Offa* (J Grimsdick, OS, P/JK 403417) sighted a U-boat on the surface, which promptly went deep on the port bow of the convoy. The Support Group proceeded to sweep down the port side of the convoy, carrying out a concerted attack, and 'hammering' was reported, allegedly from the U-boat which may have sustained damage.

At 0917hrs *Panther* sighted a U-boat on the surface, bearing 230°, probably *U-226* (Borchers). When the sighting was confirmed, all ships engaged in the hunt. *Panther* dropped a Dan Buoy to mark the diving position, while all other ships carried out a box search around the point. *Panther* and *Impulsive* each carried out one attack, followed by a second attack by *Panther*. Then sound contact was lost and *Offa* ordered the two ships to rejoin, sending *Panther* to reinforce *Penn* at the wreck of *Fort Rampart*.

Captain McCoy acknowledged he felt it wise to send two ships straightaway to investigate the *Fort Rampart* as she was bound to attract a U-boat, but he thought it better to concentrate on *Panther*'s sighted U-boat than divide forces to search for another possible submarine. Once contact was lost, he did dispatch the second ship to investigate, but too late, and *Panther* and *Penn* wisely did not persist in their hunt, since the U-boat had gone deep. Meanwhile, *Spencer* brought *U-175* to the surface, without including *Offa*, much to her crew's chagrin. '. . . Another of the wrongs of Ireland,' *Offa*'s senior officer wryly remarked in his Report of Proceedings, reflecting his keen disappointment at not being permitted to support *Spencer*.

Third Support Group then continued with HX-233, oiling from tanker *Fjordaas*, No 34, and taking up night stations around the convoy. It did sterling service running down High Frequency Direction Finder (HF/DF) and aircrafts' U-boat bearings until ordered to break off to join westbound Convoy SC-126 on 19 April, which it did forthwith, remaining with it until joining Convoy ON-178, to arrive St Johns, Newfoundland on 24 April 1943, encountering problems with pack-ice en route.

The Admiralty Naval Staff's analysis of Support Groups' operations in the North Atlantic between 14 April and 11 May 1943 shows that of sixty-seven attacks made against U-boats, eleven were made by these units, which also sank two of the eight U-boats sunk. In summary, 24 per cent of the sightings and 19 per cent of the attacks made in the vicinity of the convoys were credited to Support Groups. The report points out that the analysis does less than justice, however, to the true effectiveness of the Support Groups, because although a U-boat could already expect stiff resistance when attacking a convoy, to be harried, chased and hunted down even while keeping its distance was most disconcerting. As a result the German High Command immediately moved their U-boats into areas with less opposition, thereby lessening their threat to the North Atlantic-UK lifeline. Nine convoys shadowed by U-boats for a total of 470 hours between 14 April and 11 May were reinforced by Support Groups for 38 per cent of the period. Six Support Groups spent 700 hours with convoys, 180 hours while the convoys were being shadowed and 520 while they were not. The Support Groups were at sea for a total of 1,860 hours during the period.

Below: HMS *Impulsive,* an 'I' class destroyer and the Flotilla leader. (*Imperial War Museum*) Bottom: HMS *Panther,* a 'P' class destroyer. (*Imperial War Museum*)

12

U-Boat Transmissions, Intercepts and Decoding

The British code-breaking operations have become well-known only in recent years, since the veil of wartime secrecy was lifted about the successes of the Ultra system based at Bletchley Park, Buckinghamshire. In December 1942 the Bletchley Park facility cracked the German 'Triton' code, used specifically for U-boats operating in the Atlantic, and from then on all U-boat messages could be deciphered by the Allies. It is abundantly clear that cracking the German code systems was a crucial and determining factor in all spring convoy battles in 1943, and specifically a factor in the defence of Convoy HX-233 and the loss of *U-175*.

For a complete overview of the sinking of *U-175* it is essential to review this traffic in chronological sequence for 1943, designated by the Allies, 'Hush Secret', a very high security classification indeed. Quite clear to the Allies at the time were the following decoded messages:

On 4 January 1943, during *U-175*'s almost fatal second patrol, Bruns queried BdU: 'There is a sub in Naval Square ET 1698 (west coast of Africa). It is our own or an Italian one?' BdU responded: 'Not an Italian. Possibility of our own exists'.

On 5 January 1943 Bruns informed BdU from his West African patrol area:

> Forced underwater for two hours by persistent air [attack] bombs, search lights. Systematic air attacks attempt to starve out sub. Consider operating in vicinity of coast unpromising, since sub has no freedom of movement. Have discontinued since battery 55 degrees, Junkers Compressor out of order since 31st [December 1942]. Naval Square ET1932. 129cbm [fuel remaining].

On 6 January BdU informed twenty-six U-boats at sea of their new identifying signature groups, with 'CA' listed for Bruns in *U-175*. The following day BdU instructed *U-175* to move to WNW of ET38, operating off Freetown, reporting Trinidad convoys for Naval Square ED99 in 10 to 11-day cycles. BdU also listed several convoys at sea, clearly indicating that German radio intercepts were reading Allied convoy traffic at the time.

On 15 January BdU informed Bruns that he was free to operate to the west and southwest of his area and ordered him to report three days later. BdU also assigned *U-43* (Kptlt Hans-Joachim Schwantke) to a new area, where on 3 March 1943 he torpedoed and sank the German blockade-runner *Doggerbank* (ex-*Speybank*) 5,154grt, mistaking her for the British *Dunnottar Castle* or *Dunedin Star*. Inbound, loaded with 7,000grt of rubber, fish and vegetable oils from the Far East, *Doggerbannk*'s master Kapitän Schneidewind was making his best speed and ahead of schedule.

On 19 January Bruns signalled BdU that he was operating in Grid Square ET24 off the West African coast, that he had found nothing, had 84cbm of fuel and all torpedoes left, and that his Junkers compressor was still out of order. On 23 January 1943 he reported sinking the US Liberty ship *Benjamin Smith*, '7,000 tons'. BdU responded by ordering him to return to Lorient, with provisioning en route scheduled. This, however, was altered by a message on 29 January to return to base, 'directly without refuelling'. Four days later, on 2 February, three days after *U-175* had been attacked with nearly disastrous results, Bruns signalled BdU as follows:

> On 30th about 32cbm of fuel lost as result of severe depth bomb attack by aircraft in [Naval Square] EJ9677. Charging and discharging battery-halves now only one at a time. High rate of self-discharge. Port shaft of diesel out of order. With increased load [the] vibration is unbearable. Limited diving readiness. Because of increased fuel consumption [loss?], need refuelling urgently. EJ6141, 20cbm [fuel] remaining.

U-175 survivors recall the coincidence of severe, disabling aerial attacks coming exactly on the day their refuelling had been scheduled, which seemed an incredible coincidence until they learned, years later, of the decoding.

BdU responded on 2 February with instructions to proceed to 'LO20' (rendezvous position) with 'economical speed', and that provisioning and refuelling would take place from *U-118* (KK Werner Czygan). The following day BdU instructed *U-118* to meet *U-175* and send an arrival 'short signal'* and 'add day of completion of special task' (ie refuelling *U-175*). On 4 February BdU reported to all U-boats in 'Series 1 and 3' that Bruns was in Naval Square DT97 with a day's run of 95 miles. On 5 February Bruns informed BdU that he had an oil leak, so that his fuel estimate was inaccurate, but he confirmed his day's run was 95 miles. On 8 February, Bruns signalled that he expected to reach the rendezvous with *U-118* at 0800hrs on 11 February. BdU, in turn, informed all U-boats in the same general area (Series 1 and 3) of Bruns' location.

Via a signal dated 14 February Bruns informed BdU that provisioning had been completed from Czygan (*U-118*) and that Czygan had 293cbm of fuel remaining, and was located in Square DH2132, west of the coast of Morocco. BdU instructed *U-175*, *U-217* (Kptlt Kurt Reichenback-Klinke) and *U-108* (KK Ralf-Reimer Wolfram) to go on the 'Irland Schaltung', or Ireland circuit, one of eight operational communications circuits for U-boats operating in enemy areas. This was changed for *U-175* to the

* A compressed text out of a special, short signals code book. Used to reduce risk of revealing a U-boat's location with longer transmissions.

coastal ('America 2') circuit the following day. On 16 February BdU signalled *U-108*, *U-175* and *U-125* (Kptlt Ulrich Folkers) to return to Lorient.

On 22 February BdU informed *U-175* that an escort would meet them at rendezvous position 'Point Laterne' on 24th at 0900hrs, and informed all U-boats that *U-175* would arrive at 'Point Laterne' on 24 February at 0900hrs, the message being received off 54m, signal strength 5. Next day at 2343hrs the 10th U-Flotille instructed *U-175*: 'Radio beacons [for homing] Group 1 will run from now until daybreak'. Bruns had requested the beacons, and *U-175*'s safe return followed, after a harrowing and not entirely successful second patrol, with only one sinking, the US Liberty ship *Benjamin Smith*.

On 10 April *U-175* departed Lorient at 6pm on her third and last patrol. Next day BdU signalled new headings for *U-552* (Popp), *U-628* (Hasenschar), *U-465* (Wolf), *U-265* (Looks), *U-262* (Franke), Bruns in *U-175* and Borchers in *U-226*. While no convoy was mentioned in the message, B-Dienst intercepts suggest that U-boat Command may have already been aware of the approach of Convoy HX-233 along the general latitude of Lorient and directed out-bound boats in the direction of its expected approach to intercept. Bruns signalled his position as BE59 (46°05'N 16°45'W) to BdU on 15 April, reporting 223cbm of fuel, wind NW Force 3, sea state 2, overcast with mist and barometer falling.

Later the same day BdU signalled 'all subs concerned', a total of nine of which *U-175* was one, to alter course for 'area JX65', which British intelligence interpreted as: Naval Square AK15, position 58°39'N, 36°24'W (in mid-Atlantic), and *U-197* (KK Robert Bartels) to report his position at once.

At 1859hrs on 15 April BdU signalled *U-175*, Bruns, as follows:

> For Machinist's Mate Second Class Karl Keutken in recognition of your services as machinist's mate second class on a sub, I award you the German Cross in Gold in the name of the Führer and Supreme Commander of the Wehrmacht. (signed) Commander-in-Chief. Hearty congratulations of Com subs West.*

That evening, at 2327hrs, Bruns signalled BDU: 'One destroyer [probably *Spencer*] in Naval Square BE4542' (47°03'N 23°15'W), who in turn reported it to all U-boats 'in Series 1 [with a] Signal Strength 5.'

B-Dienst (Funkbeobachtungsdienst, the German radio-monitoring and cryptographic service) had apparently intercepted the Allied traffic and noted the departing Convoy HX-233. BdU's KTB indicates they were well aware of the North Atlantic convoy cycles and when to expect the next series, so perhaps were only partly taken by surprise to find the convoy so far south of the usual North America-UK track and thus able to react promptly to deploy several additional, nearby, outward-bound U-boats against it. When *U-262* (Kptlt Franke) was driven off and resumed course for

---

* Deutsches Kreuz: German Cross in Gold. This was the highest German Order awarded in the Second World War. In three classes, gold with diamonds, gold, and silver; the gold being awarded for courage in the face of the enemy. It was normally awarded in recognition of several outstanding achievements rather than a single gallant deed. The Order was introduced on 28 September 1941 as an attempt to bridge the gap between the Iron Cross First Class and the Knight's Cross of the Iron Cross.

'Operation Magpie', BdU ordered Koch to assume contact.

On 16 April at 1903hrs BdU requested a weather report from Bruns by 0500hrs. Next morning, 17 April, at 0336hrs Bruns dispatched a short weather report. At 1057hrs he radioed BdU: 'Halte Fühlung' [I am keeping contact]. This was the last message from *U-175*. BdU signalled all Series 1 U-boats: 'Bruns is keeping contact with convoy [HX 233]'. A signal from BdU next morning, giving Bruns instructions to break off contact and steer for Grid Square BD51, followed by a request at 2144hrs for a weather report, went unanswered. It came too late. Bruns was dead, *U-175* was lost, and her surviving crew were prisoners of war.

BdU was not aware of *U-175*'s loss for some time. Next day, 18 April, BdU signalled new headings for eight U-boats including *U-175*, instructing them: 'Operation will be discontinued on 18 April in the forenoon. Subs which cannot attack anymore in the night or stand ahead [of the convoy] discontinue. Report position and fuel, and head for square as ordered in paragraph 2' (ie, AK51, in position 55°55'N 34°45'W).

On 25 April BdU, apparently still unaware of the loss of *U-175*, sent a signal informing Bruns that his 2nd WO, Paul Möller, had been promoted to Lieutenant and forwarding congratulations from the 10th U-Flotille. Later notes in BdU's file show that *U-175* was sunk by US Coast Guard cutters, *Spencer* and *Duane*, escorting HX-233 on 17 April 1943, in position 47°58'N 21°12'W, and, 'The only information on Bruns from traffic before his sinking was that he was outbound from France. *Spencer*'s sound contact on Bruns while he was practically in the middle of convoy led to his sinking.' (Dated 14 February 1945.) One further note reports that Bruns did not survive and lists surviving officers as 'Verlohr, 1st Lt. P/W; Möller, Paul, 2nd Lt. P/W; and Nowroth, Ing. P/W'.

As the Allies became ever more adept at reading U-boat traffic, successes of the U-boats against earlier convoys became ever more difficult to sustain in the face of steadily increasing technical and material superiority.

Radio HF/DF intercepts and the Admiralty's U-boat plots indicated that German submarines were in contact with Convoy HX-233 from 15 April 1943. This would have been *U-262* (Kptlt Franke) outward-bound, who reported to BdU, who in turn directed seven more U-boats to attack, all outward-bound, all in the vicinity of the convoy: *U-614, U-382, U-264, U-358, U-226,* and *U-628,* all Type VIIC, and *U-175,* the larger Type IXC.

BdU reported in its War Diary that *U-262* was driven off and lost contact. *Spencer* recorded U-boat transmissions intercepted on 15 April, probably *U-262*, but deemed not close enough to warrant direct escort action. In fact, the HF/DF log shows interceptions as early as 1000hrs on 11 April which were ignored. The record summarises forty-six U-boat transmissions during the passage of Convoy HX-233, thirty of sufficient strength to obtain a bearing and twelve first-class bearings identified as submarines in the immediate vicinity of the convoy, 10 to 25 miles distant. Seven were obtained within four hours of the attack on 17 April and all seven were described as messages 'of highest German priority' or 'Enemy Attack Traffic'.

On 17 April the seven bearings placed four U-boat transmissions on the port beam of the convoy: one on the port bow, one almost dead ahead and one off the starboard bow, while another signal astern indicated a U-boat shadowing the convoy. The transmission intercepts allowed several escort counter-attacks. It is worthwhile noting that with Support Group Three reinforcing the preceding convoy HX-230, the use of radio direction-finding enabled the escorts to find and force under the reporting U-boat, thereby leaving a hole in the extensive patrol line through which the convoy passed safely. Of the fast convoys that followed, HX-231 (sixty-one merchant ships) was attacked by wolf pack 'Löwenherz' of fifteen boats, reinforced by an additional seven.

Some ninety-eight new U-boats had arrived in the Atlantic during April, which meant a concentration of many inexperienced commanders and junior officers, as well as a high proportion of raw crew members whose training had been telescoped into a few intense months. According to one source:

The US Coast Guard cutter *Spencer* as she appeared in 1943. Her HF/DF antenna is visible on her foremast. *(US Navy Photograph)*

It was from the last days of March that, in the course of convoy operations by the U-boat Command, the Allies obtained the first substantial evidence of a decline in U-boat morale.

This is perhaps disingenuous, as rather than a decline in morale, which remained high to the end, there was a marked decline in U-boat efficiency due to new boats and untried crews, coupled with the infinitely greater strength and efficiency of the enemy. HX-231 was escorted by crack Escort Group B-7, led by Commander Peter Gretton RN, who with the help of VLR aircraft not only beat off the wolf pack attacks, losing only three ships and three stragglers, but sank two U-boats and severely damaged several others. This could be deemed perhaps the 'end of the beginning', as the U-boats were never again able to repeat the successes they harvested against Convoys HX-229/SC 122. That battle had cost 292 officers and crew of the merchant service, the vast majority of whom, as always, were British. HX-231 was dubbed the 'crisis convoy'. The convoy that followed, HX-232, lost three ships, and HX-233, as we have seen, only one. The corner had clearly been turned by 17 April 1943. By this time BdU seems to have finally become aware of the dangers of excess radio chatter from U-boats, as a signal decrypted about this time by the Allies contained a reprimand for excessive wireless transmissions. Yet BdU still relied on its 'Enigma' cipher machine which they were certain was impenetrable. For the Allies the worst was over as losses for April fell to fifty-six ships of 327,943grt sunk by U-boats, only slightly more than half the losses of the previous month.

There were innumerable mistakes and errors in judgement on both sides, of course, and the U-boats were defeated by a combination of advancing technology and the mustering of an overwhelming force. The deciding factor seemed to be that the side making the least number of mistakes wins in the end, and the Allies could afford more mistakes.

The failure of BdU to detect the use, or suspect the capability, of the Allies' HF/DF was unquestionably one of several decisive factors. It seems never to have occurred to the Germans that Allied escorts could be locating U-boats by their radio transmissions in the vicinity of the convoys. The U-boats' attention was riveted, instead, on the efficiency and accuracy of enemy radar, so they did not notice the connection between their radio signals and immediate reaction of the escorts making straight for them.

This was despite the fact that Oblt Otto Ites of *U-94* suggested the possibility as early as June 1942 after being heavily depth charged, although a BdU analysis in May 1943 does not mention his suspicion. Furthermore, German intelligence had absolute proof of the presence of short-wave, direction-finding equipment in the escorts. In passing, unobserved, by Convoy ON-175, a U-boat patrol line reported to German B-Dienst on 4 April 1943 that an escort (*Spencer* senior escort in Task Unit 24.1.9) was equipped 'mit Kurzwellenpeiler', or 'short wave antenna,' and two similar reports followed. The U-boat had observed, without being aware of its purpose, *Spencer*'s HF/DF antenna, which can be clearly seen on her foremast on page 129.

German agents operating in Spain across from Gibraltar photographed a number of British destroyers entering or leaving with HF/DF antennae clearly visible, but they failed to recognise their significance. Had BdU realised the vital importance of this new technology, they could have taken immediate counter-measures, including at least eliminating U-boat radio chatter. Or, as Prof Dr Rohwer suggests, a radio buoy could have misled the escorts into more exposed positions where, particularly after a new acoustic homing torpedo ('der Zaunkönig', 'the wren') came into service in the fall of 1943, they would have been dangerously exposed.

On the other side, the Allies also overlooked opportunities. On 15 April four radio transmissions from *U-262*, after acknowledging receipt of BdU's order to execute Operation Magpie, requested permission to attack convoys. The U-boat was in nearby Grid Square BE7274, on a westerly collision course with the convoy. *Spencer* intercepted *U-262*'s (Franke's) signal to BdU that he had sighted Convoy HX-233 at 0434hrs on 16 April 1943 and an hour later forced *U-262* underwater, where she was compelled to stay through repeated, heavy attacks for six hours. Finally, Franke had to break off his attack. Numerous other HF/DF intercepts were ignored, however.

13

The Final Leg for Convoy HX-233

Convoy Commodore O H Dawson RNR, in *Devis* reported that fifty-one ships sailed from New York and seven from Halifax, at an average speed of 9.5 knots. The US Liberty ship *James Fenimore Cooper* with a general cargo was assigned position 95, and the US freighter *Lena Luckenbach* (ex-*Eastern Sailor*, 5,238grt, built 1920 Japan, owners Luckenbach SS Co, New York), also with a general cargo, occupied station No 81. She was abeam to starboard of the Commodore's *Devis* and had difficulty maintaining station, whether from engine or steering problems or lack of experience by her deck officers. The Commodore, aware of her poor station-keeping, which created a hazard to nearby ships, shifted her to vacant position 105, the last ship in the tenth column. He also ordered *James Fenimore Cooper* to take up a new position, No 102, on 20 April 1943, with no reason stated.

In the early morning hours of 20 April, shortly after *Spencer* and *Duane* had left the convoy, *Lena Luckenbach* and *James Fenimore Cooper* reported themselves in collision; fortunately neither had the explosive cargoes that so many ships carried in this convoy. HMCS *Wetaskiwin*, then senior officer, ordered HMS *Dianthus* to close, investigate and stand-by as required.

Dianthus reported that *James Fenimore Cooper* had her stern stove in and her forepeak flooded, and that she 'might not remain afloat but was able to make 6 knots'. Having no suitable charts, the *Cooper* was escorted into the River Clyde by HMS *Arvida*.

Dianthus closed *Lena Luckenbach* and reported her well down by the head. Two hours later the master of the *Luckenbach* considered abandoning, as water had reached her engine-room bulkhead. *Dianthus* informed the Master that tugs were on their way and encouraged him to remain aboard, but that if he were to abandon, he should secure the confidential books and leave a working party aboard to aid in rigging a tow. The US freighter M/S *Lightning* nearby, bound for Liverpool, was asked to pick up *Lena Luckenbach*'s boats after it was known her crew had abandoned her. *Lightning* picked up her lifeboats with sixty-three crew and at 1300hrs departed for Liverpool. No working party was left on board the *Luckenbach* to facilitate a tow.

On the morning of 20 April HMS *Bergamot* had received orders to search for *Lena*

Lena Luckenbach which was in collision with the Liberty ship *James Fenimore Cooper* on 20 April 1943, and was salvaged by HMS *Bergamot*. *(The Steamship Historical Society of America)*

Luckenbach and found her after some time, well down by the head, abandoned and wallowing in heavy seas. Although the master had failed to leave a line handling party aboard as ordered by *Dianthus*, the possibility of salvage was still clearly evident. *Bergamot* had sent a boarding party across to rig a tow. A large sea was running and *Dianthus* circled, providing an asdic screening sweep and an oil slick to help moderate the rough seas.

Boarding and rigging the towline were successful and, as one crew member recalls, 'Considering the weather and the circumstances, a very good job was done by all to get our 11in towing hawser across . . ' However, as the tow began, a large sea hit the wallowing freighter, causing her to surge, and 'the tow rope parted with a sharp crack as the slack was jerked straight'.

Bergamot's boarding party reported the *Lena Luckenbach* had obviously been abandoned in unseemly haste, if not in outright panic. All the lifeboats were gone, and unfinished meals, cards and money scattered around on the mess room tables, were further evidence of a hasty departure. On reboarding *Bergamot*, the boat's crew were handing up souvenirs collected on the *Luckenbach* when the commanding officer observed them and ordered everything be returned immediately, which was promptly done.

Later, to *Bergamot*'s crew's vexation and annoyance, when HM Tug *Growler* of the *Bustler* class arrived next morning at 0735hrs, the sea had abated to an almost flat calm,

James Fenimore Cooper was in collision with *Lena Luckenbach*. Despite damage to hers bows she made port safely, under escort. *(The Steamship Historical Society of America)*

and the tug first positioned herself under the stern of the abandoned vessel while the crew busied themselves throwing everything movable down onto their own vessel.

Bergamot screened until a second tug, *Destiny*, arrived and the two tugs finally managed to get the *Lena Luckenbach* underway, ultimately to be beached as described elsewhere. Despite nearly losing her once, when she lurched and settled 2ft by the head with a 5° port list, the tugs towed the *Luckenbach* safely to Rothesay. Then *Bergamot* returned to her base at Gladstone Dock, Liverpool.

Bergamot's recollections of the damaged ship were vivid from the outset. During one night in convoy the after-lookout suddenly saw her bows rear up out of the blackness, threatening to ram them astern. After a frantic report to the bridge, and with the whole ship vibrating madly, they went full ahead to avoid the rampaging freighter. *Bergamot*'s lookout reported two men on the bows of the vessel shouting and waving their arms wildly, to indicate that they were out of control.

The collision between the *Lena Luckenbach* and *James Fenimore Cooper* had occurred in 55°10'N 09°W, and Armed Guard CO Lt jg J J Stevenson on *Lena Luckenbach* reported the vessel straggling initially, before rejoining the convoy on 14 April 1943. He further stated that,

> . . . the ship was rammed on the port side between No 1 and No 2 hatches by another cargo ship, the *James Fenimore Cooper*. The *Luckenbach* was badly damaged and began at once to settle by the bow. The other ships of the convoy proceeded, but the attention of a corvette was finally attracted by signalling and it stood by. At about 1045hrs, in view of the apparent hopelessness of the situation of the ship, together with the heavy sea, and after conferring with the corvette, the captain ordered the abandoning of the ship. This was accomplished in good order, the entire crew being picked up later by the M/V *Lightning* and taken to Liverpool, England. The Navy

Lena Luckenbach with the boarding party from HMS *Bergamot*
preparing towing hawsers. Note the damage to her gun platform.
(T F J Rogers)

gun crew were then sent to Londonderry. The ship was later salvaged, and the
gunnery officer with five men reported back on board May 10, the remaining
members of the Gun Crew remaining in Londonderry awaiting further orders.

Ensign William E McCarthy, gunnery officer on the *James Fenimore Cooper*, reported that 'on the twentieth of April at 0600hrs we had a collision with another
merchant ship doing considerable damage to our bow. We cut our speed to half. One
of the escorts dropped back and stayed with us until we reached port.'

In an attached, separate and undated report Ensign McCarthy reported in three
paragraphs the scant details of the collision as follows:

On the morning of April 20th 1943 we were in collision with the *Lena Luckenbach*.
When I heard the general alarm I went up on the bridge. At that time the merchant
ship was off our starboard bow and appeared out of control. The time was 0600hrs.

One of the men that was on watch on the 3in 50 platform at the time has given to
me an account of what happened. This man is Forte, R J, S 2/c. The merchant
vessel that was in collision with us was crossing our bow port to starboard at a
distance that appeared safe. Then a heavy spray came over the bow which caused
him to lose sight of the ship for a moment. The next time he saw her was when she
was coming head on. He immediately left the gun deck and proceeded as far as the
forward 20mm gun turret on the starboard side before lying down to protect himself.
While he was coming down, the mate blew the whistle for a port turn. It seemed
quite a while before the collision took place. After the collision he moved back to

midships. He wasn't there long before her stern collided with us. Then she appeared out of control as she drifted away from us.

The damage that resulted from the collision was a flooding of the forepeak. It also tore loose the hawse pipe. There could also be some damage done to the underpinning of the 3in 50 mount. The damage that took place after the stern hit our side was a buckling of the plates. There were no casualties as far as I know.

While the reports of the two gunnery officers fail to clarify exactly what occurred, especially aboard the *Luckenbach*, the complaints registered by Convoy Commodore Dawson regarding her station keeping, seem to confirm that she may have experienced engine and steering problems from the outset. An old ship, she had been engaged in intercoastal North American trade for many years, undoubtedly with minimum maintenance. Years of neglect, as with many of the prewar coastal fleet, had taken their toll, leaving the vessels barely able to cope with the strains of North Atlantic weather and convoy duty. The miracle is that there were not more breakdowns and collisions, especially with hastily trained, inexperienced officers to replace those lost during the opening months of full involvement in the War.

Lena Luckenbach appears to have lost steering control and in heavy seas collided with *James Fenimore Cooper*, right forward, opening the latter's forepeak to the sea by striking her well forward of No 1 hatch, and causing her to take on considerable water. She struck the *Cooper* again with her stern before drifting clear. While the *Lena Luckenbach* did not sink, it is evident there was considerable danger she would do so and, significantly, she had to be beached after finally being towed to safety in Kames Bay.

Following two months' repair *Lena Luckenbach* returned to the US via Convoy

HMS *Bergamot* with the US freighter *Lena Luckenbach* in tow from an original painting by T F J Rogers *(T F J Rogers)*

A close-up of *Lena Luckenbach* with the tug *Growler* coming alongside.
(*Jim Morris*)

ON-196, departing UK 9 August 1943. Departing New York on 10 December 1943 via Convoy HX-270, she arrived in the River Clyde, Scotland, and on the 4 August 1944 was condemned and deliberately sunk as part of Gooseberry I breakwater, the artificial, harbour, Mulberry A, off the Norman coast of France at Arromanches, consisting of old or heavily damaged vessels deemed of no value in any other capacity and thus redeeming herself with an honourable discharge of an essential duty.

On 20 April 1943 at 0500hrs, *Spencer* and *Duane* left Convoy HX-233 in 55°05'N 09°54'W and made for Greenock Naval Base. The convoy escort SO was assumed by HMCS *Wetaskiwin*, Lt Cdr J R Kidston RCNR, who dispersed the convoy to their various destinations that afternoon. This consisted of six vessels for Loch Ewe for forwarding, including one scheduled for the Russian convoys, six for the Clyde ports and the remainder for the Mersey, less several for Belfast, diverted earlier. Of these many carried explosives or grain, and the majority of tankers were laden with aviation fuel for support of the air offensive against Germany by Bomber Command, who, ironically, had so steadfastly refused to provide VLR aircraft to protect the convoys.

14

Epilogue

We will follow the fate of two of *U-175*'s crew, one on each cutter, into captivity and eventual repatriation to their homeland after the War ended.

Mechanikergefreiter Peter Wannemacher celebrated his 19th birthday on 17 April 1943 and was the last man up and overboard from the sinking *U-175*, jumping from the port side of the main deck away from the hail of gunfire, utilising what shelter the already badly damaged conning tower had to offer. At one point he considered returning to the sinking sub, as the rescue cutter looked so far away. Held up by his Dräger escape apparatus and accompanied by Matrosenobergefreiter Dieter Wolf, the two finally reached the scramble net hanging over the side of *Duane* and were helped aboard. Their wet clothes were removed, dry blankets provided and survival kits issued. Objects of considerable curiosity to the Coast Guard crew, they were well treated and provided for during their time aboard the cutter. They arrived in Greenock, Scotland, on 20 April and were turned over to the custody of the British Army guards and entrained for London and the interrogation centre for German POW survivors. Those who had been aboard *Duane* were nonplussed to learn their shipmates on *Spencer* had been placed in irons.

It was more expedient to bring survivors to the UK, since *U-175* was sunk within four days sailing of England by an inbound convoy, so an agreement was reached with the US naval authorities to have the prisoners interrogated in the United Kingdom by experienced interrogators, probably a far more effective choice. The survivors remained at the London facility until 15 May, when Wannemacher was forwarded to the American ETO-POW Camp No 1 near Oxford, in transit to the USA, and then sent onwards to Liverpool on 2 June, departing via a troop ship the next day. The POW's arrived in Norfolk, Virginia, on 12 June and were then sent by train to a huge German POW camp outside Trinidad, Colorado, in southern Las Animas County, just north of the New Mexico boundary. The vast majority of German POWs in this camp were either airforce pilots, downed over the British Isles, or Afrika Korps, captured in North Africa.

Wannemacher remained in Trinidad until 16 January 1944 when he was sent to Camp Warner, Utah, arriving 19th and remaining until 26 March. He was then forwarded to Fort Ord, California, and on 1 May to Camp Papago Park, Arizona, a camp strictly for captured naval personnel. There he remained until 30 September, when he was sent to Idaho Falls, Idaho, to help with the potato harvest, moving to Pocatello on 6 October 1945.

During the potato harvest the prisoners were sent each day by truck to a farm to work. Wannemacher's farmer was a German-American, whose harsh ways may have reflected his own rejection during the War. At noon on the first day the farmer's wife brought a steaming pot of lunch to the barn, but Wannemacher went straight outdoors, took a sandwich from his pocket and sat on the grass to eat, telling the farmer that he had no compunction about refusing the farmer's lunch, as he would not eat in a barn full of animals. To his surprise the farmer invited him to his dining table.

Finally, Wannemacher was among prisoners sent, on 8 February 1946, to Oakland, California, to board the 8,007grt, C-3-S-A1 type transport, *Sea Eagle*, recently returned to the US Maritime Commission after wartime service as a Navy attack transport. Calling at San Pedro on 28 February, the *Sea Eagle* passed through the Panama Canal on 17 March.

While lying anchored on the Pacific side of the Canal, waiting their turn to transit, at 0800hrs on 17 March, the German POWs could scarcely believe their eyes. The

German POWs from *U-175* being marched away in Scotland from the US Coast Guard cutter *Duane*, in custody of the British military authorities. *(US National Archives)*

huge, graceful German cruiser, *Prinz Eugen*,* was steaming toward them, out of the Panama Canal. Waving and shouting, they soon realised her crew was a mix of German and American. Then from the cruiser, loud and clear, came the familiar greeting: 'Hummel! Hummel!' The POWs, overcome with joy, responded still louder with: 'Mors! Mors!' the traditional seeman's greeting in north German dialect. Years later the American who had been captain of the *Prinz Eugen* that day came to Germany to tell a U-boat veterans' meeting about the encounter on 17 March 1946, confirming an incident that many of their comrades had thought till then was a product of their imagination. The *Prinz Eugen* was sailing to the Pacific as a target in an atomic test on Bikini Atoll, 17 June 1946. She was sunk in November the following year during another test, but her propellor, which survived both blasts intact, can be seen today in the grounds of the German Naval Museum in Laboe, on the Kieler Förde near the Baltic Sea.

Making only a brief call at Jamaica, the *Sea Eagle* arrived at Liverpool on 1 April 1946. From there Wannemacher was forwarded briefly to POW Camp 180 at Northwich before being sent to Manin Camps 76 and 86 at Brampton, Cumbria, south of Carlisle. At Camp 76 Wannemacher worked in a quarry and headed a platoon of fellow POWs because of his fluent English. His assignment in Camp 86 was laying pipes for swamp drainage.

One day at the quarry the English captain told Wannemacher he had seen some of his men stealing coal from the railway wagons, and he knew Wannemacher would take care of the matter. The men relinquished the coal, which Wannemacher and another prisoner took back, but as they were returning, a guard spotted them. Not believing their story, he took them to the captain, who said they would have to go to court. Before the court session took place, however, the captain sent a British officer fluent in German to tell the prisoners not to fear the trial or his questioning. It simply had to be done. The 'harsh' sentence imposed at the end of the trial was 'Forbidden to work for fourteen days', a good example of British fairness that all former prisoners recall.

In America, to pass the time, Wannemacher had tried his hand at making ships' models – destroyers, U-boats, ships in bottles, etc, and brought a few with him to England. A grocer in Brampton, a former sergeant, admired Wannemacher's ships and offered to sell them in his shop. The models sold 'like hotcakes', says Herr Wannemacher. He could scarcely keep up with the grocer's demand for them, and proceeds in pounds sterling were a good incentive.

On 18 June 1947 Wannemacher embarked at Hull for Cuxhaven, arriving next day, and was forwarded to the British Army facility at Munsterlager before being sent to Dachau near Munich. He was finally released from Dachau on 2 July 1947, at last free and able to return home.

---

* Heavy cruiser, built Germania Werft, Kiel, launched 22.8.38. 13,900 × 654 ts; armour: sides 5in, deck 4in, turrets 5in; armament: 8–8in, 12–4.1in, 12–37mm AA, 28–20mm AA, 12–21in TT, 3 aircraft. Complement: 1,600. Supported Baltic front 1944-5, surrendered Copenhagen May 45, allocated to USA. Damaged by atom bomb explosion Bikini Atoll 17.6.46. Sunk Kawajalein Atoll 15.11.47.

We will now track the fate of one of those picked up by *Spencer*, following the loss of *U-175*: Maschinenobergefreiter Werner Bickel of Zehla-Melis, Thuringen, whose written evidence was invaluable in reconstructing these events. He was stationed in the 'Zentrale des Bootes', or command centre on the morning of 17 April 1943, so fully aware of events aboard *U-175* prior to abandonment.

Having overtaken and gone ahead of Convoy HX-233 during the night of 16–17 April, *U-175* submerged ahead after a high speed run of some 10 hours. At 0830hrs, at battle stations, the convoy came into the view of the periscope and Bruns selected his target. Suddenly, the hydrophone operator reported propeller sounds bearing 120°, coming rapidly nearer. Bruns had already given the order to prepare to fire a spread of three torpedoes at the largest ship in the convoy, the Esso tanker *G Harrison Smith*, and the torpedo man had entered the data into the 'Torpedo-Schuss-Empfänger' and 'Vorhaltrechner'. He only awaited the order 'Torpedo los!', as the propeller sounds grew in intensity. Too late Bruns realized the danger. At that moment eleven depth charges exploded around, above and below *U-175* with terrible and devastating effect. As described earlier, badly shaken she plunged down at 40°, with all the loose gear cascading forward, to a depth of some 350m. Water entered the battery room, creating deadly chlorine gas. The chief engineer reported to Bruns that the boat was no longer controllable. Then came the order 'Anblasen!' (Blow all tanks!), as the depth gauge

The last view of *U-175* as she slips beneath the surface at 1227hrs on 17 April 1943. In the battle of the Atlantic the tide had turned in the Allies' favour. *(US National Archives)*

('Tiefenmesser') recorded 200m, 150m, 100m, 60m, 30m, 20m, 7m, and the boat surfaced. Bruns opened the conning tower hatch and fresh air flooded in, countering the poisonous chlorine fumes.

Then came the first shell hit on the conning tower, followed by another. As Bickel mounted the conning tower, he found Bruns, first man out, lying in his own blood next to the periscope. Behind lay two other bodies, so mangled he was unable to identify them. With the storm of shot and shell coming from starboard, Bickel took shelter on the port side. Then during a brief lull in the firing he sprang overboard into the cold, unwelcoming Atlantic with the convoy still in sight on the horizon.

His last view of *U-175* was of her bow jutting out of the water as she sank stern first, and the survivors struggling in the cold, trackless ocean. Bickel was one of six crew picked up by *Spencer*'s boat, and they boarded the cutter via a scramble net. As a black steward's mate approached with a knife, the shocked, gassed and fearful *U-175* survivors, now prisoners of war, thought their end had come. Instead, their cold, soaked clothing was cut off and they were wrapped in warm blankets marked 'US Navy', and provided with hot coffee, brandy and welcome cigarettes. They were then herded into an empty room overseen by armed guards, and soon fed a hot meal. Suddenly, a nearby explosion of depth charges shook the ship, quickly spoilt their appetites, and they were hastily herded back to their prison cell under guard.

The following day each man was issued with a survival kit, and when dressed they were handcuffed in pairs to go on deck. There Bickel noted a 5–10cm hole in *Spencer*'s motor boat, caused by the stray shell of 'friendly fire' that killed one man and wounded fourteen of *Spencer*'s crew.

Maschinenmaat Herman Küffner, something of an artist, sketched Alpine scenes on US Navy letterhead stationary for the souvenir-hungry Americans, receiving a carton of cigarettes for each sketch. On the third day *Spencer* arrived in Greenock and moored at the naval base there. The prisoners were marched ashore, shackled together, behind the prisoners on *Duane*, and handed over to the British officer who ordered the men freed at once.

From Scotland the POWs from *U-175* were taken by train to London and held in English custody for interrogation from 21 April to 13 May, and Bickel was questioned on four occasions by different British officers on various subjects. On 13 May the prisoners went by train to US Army ETO-POW Camp No 1, APO 871, a Nissen-hutted camp near Oxford behind double barbed wire, already occupied by about 1,000 Luftwaffe paratroopers and Wehrmacht armoured troops, mostly captured in North Africa. Food was described as good and a sports field allowed various games, including volley ball.

Photographed, finger-printed and assigned serial numbers, Bickel's prisoner of war record (ISB-ETO-709-Na) shows that Section II, POW Cir 3, WD 1943 US Army (ie, initial issue of toilet articles) was complied with on 7 July 1943 and no personal effects were taken from him.

Each POW was issued $3 per month in 'Lagergeld' (POW camp chits or coupons) with which he could purchase cigarettes, soap, writing paper and other necessities. A

German POWs from *U-175* onboard *Spencer*. From left to right,
Hermann Küffner, Werner Kahmann, Erwin Geimeier, Helmut
Schlosser, Hermann Kohler, Walter Wepplemann, and Max Klinger.
(US National Archives)

pack of twenty cigarettes cost a mere 12 cents. The German camp commander
('Lagerführer') was a senior NCO ('Oberfeldwebel') from an airborne division. A
Berliner, he had earlier been a policeman, and was an athletic, well-built man,
completely trusted by the entire camp.

A secret tunnel was begun, inspired by a Luftwaffe pilot with the idea of stealing an
aircraft. He enticed the prisoners with the idea of escape under the wire. The tunnel
began under the floor of the hut nearest the fence, beneath the barrack stove, but
before the plans came to fruition Bickel was loaded into a lorry along with hundreds
of others and transported to the nearest railway station, en route to Liverpool on 3
June 1943.

Loaded aboard an 8,000grt American trooper, otherwise unidentified, they were on
their way to America, sailing the following day, alone. Following a zig-zag course at
high speed to thwart any lurking U-boats, the vessel arrived at Norfolk, Virginia, on
12 June. The prisoners were disembarked, marched into the railway station and seated
on stools. They were then given brutally short hair cuts under the eyes of numerous
heavily armed guards, until the intervention of an officer who put a stop to the
needless humiliation. Disinfection afterwards sufficed. Their clothing was replaced

with US Government (GI) issues with a large, black 'PW' stenciled on the jacket and the trouser legs.

Marched aboard 'Pacific Express' pullman cars with an armed military policeman at each end of the coaches, the prisoners rolled westward at 1800hrs the same day via Richmond, Cincinnati, Indianapolis, St. Louis, Kansas City to Pueblo, Colorado, thence south to Trinidad, arriving on 14 June for a 2km march from the railway station to the camp. Located on a plateau at 2,000m at the foot of the Rocky Mountains, the camp offered a breathtaking mountain panorama to the weary and anxious prisoners.

The camp consisted of five sections for enlisted personnel and one for officers, surrounded by double barbed wire fences and double gates, surmounted by well-spaced guard watch towers. Wooden barracks accommodated 250 men each. Food was described as equivalent to a three-star hotel ('einen drei-sternen Hotel'). Two months later, in August 1943, came a large influx of additional Afrika Korps prisoners, captured following the capitulation in Tunisia in May of that year. This rapidly filled the Trinidad camp.

Bickel volunteered to work in the officers' compound, earning an extra $12 a month 'Lagergeld', which with his regular $3 provided substantial income, which he started to save. He also took courses offered in basic English and shorthand. The German prisoners devised regular in-house theatre performances, and the U-boat POWs

Maschinenobergetreiter Werner Bickel.
(Peter Wannemacher)

formed a shanty chorus under the leadership of Uffz Küffner. Their rendition of 'Rolling Home' brought thunderous applause from appreciative fellow captives.

On 13 March 1944 Bickel, along with four other *U-175* crew and twenty-two others, was transferred to the POW camp in Papago Park, Arizona. Here Bickel remained until 31 May when he was transferred to Camp Beal, California, returning to Papago Park Camp from 22 October to 2 December 1944, then to two tent camps, first at Mesa, then at Queen's Creek, Arizona, picking the cotton harvest, then returning to Papago Park until 27 September 1945. On 30 September he was sent to Camp Rupert, Idaho, to harvest potatoes, returning to the Arizona tent camps and finally to Papago Park until 19 February 1946. Two days later he was dispatched to San Francisco, California, on the first long leg of his repatriation, homewards and freedom.

The homeward-bound voyage, on the C1-A ship *Cape Douglas*, commenced in the early hours of 21 February 1946, as the lines were cast off and the vessel steamed out past Alcatraz Island and through the Golden Gate. The passage south was marked by boiler problems, with repairs necessary in Panama. The Canal was a source of considerable awe and wonder to the prisoners. Whilst crossing the Atlantic, Bickel celebrated his twenty-fourth birthday and third year in captivity. The vessel arrived in Liverpool on 21 March 1946, where the former crew from *U-175* found themselves back in English custody, to be transported to a POW camp near the small village of Barlow, east of Leeds in the Midlands, freedom seemingly as far away as ever. They were compelled to work at the railway depot, whilst housed in ten-man wooden barracks behind barbed wire; their utensils were engraved with 'Hotel Astoria Hamburg', perhaps some British army's wartime booty.

Finally, on 22 February 1947, Bickel was transferred to the POW repatriation camp at nearby Snaith, headed, at last, homewards after four long and wasted years. Here prisoners were separated according to their original homes and on 13 March Bickel celebrated his twenty-fifth birthday and fourth year in captivity. The following day, as a belated present, he was ordered to pack for the trip to the port of Kingston-upon-Hull the next day, where the prisoners were marched aboard the transport *Empire Spearhead* for the short voyage to Cuxhaven in north Germany.

By coincidence *Empire Spearhead* was a sister ship to *Cape Douglas*, which had brought Bickel from California a year earlier.

Arriving in the early morning hours of 16 March in Cuxhaven, the prisoners were taken by rail to former Kaserne Munsterlager, south of Hamburg in the former Wehrkreis X, or the German Army Corps' administrative, manoeuvre and proving grounds area. Here they remained two days before being again entrained for transportation to the 'Flüchtlingslager Friedland' (refugee camp). Here Bickel underwent a physical examination which certified he was 'not verminous or suffering from any infectious or contagious disease', signed by a Dr Beudel, and he was issued with a certificate of discharge ('Entlassungsschein') on Control orm D2, dated 17 March 1947, signed by CSM W Cahill of the Irish Guards, British Army. Bickel was then moved to the village of Arenshausen, thence over the boundary of the Russian

Occupied Zone to Hermsdorf, where he was quarantined from 22 March to 3 April. With home so near Bickel commented that those 14 days were the longest of his entire four years of imprisonment, a final and gruelling test of patience and fortitude. Released on 3 April 1947, he boarded a train via Erfurt for home, arriving at Zella-Mehlis on the evening of 4 April to the welcome of his dear mother and betrothed Ruth after four years and one month of captivity and six years and two months of naval service. Looking back, Bickel, like all *U-175* survivors, regards 17 April 1943 as his second birthday, when he was fished from the cold North Atlantic seas. His was the greatest good fortune to have survived near death and the inferno of war, but he returned, however, to yet another brutal military dictatorship.

It was years before the U-boat crew began to find one another again, but after diligent pursuit and several strokes of good luck they began to meet, first individually, then biannually as a group, including wives and families, and finally the yearly 'Treff' in the hometown of one of them. In 1991 it was Max and Anni Klinger's turn to host the group in Aichach, Bavaria, and the year was a special one to commemorate – the 50th anniversary of their boat's commission – and a number of the original crew were among those celebrating.

*   *   *

Escort Ships and Commanders

At 1845hrs on 18 April 1943, all off-duty hands on *Spencer* were piped to quarters in dress uniform for the funeral service of Julius T Petrella, RM 3/c, USCG, killed 'while this vessel was engaging the enemy on 17 April 1943'. At 1855hrs speed was reduced to 63rpm and the national ensign lowered to half mast. The commanding officer read the brief burial service and the body was committed to the deep as a firing squad firing a volley of three rounds. Four minutes later all hands resumed ship's routine.

On 20 April at 0500hrs HMCS *Wetaskiwin* assumed escort commander duty, and *Spencer* and *Duane* departed Convoy HX-233 in accordance with orders from CINCWA. At 1800hrs both Coast Guard vessels were moored outboard alongside HMS *Eclipse* at North Pier, Greenock, and one hour later the German survivors of *U-175* were handed over to the custody of British Army Officer-in-charge.

At 1442hrs, 24 April 1943, *Spencer* and *Duane* departed for US Naval Operating Base, Londonderry, North Ireland, where they arrived at 0910hrs the following day, and on 30 April they departed from Londonderry en route to Boston, via the Great Circle, course at best speed. On 3 May *Duane* parted company, having been diverted to Argentia, Newfoundland.

Spencer arrived Boston, 6 May 1943, 1123hrs at Pier East, US Naval Drydock, South Boston, signalling the end of her service in Escort Group A-3 which had been disbanded. During her service with A-3 in the North Atlantic *Spencer* sank two

U-boats: *U-225* on 21 February and *U-175* on 17 April 1943. Her subsequent career included convoy escorting in the Mediterranean and Caribbean in 1944. She was then converted to an AGC, or amphibious force flag ship, with greatly increased and more sophisticated communications equipment, and served in the landings at the Philippines and Borneo through 1944-45. *Duane*'s career followed that of her sistership except that following AGC conversion she served in the Mediterranean and was with the Eighth Amphibious Force flagship during the 1944 invasion of Southern France.

Spencer served on after the War, including a tour in Vietnam in 1969. She was decommissioned 15 December 1980 to become an Engineer Training School and sold on 8 October 1981.

Duane's end was rather ignominious, being decommissioned 1 August 1985 and deliberately sunk as a fishing reef on 27 November 1987.

The Esso tanker *G Harrison Smith*, the target of *U-175* on that memorable North Atlantic day, her hull, cargo and luck intact, delivered her cargo to Bowling on the Clyde, on 22 April 1943. She returned safely to New York to survive the War, losing one man en route as the result of an engine-room accident. She delivered a total of 10,334,870 barrels of fuel cargo to the various war fronts between 1939 and 1945.

Of the major players Captain Heineman, in command of Escort Group A-3, performed somewhat better than his predecessor despite serious friction with British and Canadian naval authorities, perhaps caused by the attitudes of his US Navy superiors. He was fortunate in having the Support Group of four powerful and experienced British destroyers arrive at a critical moment in the battle around Convoy HX-233. The British part of his command had all seen long, hard service in the Arctic and North Atlantic and had already sunk several U-boats. HMS *Bryony* had three Russian convoys to her credit, including hard-fought PQ-18; HMS *Daniella*, in eight such convoys, had been in the disastrous PQ-17; and HMS *Bergamot*, with four Russian trips had defended Convoy PQ-15, the first convoy to be attacked by torpedo planes. The Third Support Group included HMS *Offa*, veteran of twenty-five Russian convoys including both PQ-17 and PQ-18; and HMS *Impulsive*, who escorted thirteen convoys, unmatched anywhere else except in the Malta relief efforts. Five of HX-233's merchant ships were also veterans of those most dangerous convoys, for a total of nine trips to Russia. The number of likewise experienced merchant navy crew cannot be calculated.

After the disbanding of Escort Group A-3, Captain Heineman served first as Atlantic Fleet 'Analyst Officer' and on 19 July 1943 became 'Vice Chancellor of the US Anti-Submarine University' near Norfolk, Virginia. Although his anti-submarine career was no match for those of his several British counterparts, he had the advantage of highly experienced British and Canadian escorts within his brief command. He became naval anti-submarine 'Co-ordinator' on 22 September 1943 and was rated by one US Navy author as 'among the best in either navy'.

In 1944 Captain Heineman was posted as commanding officer of the newly commissioned (23 March 1943) light cruiser USS *Biloxi*, CL 80, shortly before she joined the Pacific TG 38.4 as part of the US Third Fleet for the Leyte invasion, 17–25 October 1944.

Commander John B Heffernan, USN, Heineman's predecessor, was promoted to Captain after serving in Destroyer Squadron 13 in USS *Buck* during the occupation of Iceland in Task Force 37, then in convoy AT-17, which inadvertently delivered 20,000 British troops directly into the hands of the Japanese at Singapore. At the North Africa landings on 8 November 1942 Captain Heffernan commanded Destroyer Squadron 13 (Comdesron 13) in the new destroyer USS *Bristol* (DD 453) (*Livermore* class) as part of the Center Attack Group TG-34.9, Task Force 34 under Rear Admiral H Kent Hewitt, at Cape Fedhla, Morocco. *Bristol* made an unsuccessful counter-attack on *U-173* (Schweihel) sister of *U-175*, after she torpedoed the tanker USS *Winooski* (AO-38) and destroyer USS *Hambleton* (DD-455) at anchor off Fedhla. He later commanded Trans Div 38 in *Lamar* (APA-47) in the 1944 invasion of Guam in the Pacific. He next appeared in command of the old battleship, USS *Tennessee* (BB-43) at the Battle of Surigao Straits, 24 October 1944, and as fire support at the Okinawa landings on 1 April 1945. Promoted to Rear Admiral, he became Director of Naval Records and History in Washington, DC.

Captain H G Bradbury, USCG (class 1920), of *Duane* had commanded the transport USS *Wakefield* which caught fire at sea in the North Atlantic whilst in Westbound Convoy TA-18 and was abandoned 3 September 1942. The wreck, burning for

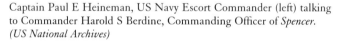

Captain Paul E Heineman, US Navy Escort Commander (left) talking to Commander Harold S Berdine, Commanding Officer of *Spencer*. *(US National Archives)*

eight days and, virtually gutted, was beached off Halifax, later refloated and restored to service by 1944. Captain Bradbury was in convoy AT-17, transporting British troops to the Far East, in command of the transport USS *Leonard Wood* (AP 12). She fell out with boiler trouble but later rejoined. He retired a Rear Admiral as did the former *Spencer* executive officer, John B Oren, USCG (class 1933).

The two admirals engaged in a somewhat acrimonious disagreement over the events surrounding the sinking of *U-175*, which were published in the USCG Alumni bulletin in 1981.

Commander Harold S Berdine, USCG, was promoted to captain and posted to the old flush-deck destroyer *Decatur* (DD-341), in command of Escort Group TF-64, composed of seven Coast Guard-manned destroyer escorts and three old destroyers. On 1 April 1944 while escorting Convoy UGS-36, consisting of seventy-two ships eastbound with eighteen LSTs in company and supported by British 37th Escort Group, two U-boats were driven off and an attack by twenty German aircraft managed to damage only one US Liberty ship, *Jared Ingersoll*, west of Algiers.

Of the other players, Captain J W McCoy RN, of the 3rd Support Group, was SO commanding the vital escort for North Russian Convoy JW-55B, composed of nineteen ships which departed Loch Ewe 20 December 1943. The convoy became the focal point of the subsequent Battle of North Cape on Boxing Day, resulting in the

Captain H G Bradbury, Commanding Officer of *Duane*, on the bridge during the battle around Convoy HX-233. *(US National Archives)*

loss of the German battle ship *Scharnhorst*, the most active and successful of the German fleet. Shelled heavily by HMS *Duke of York* and hit by at least fourteen or fifteen torpedoes, the *Scharnhorst* sank on the evening of 26 December. British destroyers were able to rescue only thirty-six of her crew (none of them officers) of nearly two thousand from the black, icy Arctic Ocean.

Of the eight U-boats around Convoy HX-233 four were lost in 1943, including *U-175*, two the following year and two survived into 1945, one to be scrapped and one to endure a collision and salvage, only to be scuttled at the end of the War. Two were sunk by aerial bombing and the rest fell to ships of the Royal Navy. Of the eight, *U-175* was the most successful, having sunk ten ships before her own loss. The only other coming close was *U-628*, which destroyed six ships before her own sinking only a few weeks later in the Bay of Biscay. This was credited to aircraft.

Many U-boats were surrendered to the Allies. Here, *U-532* is seen at Liverpool in May 1945. *(Imperial War Museum)*

The escorts were quickly sold off after the war and have long since passed into history and scrap. Winston Churchill wrote after the War ended:

> Battles might be won or lost, enterprises succeed or miscarry, territories might be gained or quitted, but dominating all our power to carry on the war, or even keep ourselves alive, was our mastery of the ocean routes and the free approach and entry to our ports . . . the only thing that ever frightened me during the war was the U-boat peril.

Allied and neutral merchant men's wartime casualties were 62,933, and 24,000 of their names appear on the Tower Hill Memorial in London, with others scattered on memorials around the world. The 6,000 American merchant seamen's deaths exceeded in percentage those of any branch of the US armed forces. The great majority of the Royal Navy's losses of 50,758 dead and 820 missing occurred in the Battle of the Atlantic. The worst rate losses were among the German U-boat crews, whose life expectancy was less than 50 days.

As prisoners of war, *U-175* survivors sat out the War in camps located in Colorado, Arizona, Utah and California, participated in escape attempts and were employed mainly in picking cotton and harvesting other crops for local farmers. They ultimately returned to a shattered, devastated, occupied country, where many loved ones were missing, even if only by being displaced, to try to rebuild their homeland and their own lives.

Surviving seamen on both sides continue to be enormously proud of having taken part in that prolonged conflict, now known as 'The Battle of The Atlantic'. The real story was best and most succinctly described by Rear Admiral Leonard Murray, RCN, C-of-C, NW Atlantic, when he wrote: 'The Battle of the Atlantic was not won by any navy or air force; it was won by the courage, fortitude, and determination of the British and Allied Merchant Navy'.

Some authors contend that the safe transportation of 250,860 US troops to the UK during 1942 was a major Allied victory, and so, of course, it was. But had the 1942-3 bridge of ships from the New World to the Old been severed by the U-boats, that victory would have only added that many additional mouths to go hungry amid the British civil population, already on a precarious ration system, and they as well as the Americans would have faced possible abject surrender, with no North African operation or Normandy invasion possible. We had to carry on.

END

Appendices

1 Armed Guard Commanders' Reports to Vice CNO
2 Sailing Telegram of Convoy HX-233
3 Composition of HX-233
4 Notes on Ships of Convoy HX-233
5 Escorts
6 Support Group Vessels
7 Convoy HX-233: 0800hrs Positions
8 Casualties on US Coast Guard Cutter *Spencer*
9 Casualties on SS *Fort Rampart*
10 German POWs on *Spencer*
11 German POWs on *Duane*
12 Casualties on *U-175*
13 U-Boats Operating against Convoy HX-233
14 Technical Details of *U-175*

1   Armed Guard Commanders' Reports to Vice CNO

1. Ensign Ray A Dyke, Commander of the Armed Guard Unit on US Liberty *James Jackson* described the vessel as 'Cargo Model EC-2 with general cargo, owned by the War Shipping Administration of the Maritime Commission, operated by the South Atlantic Steamship Lines', departing New York 1200hrs GMT, 5 April and arriving Liverpool, UK, 0950hrs GMT, 21 April 1943. Report dated 21 April 1943 was classified 'Confidential'.

On 17 April 1943, at 0600hrs GMT in 47°05'N 27°16'W, course 047°, wind NE4, fair visibility, Ensign Dyke reported:

> The lead ship in the first column [*Fort Rampart*] was torpedoed two times. The ship dropped out of the convoy in an orderly manner and fell astern the port side of the convoy. An escort [HMS *Arvida*] closely followed the vessel. It is not known if the vessel was lost. It remained afloat until no longer visible.

Later he described the role of his vessel and gun crew as follows:

> 1235hrs GMT, April 17, 1943, Lat 47°48'N Long 21°06'W. Conditions: Course 047°, Wind NE 4, Visibility very good, partly cloudy and calm sea. Submarine surfaced 5,000yds abaft the convoy, one point off the starboard quarter of this ship. The submarine was apparently forced to the surface by depth charges of two escort vessels.
>
> Welch, John M, 709–30-58, S1/c, V-6, USNR, plugman on the 5in-51 gun, spotted the submarine and fire was opened immediately. The entire gun crew was in the vicinity of the gun on alert standby watch at this time. Two rounds were fired by the crew of this vessel before the escorts changed course and headed for the submarine. The S/S *James Jackson* was the first ship to fire at the submarine. The No 1 pennant was run up immediately upon sighting the submarine. Eight rounds were fired, the first seven short and the eighth one a hit on the base of the conning tower. From this observer's position this appeared to be the second hit scored on the sub. The range of the eight rounds fired was 5,700yds and the deflection 49mils. Fire was halted when the escorts had reached the area of fire within several hundred yards of the submarine. Several other merchantmen joined in the firing. From the telescopes it was apparent that the submarine was permanently demolished. No insignia was visible on the submarine at this distance. It was evidently one of the larger models.

Regarding the problem of misfits Ensign Dyke, under his 'Recommendations', wrote:

> The Commanding Officer of the Unit should have the authority to request the transfer or replacement of a member of his crew who is unfit for this type of detached duty. The Port Director's staff should do all in their power to support the judgment of the Officer and assist him in this respect. A properly timed transfer or replacement could have prevented disciplinary action and a bad conduct record for the misfit.

Ensign Dyke was not the only Armed Guard Commander from ships in this convoy to complain about misfits and serious personnel problems. He reported several alleged incidents of apparent sabotage and possible breaches of security while in England and on their return voyage. On the vessel's return to the United States she was boarded by an unnamed 'Boarding Officer' of the Third Naval District at Pier 2, Staten Island, New York, on 18 May 1943. Ensign R A Dyke and Second Officer F Cogswell were interviewed but added nothing to the initial report submitted in Liverpool. However, the Boarding Officer added: '. . . credit for the submarine sinking was awarded to one of the escort vessels. It was Dyke's belief that S1/c Welch should be commended in some manner as it was believed he was the first man who sighted the submarine as it surfaced.'

Captain Robert L Chaplin, Master of the *James Jackson* wrote the New York Port Director in an undated memorandum, commending 'Lieut (jg) Dyke and his men for courage and prompt defensive action taken when our ship was attacked [sic] by a submarine'.

> 'Our gun crew was the first to sight the sub and the first of the merchant ships to open fire. After several rounds Mr. Dyke's men scored a direct hit [sic], which contributed to the destruction of the enemy.'

The Commandant, Third Naval District (Port Director) F G Reinicke wrote a memorandum dated 2 June 1943 to the Secretary of the Navy's Board of Decorations and Medals, stating that:

> At 1233hrs GMT, April 17, 1943, a submarine attacked [sic] the convoy, of which the 7,176grt merchant ship S/S *James Jackson* was a member, at Lat 47°48'N Long 21°06'W.
>
> It is recommended that a commendation be granted to Lieut (jg) Ray A Dyke Jr D-V (S), USNR, commanding officer of the Navy gun crew, for prompt and decisive action in directing fire on the attacking [sic] submarine when it surfaced 5,000yds abaft the convoy. Lieut (jg) Dyke and his men were the first ship's gun crew to open fire and on the eighth round succeeded in making a direct hit [sic] on the exposed conning tower. Later fire from all ships demolished the enemy craft.

Mr James E Bentley Sr of Tennessee, USMMA engine cadet on the US Liberty *James Jackson* from 21 March 1943 to 26 February 1944, recalls:

> When the action started on the day in question [17 April 1943] I was on watch in the engine room. Just before my watch was over, we heard our 5in stern cannon fire 3 rounds. When I made it to the deck, I saw to our aft the US Coast Guard Cutter *Spencer* racing towards a disabled submarine. I was told the *Spencer* had directed us to cease fire. Our gun crew said they had made a direct hit on the sub. After the submarine sank, the *Spencer* returned to the convoy with survivors on deck.

Mr Robert D Mattox served as USMMA deck cadet in the same vessel from 21 March to 28 August 1943 and recalls it was his first convoy experience, fresh out of basic school at Pass Christian, Mississippi. He further recalls the ship departing from a US east coast port for Liverpool, UK, after being fitted with a barrage balloon and winch for air raid protection.

> As a cadet in training, I was not aware of our convoy or position number in the convoy, but I do remember that we were in a spot called 'coffin corner', lead ship in the outboard column. For some reason, the convoy was narrowed down sometime into the voyage and the *James Jackson* moved to the last position [from position No 11 to position No 125] in one of the other columns and was in that position when the German submarine, damaged by escort depth charges, surfaced well astern of the convoy. The US Navy armed guard crew aboard the *Jackson* began shelling the submarine with our 5in gun until ordered to cease fire by the escorts.

2. Ensign Farris D Weigel, Armed Guard Commander on S/S *Alcoa Cutter*, Convoy Position No 75, reported that they sailed from the New York's North River, arriving Swansea, Wales at 9am on 22 April 1943. He further stated:

> The first contact we had with the enemy was on April 16, 1943 [sic]. Nothing was visible to us but the escorts dropped a series of depth charges. At 1045hrs on April 17, 1943, one of the escort vessels dropped several depth charges just ahead of the column leader on our starboard

side. Four of the escorts started through the convoy and attempted to form a mousetrap [sic] about 200 yards off our port quarter. At 1145hrs a submarine was seen to surface 2 points abaft our port quarter at a distance of approximately 4,500yds. Two of the escorts were between us and the submarine; therefore, it was necessary to hold our fire. Other ships on our port side opened fire, however, as did the two escorts. Gunfire ceased at 1200hrs. The escorts evidently captured the submarine's crew and at 1220hrs the sub was seen to sink, possibly from a shell from one of the escorts. The distance had increased between us and the details were not clear to us.

3. Ensign William F Milligan on the Sun Oil Company tanker, *Sun* (9,002grt), Position No 82, reported that his ship had no direct contact with the enemy.

> As a whole the voyage out and return was routine. On two occasions escorts had successful contact with enemy underwater craft. At 1140hrs convoy time April 17, 1943, an escort dropped depth charges near the head of the convoy while manoeuvring in close circles. After the convoy passed over the spot, a submarine surfaced and was fired on by two escorts. From a distance of over 3 miles, it appeared to be a 'U' boat of the 500grt class.

Ensign Milligan also reported: 'On April 18, 1943, the escort forced another submarine to surface approximately six miles behind the convoy. Lack of gunfire would lead one to believe prisoners were taken.'

4. Ensign S J Marzullo, USNR, Armed Guard Commander on the US Liberty S/S *Roger Williams*, Position No 83, was terse in reporting: 16 April 1943 'Depth charges dropped by escort.' and on 17 April – 'Depth charges dropped by escort from 1100hrs to 1200hrs with probable sinking of one submarine. Submarine surfaced behind convoy, disabled. More depth charges dropped during evening.'

5. Ensign James Sherman, USNR, on Liberty *George Handley* was even more terse, as were several others, in reporting merely: 'No contacts with the enemy'.

6. Ensign Chester C Kasiea of the big Esso tanker *G Harrison Smith*, target of *U-175* and probably also *U-628*, wrote a bit more detail, stating:

> We departed from New York at 1030hrs, 4.6.43 in a convoy of fifty-three ships and five escorts. Later we were joined by five ships and two escorts from Halifax . . . We arrived in the Clyde at 1512hrs, 4.21.43.
>
> At 1650hrs, 4.17.43, the ship adjacent to us on our port side suffered an explosion at its stern. The three lookouts on the port side said the whole after end of the ship seemed to lift out of the water. One believed he saw a greenish glow in the water just before the explosion. [phosphorescence from the torpedo?] The ship showed all kinds of lights and ended up showing a single red torpedoing light and a white light. About twenty depth charges were noted between the incident and slightly past noon.
>
> Gunfire was observed at 1145hrs of the same day from 4 or 5 ships about 2,500yds from us, astern, as well as from 2 destroyers which immediately arrived on the scene. Suddenly we sighted an object between the two destroyers which was carefully guarded by the latter till lost to view. Obviously, the object was a submarine forced to the surface.

It is interesting that Ensign Kasiea does not mention in his report witnessing the German POWs being marched away in Scotland, nor the death of a merchant crew member on the return voyage, possibly because neither incident required armed guard involvement.

7. Ensign Edward S Wise, on board the US Liberty S/S *Jonathan Worth*, Position No 24, reported in some detail, confirming that the convoy was reformed on 15 April 1943 when Column Number 1 was eliminated for unknown reasons, making Column Number 2 outboard on the port side. The US Liberty *James Jackson*, No 11, was repositioned to No 125, or the last ship in Column No 12, and the Panama flag freighter *Yemassee*, No 12, was shifted to a position vacant on the starboard side of the convoy. It is not clear where the remaining ships were moved, but presumably to the vacant positions in Columns originally No 2–3-4, and 11 and 12. It is curious, but unexplained anywhere in the official documents including the commodore's report why the ships were repositioned.

Ensign Wise described the attack on HX-233 as follows:

At 0550hrs GMT, April 17, 1943, at 47°20'N 22°29'W, while off watch duty and proceeding to morning general quarters, MacSorley, Coxswain, reported to the Armed Guard Commander in the wheel house that he heard a noise that sounded like ship No 21 firing her 4in gun. General Quarters were sounded, and from the flying bridge the Armed Guard Commander observed ship No 21, the *Fort Rampart*, British, with a cargo of lumber and general, athwart the column, with bow pointed outboard and toward the forward end of the column. Ship's broadside guns were ordered trained to 270°. Visibility was good, and the sea was calm. Ship No 22 [*William D Pender*] turned to port to pass the stricken ship, and was almost parallel to her for about 30secs. Ship No 21 hoisted a white light in her rigging and showed a red light ['I have been torpedoed'] on top of her bridge. Lights could be seen moving about her after deck. Ship No 23 [*John Bakke*] passed astern and subject ship and ship No 125 [*James Jackson*] passed across her bow. She did not appear to be settling, but her crew was lowering boats. No further attack was made. Two corvettes left the screen and began to search the area as the torpedoed ship dropped astern. One corvette rejoined the convoy screen at about 0630hrs GMT, while the other continued its search. At 0715hrs GMT Ship 21 was almost hull down below the horizon, but appeared to be sinking slowly, very slowly. Members of the forward 3in gun crew, who were nearest the explosion, described it as consisting of a red ball of fire apparently as high as a loaded vessel's bulwarks accompanied by a higher cloud of greyish-white smoke which went much higher. The noise, to those on the bow, was like a muffled report of a 4in gun. Immediately after the attack four British destroyers [Support Group B-3] appeared over the horizon and passed astern, apparently searching the area of the attack.

The loss of *U-175* is described by Ensign Wise later in the same report:

At approximately 1210hrs GMT . . . at Lat 47°51'N Long 21°00'W, the Armed Guard Commander went to the flying bridge after a USCG cutter had dropped depth charges in the area just forward of columns 3 and 4. At about 1215hrs GMT the same cutter dropped a pattern of depth charges about 300yds in front and to starboard of Ship No 31 [*G Harrison Smith*] then went to the rear of the convoy and took up a position there. The Armed Guard lookout on the flying bridge sighted an oil slick between Columns 2 and 3. At 1240hrs GMT ship in position No 125 [*James Jackson*] opened fire on an object bearing 170° from subject ship. The object was immediately identified as a submarine partly surfaced. At 1242hrs subject ship opened fire with the after 3in gun. Four rounds were fired before the order to cease fire was received from the convoy commodore. The first three projectiles fell short, but the fourth, with a drum range of over 6,000yds, appeared to fall within the target area. Other ships, including the two Coast Guard cutters were dropping shells into that area so rapidly that it was impossible to distinguish individual splashes. After the cease fire order was given, the two USCG cutters bore down on the submarine, one on each beam, at point blank range. Evidently they were giving the survivors a chance to surrender. The submarine was undoubtedly damaged by shell fire as well as by depth charges which forced it to the surface, for ship No 125 [*James Jackson*] scored at least one hit. The convoy held course and speed, and the submarine, wallowing in the trough of the sea and *making no attempt to do battle* [emphasis added] dropped astern with the Coast Guard cutters trained on it. At about 1400hrs GMT one of the cutters rejoined the convoy, and the other returned later.

Ensign Wise complained bitterly about poor station-keeping by ship No 22 (*William D Pender*) as her manoeuvres caused other ships considerable trouble and some degree of danger. He also commented caustically about the problems he was having with a member of his crew, recommending that he be transferred to other duties as soon as possible.

8. The Armed Guard Commander on the US Liberty *William D Pender* reported no contact with the enemy, although he acknowledged that the escorts dropped depth charges on several occasions and that he learned from the 'British Naval Control Officers at Loch Ewe' that an enemy submarine had been 'blown to the surface and sunk by gunfire. The action is supposed to have occurred at the rear of the convoy and cannot be confirmed by the S/S *William D Pender* whose position was near the front.'

Mr Perry Jacobs, USMMA, was an engineer cadet aboard the *William D Pender*, Position No 22, directly astern of the *Fort Rampart* when the latter vessel was torpedoed in the early hours of 17 April 1943. He writes:

I recall very early in the morning that it was gray, misty, chilly and about 0500hrs. Most everyone in the *Pender* slept in their clothes except Ray Smith, the Deck Cadet I was with. When the General Alarm sounded, Ray jumped out of his bunk [he had the upper] and ran out on deck, stark naked but clutching his rubber survival suit under his arm.

All I can recall is the ship with the red [out of control] light passing from ahead to astern of us, listing to starboard and we taking her place in the column. I heard no explosions and as I recall it was the ringing of the general alarm that awakened us and we went to our stations.

9. The Esso tanker *Wallace E Pratt* (7,991grt) in Position No 102, as reported by the Armed Guard Commander Lt (jg) Walter S Grimala, USNR, had no contact with the enemy until 17 April 1943, when he felt some nine depth charges at 0500hrs. The report goes on to say:

1005hrs: approximately 20 depth charges dropped by starboard escort. Approximate dropping of above was 1018, 1025, 1055hrs. Senior escort on port bow about 1/2 mile away dropped 16 depth charges. These charges were responsible for forcing the submarine in question to the surface. The senior escort maintained the contact while the convoy passed over the area. Another escort was requested by blinker to come over and assist when the submarine surfaced. Two escort destroyers [sic] closed in the begun [sic] to shell the sub. This firing was assisted by 2 or 3 merchant ships in the stern columns of the convoy. . . . According to my observations the surfaced submarine was destroyed and at least one other may have been damaged. The observation of the damaged submarine is based upon the dark collar of the swell forced by the depth charges. [Since *U-226* reports depth charges very near and doing damage during the time of the sinking of *U-175*, Armed Guard Commander Grimala's conclusion could possibly be accurate.]

10. Lt (jg) J J Stevenson was Armed Guard Commander of the old US freighter *Lena Luckenbach*, originally in Position No 81 but relegated by the Convoy Commodore for poor station keeping to Position No 105 astern. Lt Stevenson reported the ship was under charter to United States Lines with a cargo of phosphate, tobacco, wire, wheat and steel billets and described the sinking of the *U-175* as follows:

During the voyage depth charges were dropped occasionally by the escort ships but no enemy vessels were sighted until the morning of April 17 at about 1130hrs when a submarine, badly damaged by depth charges which had been dropped immediately ahead of the convoy, surfaced about 800yds off the port quarter of the *Lena Luckenbach,* whose position at that time was in the last row [sic] of the convoy on the starboard side [Position No 105]. The 4in-50 gun on the stern and the two 20mm guns aft, which had been manned previously, were immediately trained on the submarine, but fire was held because of the position of two destroyers between the ship and the target which ships had the situation well in hand. The destroyers shelled the submarine, having little opposition, and eventually captured it. The action was clearly visible from this ship. General Quarters were maintained, a careful lookout being kept to prevent a surprise attack from any other direction by other enemy vessels. During this time the convoy continued on its course and the final disposition of the submarine and its crew is not known. The weather was moderate, sea moderate.

The section of Lt Stevenson's report describing the collision and abandonment of the *Lena Luckenbach* will be found under 'Damage'. Interestingly he reported, 'Relations between the merchant crew and the navy crew were very good.'

11. Ensign William E McCarthy, USNR, Armed Guard Commander of the US Liberty *James Fenimore Cooper,* Position No 95, reported the sinking of *U-175* to CNO on 21 April 1943 as follows:

> There was no cause for alarm during the voyage until Saturday the 17th of April. On that morning at 1005hrs the gun crew and myself were called to our stations. On reaching the bridge the man at the controls, i. e. officer of the watch, pointed out to me a black pennant [i e, flag] on an escort vessel on the starboard quarter. The escort vessel dropped 12 depth charges. Gun crew was secured after the black pennant was hauled down. At 1050hrs we were called again and the escort vessel was dropping depth charges at 3 points on the port bow. Gun crew was secured after the black pennant was hauled down. At 1140hrs sub surfaced at 2 points abaft the port beam. I kept the crew at standby while the two escort vessels fired at the sub who in return fired back. After a few moments firing ceased and the sub appeared to surrender as the two escort vessels stayed with it while we went on. At 1220hrs the escort vessel dropped 4 depth charges 2 points abaft the beam. Gun crew secured at 1230hrs.

Ensign McCarthy also stated that the ship's cargo consisted of 'gasoline, steel, grain and general cargo', and that she was 'operated by American President Lines but owned by U. S. Lines', which was incorrect.

2   Sailing Telegram of Convoy HX-233

To: CTU 24.18.17 (R) Admit COMMENT CF 24
For Commodore HX-233 51 ships including added starter *Thorsholm* sailed out gate by 13 hours Q. Tanker *Voco* arriving from Delaware expected to join you at point Z. *Esso, Nashville* and British *Harmony* did not sail. Total 52 when *Voco* joins. *Voco* employed in port will not join.

Route HX 233
   (1) C 40 07 N 72 58 W AT 1900 Z / 6 April
        D 40 10   67 49
        E 42 28   64 24
        F 42 50   55 01
        G 43 13   45 38

Westchop 1300 Z / 8 April

(2) HOMP 42 35 N 60 58 W 1400 Z / 9 April
Westomp 44 28 N 45 01 W at 1900 Z / 12 April

(3) H 48 48 N 41 22 W
J 54 03   35 48
K 55 20   25 57
L 55 59   15 01
Chop 2000 Z / 15 April 36°W

(4) Stragglers route N 48 48 N 42 22 W
O 51 19   41 11
P 54 48   36 04
Q 56 09   26 10
R 56 47   15 03
S 55 50   08 00
FOIC Iceland pass to NOIC Iceland for Information

Convoy HS 233 Internal Organisation
(1) Commodore Convoy and Div 3 Commodore O H Dawson RNR in *Devis* Vice Commodore H C Smith in *Empire Pakeha* Rear Commodore E Garner in *City of Delhi* Com Div 1 W S Stein in *Fort Rampart* Com Div 2 P W Barry in *Empire Wordsworth* Com Div 4 W Pittman in *R F Hand*

(2) Sound Repeaters Column Leaders and Ships in positions 32 33 34 35 72 73 74 75 102 103 104 Light repeaters will be assigned at sea

(3) 12 Columns single
4 3 4 4 5 5 4 5 5 5 4 3
Pennants available Halifax 23 73 123
CESF Pass to CINCONWA for action
Hx 233 CTU 24.1.3 in *Spencer*
1. Take *Spencer*, *Duane*, *Arvida*, *Wetaskiwin*, *Bergamot* and *Bryony* under your orders and sail at 0830Z April 11th
2. Rendezvous with HX 233 in position 44° 28' N 45° 01' W at 1900Z April 12th. Approach course and speed of HX 233 022° 9.5 knots
3. Signals attached CESF 022025/4 061515Z/4 Com 3rd USND NY 061721/4 062101Z/4 PD New York 062216Z/4 062252Z/4 CINCCNWA 081407Z/4
4. Western Local Escort with HX 233 TU 24.18.7 *Lincoln* (SO) *Oakville Brockville Lethbridge*
5. To avoid ice en route to rendezvous pass through position 10 miles 090 Cape Race
6. *Rosthern Dianthus* will sail to overtake when ready

3   Composition of Convoy HX-233

Name	Tonnage	Flag	Type	Cargo	Position/remarks
James Jackson	7,176	US	Liberty	general	01; post war reserve

Name					
Yemassee	–	Pan	freighter	general	02
Kentuckian	5,200	US	freighter	gen./grain	03
George Handley	7,176	US	Liberty	general	04; scrapped 1964
Fort Rampart	7,130	Br	freighter	gen./ lumber	21; torpedoed
William D. Pender	7,176	US	Liberty	expl/gen.	22; scrapped 1960
John Bakke	4,718	Nor	freighter	expl/gen.	23; 2 passengers
Jonathan Worth	7,176	US	Liberty	general	24; scrapped 1969
G Harrison Smith	11,752	US	tanker	pool gasoline	31
Velma	9,720	Nor	tanker	Adm. fuel	32
British Pride	7,106	Br	tanker	av. gasoline	33
Fjordaas	7,361	Nor	tanker	Adm. fuel	34
Empire Pakeha	8,115	Br	freighter	gen./reefer	41; scrapped 1950
City of Khios	5,574	Br	freighter	expl/gen.	42
Cistula	8,097	Dutch	tanker	gas./kero.	43
Good Gulf	7,874	Pan	tanker	oil	44
Fernwood	4,695	Nor	freighter	expl/gen.	51; 4 aircraft
Empire Wordsworth	9,891	Br	tanker	gasoline	52; scrapped 1960
Maya	5,383	Hon	freighter	expl/gen.	53
Villanger	4,884	Nor	freighter	expl/gen.	54
John Bidwell	7,176	US	Liberty	sugar	55; scrapped 1960
Axtell Jog Byles	8,955	Gr	tanker	pool/fuel	61; see Appendix 4
Skiensfjord	5,922	Nor	freighter	expl/gen.	62
Axel Johnson	4,915	Sw	freighter	general	63; 47 passengers
Egda	10,050	Nor	tanker	av. gas./oil	64
Kronprinsen	7,073	Nor	tanker	gen./fuel	65; 4 passengers
Devis	6,054	Br	freighter	general	71; see Appendix 4
Ivaran	4,955	Nor	freighter	expl/gen.	74
Alcoa Cutter	4,965	US	freighter	general	75
Thorsholm	9,937	Nor	freighter	general	81
Sun	9,002	US	tanker	navy fuel	82
Roger Williams	7,176	US	Liberty	expl/val.	83; lost 1965, untraced
Kaituna	4,907	Br	freighter	expl/gen.	84; see Appendix 4
Santos		Br	freighter	expl/gen.	85
Esso Nashville	7,943	US	tanker	navy fuel	91; failed to join
Brimanger	4,883	Nor	freighter	general	91
Stiklestad	9,349	Nor	tanker	gasoline	92
Norsol	11,870	Nor	tanker	av. gasoline	93
Charles B Aycock	7,176	US	Liberty	expl/gen.	94; scrapped 1962
James Fenimore Cooper	7,176	US	Liberty	general	95; scrapped 1967
City of Delhi	7,443	Br	freighter	general	101; see Appendix 4
Wallace E Pratt	7,991	US	tanker	gas./oil	102
Wearfield	–	Br	tanker	gasoline	103
Brasil	12,400	Nor	tanker	pool gasoline	104
Lena Luckenbach	5,238	US	freighter	general ?	105; collision
Robert F. Hand	12,197	Br	tanker	Vapoilgas	111
G S Walden	10,627	Br	tanker	gasoline	112; see Appendix 4
Atenas	4,639	US	freighter	bombs	113

Skaraas	9,826	Nor	tanker	gasoline	114
William R Keever	5,350	US	freighter	general	121
Isaac Sharpless	7,176	US	Liberty	grain/gen.	122; post war reserve
Ville D'Anvers	7,462	Belgian	freighter	general	124

Stragglers or failed to join:

Mosli	8,291	Nor	tanker	Navy fuel	Escort tanker
British Pride	7,106	Br	tanker	aviation gasoline	
Tudor Prince	1,914	Br	freighter	gen./expl.	
Hannibal Hamlin	7,176	US	Liberty	routed independently	
Empire Lightning	6,942	Br	freighter	failed to join	
Eastgate	5,032	Br	freighter	failed to join	

NOTES

(1) Convoy Commodore O H Dawson, RNR, in *Devis*, position 71.
(2) Vice Commodore H C Smith in *Empire Pakeha*, position 41.
(3) Escort Commander Captain Paul Heineman, USN, in USCG *Spencer*, Cdr Harold S Berdine, USCG, commanding.
(4) No rescue ship attached; HMS *Arvida*, acting.

Freighters: 32 Tankers: 20 Speed: 9 knots Distance between columns: 1,000yds

4 Notes on Ships of Convoy HX-233

M/V *G S Walden*
10,627 × 149 × 22, built 1935, speed 12 knots, owned by Oriental Trade and Transport, London and Toronto. Torpedoed and damaged 3 August 1942, Convoy ON-115, 45°45'N 47°17'W by *U-552* (Topp). Repaired and returned to service. Torpedoed and again damaged 14 May 1944 by *U-616* (Koitschke), position 36°45'N 00°55'E.
    (*U-552* scuttled 2 May 1945, Wilhelmshaven; *U-616* sunk 14 May 1944, Mediterranean.)

M/V *Sun*
Speed 11 knots, built Chester Pennsylvania 1928, 9,002 × 481 × 66 × 37, Sun Oil Company, Philadelphia, owner. Torpedoed twice: first by *U-502* (von Rosenstiel) on 23 February 1942, 54 miles north of Aruba, West Indies, 13°02'N 70°41'W, whilst proceeding alone and unarmed. Returned to Aruba for temporary repairs; repaired Chester, PA, and returned to service. Torpedoed second 16 May 1942 by *U-506* (Wurdemann) off SW Pass, Louisiana, USA, at 28°41'N 90°19'W, under Captain John P Bakke. Made the Mississippi River. Repaired and returned to service.
    (*U-502* lost 5 July 1942, Bay of Biscay, no survivors.)

S/S *Atenas*
4,639 × 115 × 15.7 (metres), built 1908, was shelled by *U-106* (Ktlt Hermann Rasch, Ritterkreuz) in Gulf of Mexico while en route from New Orleans, Louisiana to Christobal, Canal Zone on 26 May 1942, position 22°50'N 89°05'W, with general cargo. Armed with 1–4in anti-submarine gun aft, the armed guard fought back gallantly. The submarine, out

of torpedoes, chased the *Atenas*, shelling from a range of about 2,000yds, hitting her seven times and starting two small fires, which were quickly brought under control as Captain Trygue Angell skilfully manoeuvred his ship to present as small a target as possible, retreating at the greatest speed the ancient power plant could produce. Prudently, the *U-106* broke off the engagement and dived, as a single hit to her pressure hull would have been fatal.

(*U-106* bombed and sunk 2 September 1943, northwest of Cape Ortegal.)

S/S *Axtell J. Byles*
8,955 × 481 × 66 × 37, built 1927 Chester, Pennsylvania, owned by Tidewater Associated Oil Company, New York, Frank Haskell, Director. Torpedoed 18 April 1942, four miles off Wimble Shoals, North Carolina, position 35°32'N 75°19W by *U-136* (Zimmermann). Vessel made Hampton Roads, Virginia, under her own power, was repaired and returned to service.

(*U-136* sunk 12 July 1942, mid-Atlantic, no survivors.)

S/S *City of Delhi*
Speed 12 knots, built 1925, 7,443 × 137 × 17 × 8, owned by Ellerman Lines Ltd, London. Participated in 'Operation Husky', the invasion of Sicily, which one DEMS gunner recalls off Augusta as one of the worst moments of his life: 'The enemy, with his Ju 88s and Stukas, was terrifying; every 1½ hours for three days and four nights they came at us at anchor . . . We finally beached off Syracuse and discharged the DUKWs (amphibious lorries) and floated off at high tide several days later.'

Following 'Operation Husky' the *City of Delhi* remained in the Mediterranean and Indian Oceans, away from home port for over fourteen months.

S/S *Devis*
Commodore ship: speed 14 knots, 6,054 × 134 × 19 × 8, built 1938, Lamport-Holt, Liverpool, owners. Bombed and badly damaged by nine Junker 88s on 5 April 1940 in Convoy , seven killed, fourteen wounded. She was at Piraeus, Greece, badly damaged and leaking when ammo ship *Clan Fraser*, blew up.

Was also commodore ship, Rear Admiral Hugh England, in Convoy KMS-18B. Torpedoed and lost 5 July 1943 to *U-593* (Ktlt Gerd Kelbing) 600 miles from Sicily beach head whilst en route with 4000grt of military stores and 2 LCM's on deck. Hit starboard side, No 4 hatch; sank in 15mins; 52 killed, survivors landed at Bougie, Algeria.

(*U-593* lost 13 December 43 off Constantine, Algeria, to USS *Wainwright* and HMS *Calpe*.)

S/S *Empire Pakeha*
8,115 × 477 × 63; built 1910, Harland & Wolff Ltd, Belfast, owned by Shaw, Savilland Albion Ltd, taken over by the government along with *Mamari* and *Waimana* of the same company and converted with a configuration to resemble capital ships, *Pakeha* as a battleship of the *Royal Sovereign* class. Anchored at Scapa Flow, they acted as decoys for enemy aircraft. When no longer needed for such deception, they were reconverted to their original roles as refrigerated cargo ships. *Pakeha* was scrapped, Briton Ferry, 1950.

S/S *Esso Nashville*
7,934 × 463 × 64 × 53, steam turbine, built 1940, Sparrows Point, Maryland. Standard Oil Co of New Jersey, owner. Torpedoed by *U-124* (Mohr) on 21 March 1942, sixteen miles

northeast of Frying Pan Shoals, 33°35'N 77°22'W, en route Port Arthur to New Haven, Connecticut, with full load of oil, alone and unarmed. The explosion broke her back, and the bow section sank. The after section was towed into Moorhead City by USS *Umpqua* (ATO-25). Later, 1 June 1942, towed to Baltimore, where a new bow was built and fitted. She was returned to service 16 March 1943, sold in 1952 to become *Joshua Hendy*, in 1958 *Helen* scrapped Onomichi 1963.

   (*U-124*, sunk 3 April 1943 off Oporto, Portugal, no survivors.)

S/S *Fjordaas*
7,361 × 129 × 18 × 7, 11 knots, built 1931, J. Mørland, Arendal, Norway. Torpedoed 11 September 1942, Convoy ON-127, position 51°16'N 29°08'W, by *U-218* (Becker), damaged and put back to Clyde for repairs.

   (*U-218* surrendered Bergen May 45; scuttled in Operation Deadlight.)

S/S *Kaituna*
4,907 × 126 × 17 × 7, built 1938, Plymouth (New Zealand) Shipping Company, owner. One of the first British merchant vessels to be armed, 17 August 1939.

S/S *Kronprinsen*
7,073grt, Norwegian, torpedoed by *U-432* (Schultze) 9 June 1942 at 42°53'N 67°11'W and damaged. Repaired and returned to service.

   (*U-432* sunk 11 March 43, mid-Atlantic, by French corvette *Aconit*.)

S/S *Thorsholm*
9,937grt, Norwegian, torpedoed by *U-118* (Czygan) off Cape Espartel in February 1943 and damaged. Repaired and returned to service.

   (*U-118* refuelled *U-175* at sea on second patrol. Sunk 12 June 1943 in the Atlantic, west of Canary Islands, by aircraft from USS *Bogue*.)

Liberty *James Fenimore Cooper*
Built Oregon Ship Building Corporation, Portland, Oregon, commissioned June 1942, named for American novelist (1789–1851), convoy Position No 95, in collision with *Lena Luckenbach*, Position No 105, on night of 18 April 1943. Damaged, she reached a UK port under her own power and was repaired. Whilst in Convoy Norfolk to North Africa, on 8 December 1944 she collided with the newly commissioned *Tacoma* class frigate USS *Huron* PF 19, badly damaging her. *Cooper* was sold commercially 1955 and renamed *Mohawk*. She became *Algonkin* the following year, *World Loyalty* in 1962, and when sold yet again was named *Faro*. On 4 January 1966 she ran aground in bad weather two miles off Nojima, Japan, position 34°53'N 139°55'E on a voyage from Muroran to Keelung in ballast. Declared a constructive total loss the following year, the wreck was sold to Japanese shipbreakers 'as she lies' and scrapped after 25 years faithful service.

5   Escorts

1. Local Escort
Oakville, RCN, corvette, 'Flower' class, built Port Arthur Shipbuilding, 21.6.41; 1946 to
   Venezuela as *Patria*.
Lincoln ex-USS *Yarnell*, RNorN Destroyer, 1,090 × 309 × 30.5; 1–4in, 1–3in, 4–20mm AA,
   3–21in TT; to Norway, 9.41; to Russia as *Druzni*, 26.8.44 to 19.8.52; broken-up 1952.

Brockville, RCN, *Bangor* class minesweeper; Marine Ind, 20.6.41; RCMP *Macleod* 1950; RCN 1951.

Lethbridge, RCN, corvette, 'Flower' class; Vickers, Montreal, 21.11.40; sold 1952 as *Nicholas Vinke*.

2. Ocean Escort

USCG Cutter *Spencer*, WPG-36, 2,216 × 327 × 41 × 12.5; 2-shaft geared turbines, SHP 6200=20kts; 3–5in, 3–3in; built. NY Navy Yard, 6.1.37; 8000mi at 12knots.

USCG Cutter *Duane*, *WPG-33*, as above; built Philadelphia Navy Yard, 3.6.36.

HMS *Bryony*, corvette, 'Flower' class; built Harland Wolf, Belfast, 15.3.41; sold Norway 1948 as *Polarfront II*.

HMS *Dianthus*, corvette, 'Flower' class; built Robb 9.7.40; sold 1947 as *Thorsley*.

HMS *Bergamot*, corvette, 'Flower' class, built Harland-Wolf, 15.2.41; sold 1946 as *Syros*.

HMCS *Arvida*, corvette, 'Flower' class, built Morton, Quebec, 29.9.40; sold circa 1946 as *La Ceiba*.

HMCS *Skeena*, destroyer, 1337 × 309 × 33, built Thornycroft, 10.10.30; 4–4.7in, 8 TT. Veteran, part of the pre-war Canadian Navy, she was an escort of Convoy SC-2 Commodore Rear Admiral E Bodham-Whetman, of fifty-three ships, attacked by the first successful U-boat wolf pack on 25 August 1940. She joined Convoy SC-42 as escort in September 1941. The sixty-five vessel convoy suffered severe losses of fifteen ships; two U-boats were sunk. Captain Bernard Edwards wrote of Cdr James Hibbard, RCN, commanding *Skeena*, 'When the battle with the U-boats started, Hibbard must have been a very tired man. His subsequent achievements, in what amounted to defending the convoy with his ship alone, were superb.'

On 31 July 1942 HMCS *Skeena* commanded by Acting Lieutenant Commander K L Dyer, DSC, RCN, and HMCS *Wetaskiwin*, commanded by Lieutenant Commander G Windeyer led *U-588* in what has been described as 'tantamount to a dance of death'. After five hours of attacks, wreckage including human remains surfaced, establishing for the Admiralty Assessment Committee that, beyond all reasonable doubt, the U-boat had been destroyed.

Wrecked Iceland, 25.10.44; sold 1945 locally.

HMCS *Wetaskiwin*, corvette, 'Flower' class; built Burrard, 18.7.40; original name *Banff*; renamed 1941; sold Venezuela 1946 as *Victoria*.

HMS *Daniella* ex-*Daffodil*, corvette, 'Flower' class; built Lewis 3.9.40; renamed 26.10.40: broken up Portaferry 1947.

6   Support Group Vessels

HMS *Offa,* destroyer, 1,540 × 338.5 × 35; 5–4.7in, 1–4in, 4 TT; built Fairfield 11.3.41; to RPN 1949 as *Tariq*; broken up 1959, Young, Sunderland.

HMS *Panther*, destroyer, 1540 × 338.5 × 35; 4–4.7in, 4 TT; built Fairfield; sunk in air attack Scarpanto Strait, 9.10.43.

HMS *Impulsive*, destroyer, 1370 × 312 × 32; 4–4.7in, 10 TT; built White, 1937; to Young, Sunderland 22.01.46, broken up.

HMS *Penn*, destroyer, 1540 × 338.5 × 35; 4–4.7in, 4 TT; built Vickers Armstrong, Tyne, 12.02.41; sold 31.01.50, broken up at Troon.

US Coast Guard Secretary Class Cutters

WPG-33, built Philadelphia Navy Yard, keel laid 1.05.35; launched 3.06.36; commissioned 1.08.36. Decommissioned 1.08.85; sunk as a reef 27.11.87.

WPG-35, built New York Navy Yard. Keel laid 11.09.35; launched 6.01.37; commissioned 1.03.37. Decommissioned 23.01.74; sold 8.10.81.

Cost: $2,486,460 each.

Hull displacement: 2,750grt, 1945. 2,216 × 327 × 41.2 × 12.5.

Main engines: 2 Westinghouse double-reduction geared turbines; 2 Babcock and Wilcox sectional express, air-encased main boilers.

SHP: 6200 = 19.5 knots.

Propellers: twin, 3 bladed.

Speed:

Maximum:	19.5 knots;
Maximum sustained:	19 knots, 4200mi radius;
Cruising:	13 knots, 7000mi radius;
Most economical:	11 knots, 9500mi radius.

Fuel capacity: 136,520 USgal.

Complement: 24 officers, 2 warrants, 226 men, 1945.

Electronics:

    (1) Special: British high frequency direction finder, 1942

    (2) Detection Radar:

        (a) *Spencer* SC-4, SGa

        (b) *Duane* SC-3, SGa

    (3) Fire Control Radar   Mk 26

    (4) Sonar   QC series

Armament:

    3 – 5in / 51 single, 3 – 3in / 50 single

    Depth Charge racks, K guns

    14 – 40mm / 60 (2 quad and 3 twin mounts)

    8 – 20mm / 80, (single mounts).

7 Convoy HX-233: 0800hrs Positions

DATE	POSITION
7 April 1943	40° N 71° 25' W
8 April 1943	40° 40' N 66° 45' W
9 April 1943	42° 28' N 62° 25' W
10 April 1943	42° 45' N 57° 10' W
11 April 1943	43° 05' N 51° 40' W
12 April 1943	43° 35' N 46° 25' W
13 April 1943	45° 30' N 42° 10' W
14 April 1943	45° 15' N 36° 58' W
15 April 1943	45° 10' N 31° 40' W
16 April 1943	45° 03' N 26° 20' W
17 April 1943	47° 22' N 22° 00' W
18 April 1943	50° 02' N 18° 00' W
19 April 1943	52° 40' N 13° 20' W
20 April 1943	55° 20' N 09° 00' W
21 April 1943	Outer Liverpool L. V.

8 Casualties on USCG Cutter *Spencer*

Name	Rating	Wounded / Killed in Action
Anderson, Harold V	SOM 2/c, USCG	multiple, general
Appel, William H	Sea 2/c, USCG	upper back
Barnett, William E	CC Std. USCG	right leg
Bugbee, William E	RDM 3/c USCG	general
Buzzell, Richard A	MATT 2/c, USCG	left leg
Croak, Robert J	MM 1/c, USCG	left hand
Fowler, Leon O	Sea 2/c USCG	ruptured eardrum(s)
Glemser, Robert	SM 1/c USCG	ruptured eardrums
Godfrey, Ernest E	Sea 2/c, USCG	abdomen
Haddon, David A	RDM 3/c, USCG	upper dorsal region
Hamilton, Marvin D	BM 1/c, USCG	ruptured eardrums
Hoggard, James M	MATT 1/c USCG	general
Hoyt, James R	Sea 2/c USCG	ruptured eardrum(s)
Hudek, Frank	Surfman USCG	flash burns
Karnis, Joseph	CY, USN	right leg w/fracture
Lee, Hampton	MAH 1/c USCG	ruptured eardrum(s)
Maxwell, Vern E	GM 2/c USCG	ruptured eardrums
Morton, Edward W	Sea 1/c USCG	ruptured eardrums
Petrella, Julius T	RM 3/c, USCG	KIA
Russell, Louis	Sea 2/c USCG	left leg
Schiewe, Wesley A	SM 2/c, USN	right leg and arm
Schuster, George	CC Std. USCG	right little finger
Stratton, Richard E	F 1/c, USCG	general
Walker, Herbert D	EM 1/c USCG	ruptured eardrum(s)
Whitt, Alfred R	Sea 2/c, USCG	ruptured eardrums

9 Casualties on SS *Fort Rampart*

Killed in Action
James Turnbull Douglas, aged 21 years, Fireman and Trimmer.
Anthony Grimes, aged 23 years, Fireman and Trimmer.
Thomas Hutchinson, aged 28 years, Fireman and Trimmer,
Gerard Lively, aged 23 years, Ordinary Seaman.
William Etherington Magee, aged 37 years, Ordinary Seaman.
Samuel Tait, aged 34 years, Fireman.

Wounded
Ambrose H. Carr, AB
Alexander Lengstone, AB
Harry Mitchell, oiler/greaser (picked up by HMS *Arvida*, transferred to USCGC *Duane*,
    1105hrs, 17 April 1943)

10   German POWs on *Spencer*

Officers

Name	*Rank*	*Date of Birth*
Möller, Paul	Leutnant zur See	29.11.10
Voelker, Karl	Fähnrich (Ing.)	22.9.23
Weppelmann, Walter	Fähnrich zur See	12.12.23

Other Ranks

Name	*Rating*	*Date of Birth*
Bickel, Werner	Maschinenobergefreiter	13.3.23
Brückmann, Gustav	Maschinengefreiter	29.4.23
Brunken, Herbert	Mechanikersmaat	13.12.19
Geimeier, Erwin	Maschinenmaat	22.8.19
Kahmann, Werner	Maschinenmaat	27.8.19
Klinger, Max	Matrosenobergefreiter	20.3.22
Klotzsch, Helmut	Obersteurmann	12.2.14
Kohler, Hermann	Funkmaat	29.8.21
Küffner, Hermann	Maschinenmaat	24.3.18
March, Rudolf	Funkobergefreiter	11.6.22
Rosenkranz, Josef	Mechanikerobergefreiter	15.8.23
Schlosser, Helmut	Maschinist	6.2.07
Schroeder, Walter	Maschinenobergefreiter	19.1.20
Schwarze, Herbert	Matrosenobergefreiter	6.3.23
Sichler, Albert	Matrosenobergefreiter	19.7.22
Urbanek, Ewald	Matrosenobergefreiter	29.4.22

11   German POWs on *Duane*

Officers

Name	*Rank*	*Date of Birth*
Nowroth, Leopold	Oberleutnant (Ing.)	28.9.10
Verlohr, Wolfgang	Leutnant zur See	21.4.21

Other Ranks

Name	*Rating*	*Date of Birth*
Bamberg, Jean	Matrosengefreiter	8.4.24
Blümling, Peter	Maschinengefreiter	31.1.22
Böhnsch, Alfred	Maschinenmaat	19.9.19
Butscheidt, Josef	Maschinenmaat	3.2.16
Grund, Werner	Maschinenobergefreiter	6.12.21
Herklotz, Werner	Maschinenobergefreiter	20.8.22
Herzke, Otto	Maschinengefreiter	12.1.22
Keutken, Karl	Obermaschinist	7.1.14

Kistler, Wilhelm	Matrosengefreiter	16.4.23
Labs, Phillipp	Maschinenobergefreiter	5.10.21
Niemann, Werner	Maschinenmaat	22.6.21
Noak, Gerhard	Maschinengefreiter	21.2.22
Petrik, Josef	Maschinengefreiter	2.1.23
Saurbach, Alois	Bootsmannsmaat	13.7.14
Stachel, Ludwig	Matrose II	5.5.24
Tepke, Alfred	Matrosengefreiter	6.3.22
Wannemacher, Peter	Mechanikergefreiter	17.4.24
Winkler, Gerhard	Matrosenobergefreiter	22.2.23
Wohlmann, Heinz	Matrosenobergefreiter	10.11.21
Wolf, Dieter	Matrosenobergefreiter	7.4.22

12   Casualties on *U-175*

Officers

Name	*Rank*	*Date of Birth*
Bruns, Heinrich	Kapitänleutnant	3.4.12
Lohmeier, Hans	Fahnrich zur See	4.7.23

Other Ranks

Name	*Rank*	*Date of Birth*
Falter, Herbert	Maschinenmaat	14.10.16
Flickinger, Wilhelm	Maschinenobergefreiter	26.3.22
Fritze, Gerhard	Matrose II	13.3.24
Kordt, Wilhelm	Maschinengefreiter	1.1.24
Krause, Victor	Bootsmannsmaat	14.12.19
Schlie, Fredrich	Obermaschinist	12.9.12
Schlüter, Kurt	Bootsmannsmaat	3.5.16
Steinle, Robert	Maschinengefreiter	3.2.16
Wienand, Walther	Mecanikergefreiter	19.11.24
Wönnemann, Fritz	Funkgefreiter	9.9.20
Zacharias, Rudi	Funkmaat	30.9.21

13   U-Boats Operating against Convoy HX-233

Type VIIC: Ocean going
First launch 1940, 769/871 × 220.25 × 20.25 × 15.75; 2 shaft diesel/electric motors; BHP
2,800/750 = 17/7.5 knots. Diving time 30 secs. Radius 10,000mi at 12 knots / 80mi at 4
kts.; 1–3.5in, 1–37mm AA, 2–20mm AA (2x1) guns; 5–21in (4 bow, 1 stern) TT, 14
torpedoes or 14 mines; complement 44–50. (NB: by 1942 pressure hull strengthened for
deeper diving, deck gun removed, AA defence increased, in some cases with 4–20mm
'Vierling' AA.)

Type IXC: Long Distance

First launch 1940, 1,144/1,247 × 252 × 22.5 × 15.5; 2 shaft diesel/electric motors, BHP 4,400/1,000 = 18.25/7.25 knots; radius 11,000mi at 12 knots / 63mi at 4 knots; 1–4.1in, 1–37mm AA, 2–20mm AA; 6–21in (4 bow, 2 stern) TT, 22 torpedoes 35 sec including deck storage of reserve; complement 48–54.

U-Boat, Commander	Type	Built	History and Career
U-262, Kptlt Heinz Franke, Ritterkreuz	VIIC	Bremer Vulcan Vegesack	sank four ships; bombed damaged Gydnia; paid off 2.4.45, Kiel, broken up.
U-628, Kptlt Heinrich Hasenschar	VIIC	Blohm Voss Hamburg	sank six ships; bombed-sunk Biscay, NW Cape Ortegal, 3.7.1943, forty-nine lost.
U-226, Kptlt Rolf Borchers	VIIC	Germania Kiel	sank one-half ship: *coup de grâce*; lost N Atlantic off Newfoundland to RN Sloops *Starling* and *Kite* 6.11.43.
U-358, Kptlt Rolf Manke	VIIC	Flensburger Schiffsbau Ges.	sank four ships; lost N Atlantic off Azores to RN frigates *Gould*, *Affleck*, *Gore*, and *Gorlies*, 1.3.44, fifty lost.
U-264, Kptlt Hartwig Looks	VIIC	Bremer Vulcan Vegesack	sank three ships; lost mid-Atlantic to RN Sloops *Woodpecker* and *Starling* 19.2.44, crew taken prisoner.
U-382, Klptlt Leopold Koch	VIIC	Howaldts Werke Kiel	damaged one ship and possibly two others, unconfirmed; collision in Baltic 1.45, raised; scuttled 3.5.45.
U-614, Kptlt Wolfgang Sträter	VIIC	Blohm Voss Hamburg	sank two ships; bombed-sunk N Atlantic, NW Cape Finistere 29.7.43, forty-nine lost.
U-175, Kptlt Heinrich Bruns	IXC	Deschmag Bremen	sank ten ships; lost North Atlantic, USCG *Spencer* 17.4.43, thirteen lost.

Total of ships sunk by above U-boats : twenty-nine ships. (NB As there were other U-boats along the mean meridian of Lorient, it is possible others also operated against Convoy HX-233.)

14   Technical Details of *U-175* Type IXC

Builders   Deschimag, Bremen
Armament   1 – 105mm (4.1in) forward, max. elevation 50°
             1 – 37mm AA (1.45in) aft
             1 – 20mm AA (0.79in) aft of conning tower
             2 – portable machine guns AA (7.9mm)
Ammunition   About 100 rounds of mixed, HE, SAP and incendiary, with 25 stowed on each side of engine room / ratings' quarters
Torpedoes   22–23 carried.   On 2nd patrol: 15 electric, 8 air-driven
                                 On 3rd patrol: 14 electric, 8 air-driven

Stowage, 2nd patrol
6 electric torpedoes in torpedo tubes
4 electric torpedoes in forward compartment
2 electric torpedoes under bow compartment floor plates
3 electric torpedoes in after compartment
8 air-driven torpedoes under main deck.
Torpedo tubes   Four bow, two stern.
Torpedo pistols   G7 H, four whiskered Pi 1s and possibly Pi 2 pistols, requiring an aiming distance of 150m.
Electric torpedoes   speed 30 knots, depth setting 0–12m. Motor operated every 2–3 days from auxiliary 24-volt battery. Each had 56 lead, acid cells connected in parallel, recharged once a week, requiring ventilation daily and charged at 23amps. The torpedo man was the only member of the crew not required to stand watches aside from the captain, so important was his function on board.
Propulsion: Diesel engines, two 9 cylinder, four stroke, type M9V, 40/46hp. engines with Buchi superchargers.
Fuel consumption   3–4 tons daily at normal cruising speed, 20 knots reached in trials but never used in operations.
Fuel capacity   total 230 tons with 32 in trimming tank.
Electric motors   Two 500hp Siemens; maximum submerged speed 8 knots. As *U-175* was found to be a very noisy boat submerged, it was difficult to determine silent submerged speed. It was finally ascertained that 90rpm, or dead slow, gave best results.
Pressure hull   2cm (0.79in) and outside hull casing 5mm (0.2in) thick.
Electrical equipment   Two main switchboards and two auxiliary, Nos 1, 2, 2A and 3. Lighting came from No 1; generators for the wireless from Nos 2 and 2A; electric torpedo charging from 2A; light and power from No 3, located in control room. The others were located in the motor room above the electric motors.
Main Batteries   Two AFA (Akkumulator Fabrik Aachen) units, each with 62 cells, total capacity 24,000amp hours with life of 2yrs.
Compressors   One Germania electric compressor with a 110volt motor, making 400amps, reportedly very reliable. One Junkers free piston compressor, which was reportedly the source of constant problems if not handled with care.
Bilge pumps   Rated for 100m (328ft), but failed at 80m (262ft).
Potable water   841gals in 4 tanks.
Wireless radio equipment   All Telefunken
Transmitters   One 200wtt short wave, one 150wtt long wave, one 40/50wtt reserve
Receivers   One short wave, one all wave
Radar detection equipment (German Search Radio)   Metox R 600 GSR with wooden 'Southern Cross' (also known as 'Biscay Kreuz') type aerial; carried on second patrol.

Metox R600 A, a new improved set with new type aerial, known as the 'wire basket', which did not have to be dismantled when boat submerged, and received transmissions over 360°. When the boat surfaced it was manned continually. (NB This is probably the device seen and described by *Spencer*'s boarding party.)

Wireless code books   Kept in a strong box or safe requiring three locks to be opened for access.

Camouflage   *Spencer* and other observers reported *U-175* freshly painted, with conning tower a light grey and hull a darker grey with black boot topping. Not surprising, since she was fresh from the dockyard, only a few days out, and the crew had not even had time to grow beards.

Conning tower badge-emblem   Two juxtaposed German paragraph signs, alluding to the well-known German Criminal Code Paragraph 175, about homosexual offences.

Field post number (Feldpostnummer)   M41704.

15   Eyewitness Account of Attack on Bridgetown Harbour, 11 September 1942, by Revd Stanley R Haskell

The German submarine that attacked the shipping in the harbour did so around 1745hrs (local time). The schools were closed for the Easter holiday, so I was at home that afternoon. My home was on the grounds of the school property, where my father taught, and at the time of the attack I was on the playing field on the east side of the school buildings. While I could not see the harbour as such, I could see jets of water going into the air as I heard the torpedoes hit. The torpedo nets and buoys that supported the nets were blown into the air and floated down like large sheets of tissue paper. The actual attack could not have lasted more than twenty minutes and occurred just as the sun was setting.

It did not take long for a large crowd to gather on the water front, among whom was an uncle of mine who was a medical doctor. Really, for them it was a blessing that no one was killed, for had any of the torpedoes managed to get through the openings made in the nets, they would have come ashore and exploded on the coral rocks of the Esplanade Shore front, with much loss of life. Also, around the time of the attack the local fishing boats were returning after a day at sea. It was said that the sub had hoisted an improvised sail on the periscope as a disguise to look like one of the returning fishing boats.

In the harbour I do believe, there were only two merchant ships, the Canadian freighter *Cornwallis* and a French freighter. The sub's captain must have had an informant on the island, as the one and only motor torpedo boat was in dry dock and the lone patrol plane had taken off for St. Lucia, so really it was the ideal time to attack in a setting sun.

The *Cornwallis* brought general supplies to the island, which in turn were transhipped to neighbouring islands by schooner, so it was an ideal target to be attacked. The supplies were mainly food. Schooners were also used for taking petrol from Trinidad in metal barrels, which were shipped back after being emptied. The Germans did not care to attack schooners with empty barrels, as they would not sink but only cause problems for them in the shipping lanes; yet they did sink them from time to time.

Neither *Cornwallis* nor the French ship was sunk. However, the *Cornwallis* was badly damaged about midship and after temporary repairs was escorted to dry dock in Puerto Rico. What happened to her after she left Barbados I have no idea, possibly she was sunk.

Sinking her in our harbour would have caused much difficulty and hardship for other boats coming to or leaving the island. The *Cornwallis* and the French freighter were both equipped with anti-submarine guns, and as the attack started they opened fire as well.

The Bridgetown natural harbour opens like a horseshoe. There was a (gun) battery on the Southeast end of the harbour and another existed at the time, I do believe on Pelican Island (i. e., the mainland) which was on the Northwest end of the harbour. That island (Pelican) is now part of the Deep Water Harbour which replaces the Natural Harbour of Carlisle Bay. Stretching from battery to battery across the harbour was a submarine net suspended by large metal buoys with gaps in it to let ships enter and leave.

After the attack it did not take long for a number of white youths to go in search of the torpedo or torpedoes, one of which they were able to locate. It is now on display at the local museum, which in early colonial days was used as a military prison.

Glossary

Adressbuch U-boat codebook of disguising Grid Square positions on a sea chart for wireless traffic.

A/S Anti-Submarine.

AB Able seaman.

Asdic Underwater sound ranging device (acronym for Allied Submarine Detection and Investigation Committee).

B-Dienst Beobachtungs Dienst (German radio monitoring and cryptographic service).

BdU Befehlshaber der Unterseeboote (U-boat High Command).

BM Boatswain's Mate.

Bold Abbreviation of 'Koboldstreich', an impish or mischievous trick. A U-boat could expel a container, 15cm diameter, containing a chemical that on contact with water created a dense hydrogen gas bubble, simulating a moving U-boat to enemy ultra-sound devices, while allowing the actual boat to move away. Dubbed Submarine Bubble Target (SBT) by the Allies.

Br British.

Capt Captain

Catalina An amphibious patrol bomber – PBY-5.

CBM Chief Boatswain's Mate.

Cdr Commander.

CINCWA Commander-in-Chief, Western Approaches, British Royal Navy.

CNO Chief of Naval Operations (US).

CO Commanding Officer.

DBS Distressed British Seaman.

DC Depth Charge.

DD Destroyer.

DEMS Defensively Equipped Merchant Ship.

D/F Direction Finding

DR Dead (i.e., deduced) reckoning position.

DSM Distinguished Service Medal (British)

EG Escort Group.

Fähnrich zur See Midshipman

FK Fregatten Kapitän (Commander)

FuMB Funkmessbeobachtungsgerät (German search radar).

Funker German Navy wireless operator (radioman). Also 'Puster'

Gefechtsstationen Battle stations

GMT Greenwich Mean Time.

GSR German Search Radar (see also FuMB).

HF/DF ('Huff-Duff') High Frequency Direction Finding.

HMCS His Majesty's Canadian Ship.

HMNoS His Majesty's Norwegian Ship

HMS His Majesty's Ship (British).

HX New York-Halifax-UK, convoy designation.

Ing. Engineer

IWM Imperial War Museum

I WO, II WO First Watch Officer, Second Watch Officer (U-boats).

KK Korvetten Kapitän (Lieutenant Commander).

Kptlt Kapitänleutnant (Lieutenant, U-boat commander).

KTB Kriegstagebuch (official war diary kept by all units of the German Navy)

Kurzsignale A special U-boat short or brief signal to BdU, a position report

LCdr Lieutenant-Commander.

Lt jg Lieutenant junior grade (US).

LV Light Vessel.

Marinquadrat German system of squares drawn on a Mercator projection chart, organising the oceans into a grid chart, whereby positions could be determined by letters and number.

Metox German electronic radar warning device replacing the earlier, bulky and primitive 'Biscay Cross' that could detect radar emissions only within a 10cm range.

M/S Motor Ship.

M/V Motor Vessel.

'Newfiejohn' St Johns, Newfoundland.

NSDAP *N*ational *S*ozialistisches *D*eutsches *A*rbieters *P*artei, National Socialist German Workers' Party, the Nazi Party.

Obersteurmann Chief Quartermaster (navigator).

OD Officer of the Deck

OL Oberleutnant (Lieutenant Junior Grade).

OS Ordinary Seaman.

Pour le Mérite Germany's highest award for gallantry in the First World War.

POW Prisoner of war.

Q-ship A disguised military ship.

RAF Royal Air Force.

RDF Radio Direction Finder.

RESD Ritterkreuz mit Eichenlaub, Schwerten und Diamanten (Knight's Cross with Oak Leaves, Swords and Diamonds, the highest German award for gallantry).

Ritterkreuz Knight's Cross of the Iron Cross

RNoN Royal Norwegian Navy

Schussmeldung The required report on each torpedo discharge, the 'shooting report' for every U-boat

SO Senior Officer.

SOE Senior Officer of the convoy Escort.

SOM Sonar man.

Sonar Sound Navigation and Ranging (American for Asdic, q v).

Sperrbrecher 'Blockade breaker,' a heavily armed escort vessel.

S/S Steamship.

Sunderland British flying boat

TF Task Force.

TG Task Group.

'T-Schu' Torpedo Schuss Empfänger, a receiver in the fore and aft torpedo rooms which fed data into the Vorhaltrechner (computer), which then fed it directly into the individual torpedo guidance system.

TT Torpedo Tubes.

TU Task Unit.

UAK U-boat Acceptance Command.

USCG United States Coast Guard.

USCGC USCG Cutter.

USCGR USCG Reserve.

USMMA United States Merchant Marine Academy.

USN United States Navy

USS United States Ship (Navy).

VLRA Very Long Range Aircraft.

Vorhaltrechner A form of computer or calculator manufactured by Siemens, located in the conning tower control room of the U-boat, which fed attack headings into the gyrocompass mechanisms of each torpedo in their tubes prior to launch.

Wabos German abbreviation for 'Wasserbombe' ('water bombs', English 'depth charges') were 250lb explosive drum projectiles, capable of exploding under water at a pre-set depth.

Westomp Western Ocean Meeting Place

WSA War Shipping Administration (US).

Sources

A full list of all the primary and secondary sources can be found at the end of this section

U-175

Much of the material is based on personal interviews with survivors of *U-175*, plus *Interrogation of Survivors,* Naval Intelligence Division [NID] 03262/43; CB 04051 (68) of June 1943; *Kriegstagebücher* for *U-628, U-262, U-226* and *U-175*; *Kriegstagebuch* of the German Naval High Command; *U-Boats* December 1942 through May 1943; *The U-Boat War in the Caribbean* (Annapolis 1994); *The War at Sea, Vol 2* (London 1956); *Axis Submarine Successes 1939-1945* (Annapolis, 1983); *Deutsche U-Boote 1906-1966* (Erlangen 1993); *British Vessels Lost at Sea 1939-45* (London 1945); *Chronology of the War at Sea 1939-1945* (Annapolis 1992); *Memoirs: Ten Years and Twenty Days* (London 1959); *German Warships of World War II* (London 1966); *U-Boats under the Swastika* (Exeter 1973); *Business in Great Waters: The U-Boat Wars 1916-1945* (London 1989); *The Submarine Commander's Handbook 1943* (Gettysburg 1989); *Bomber Command* (London 1979); and *U-Boot Krieg* (Munich 1976).

The description of *U-175*'s training period is based on personal interviews; *U-175*'s War Diary; BdU's War Diary; *U-333* (London 1986); *Iron Coffins* (London 1970); *U-628*'s War Diary; *The Boat* (NY 1975); *U-Boot Krieg* (Munich 1976); and *The Submarine Commander's Handbook 1943*.

For her actions in the Caribbean and her first patrol *The U-Boat War in the Caribbean* (Annapolis 1994) is absolutely indispensable in understanding the scope and detail of the battles fought, while Captain Roskill's *War at Sea, Vol 2*, pages 96-107, and the *Chronology of the War at Sea 1939-1945* from page 116 onward give an almost daily accounting of events. The outstanding *Operation Drumbeat* (NY 1990) provides an excellent detailed account of the German onslaughts along the US East Coast. Additionally, US Naval Operating Base 1943-45, Unit Returns Caribbean Theatre, Command History File, Royal Navy Anti-Submarine Summaries, War Diary Attack Reports and Merchant Ship Losses 1942-3, as well as *The Battle of the Atlantic* (London 1961) by Donald Macintyre, pages 126-35 proved to be valuable research tools for this section.

BdU war diary and the *U-175* war diaries as well as personal interviews are important sources. Vessel losses under the US flag are detailed in Captain Arthur R Moore's excellent and monumental *A Careless Word . . . A Needless Sinking* (Kings Point 1984) with detailed descriptions of each sinking, while *British Vessels Lost at Sea 1939-45* (HMSO 1947 London) lists those lost under the Red Duster. Vessel losses under Allied flags are listed in some detail in *The U-Boat War in the Caribbean*. Procedures and the attack on Barbados are described in the foregoing and confirmed by eye witness accounts, while the 'U-Boat Commander's Handbook' ('U Kdt Hdb') provides background on *U-175* operations. Dr Robert M Browning's excellent *U. S. Merchant Vessel War Casualties of World War II* includes many details of US flag vessels lost, gleaned from a variety of official sources, and was an indispensable reference for this section.

The descriptions of the U-boat base at Lorient are based on personal observations, survivor interviews; 'U-Boat Bases' in *After the Battle*, No 55 (London 1987); *The War at Sea Vol 2*, pages 352–3; *Business in Great Waters*, pages 256–7, 670, 354–5, 516, 615 and 648–9; Dönitz's *Memoirs*, pages 110, 112, 409, and 467; *U-175* War Diary; and *Bomber Command*, pages 99, 100, 101, 193 and 195.

The description of *U-175*'s second patrol is based almost entirely on personal interviews plus the *U-175*'s BdU war diaries. Additional details on the loss of the S/S *Benjamin Smith* are found in *A Careless Word . . . A Needless Sinking* pages 31-2, and in *The Liberty Ships* (London 1970) on page 104. Operations off West Africa are described in *Chronology of the War at Sea 1939-1945* page 183 et al; *The War at Sea Vol 1*, pages 351-3, 463, 470 and Vol 2 pages 92, 100, 108, 371; also *Business in Great Waters* pages 244, 344, 499, 593; while descriptions of crew and officers are taken from survivors, supplemented by 'Narratives: History of *U-175*, in the *Monthly Anti-Submarine Report*, May 1943, Section 4 (XC 21758), and Naval Intelligence Division's '*U-175*: Interrogation of Survivors', June 1943 NID 03262/43.

The third and last patrol is based on BdU war diaries; Signal file of US Navy with enemy radio intercepts; *Narrative: History of U-175*; personal interviews; *U-Boat Commander's Handbook*; and BdU signal files. Unpublished accounts by Gustav Brückmann and Werner Bickel, as well as personal interviews with other surviving crew members, were invaluable in recreating events on *U-175*.

Numerous sources from both sides were utilised for the chapter on the actual battle including eye witness accounts, war diaries, after action reports, log book extracts, attack diagrams, prisoner interrogations, photographs and personal observation. The description of the *Fort Rampart* and her loss is from *Wartime Standard Ships, Vol Two: The Oceans, the Forts and the Parks,* pages 7-19; *British Vessels Lost at Sea 1939-45,* page 47; *Axis Submarine Successes 1939-1945*, page 163; *Chronology of the War at Sea 1939-1945,* page 207; *The War at Sea Vol 2*, page 372, 380. Additional details are found in the various US Navy armed guard commanders' reports.

The loss of *U-175* is based on personal interviews, interrogations of prisoners, and *Narrative: History of U-175* provided the details of what transpired during the approach and attempted/aborted attack. The boarding of the abandoned wreck is in the After Action Report and War Diary of USCGC *Spencer* for 17 April 1943. Details of the attack by *Spencer* on *U-175* are also found in the above as well as in attack diagrams and personal recollections and the history of *Spencer*. Lists of prisoners are found in the log books of both *Spencer* and *Duane* with corrected data in prisoner interrogation reports in NID-03262/43 from British Intelligence sources. Again unpublished accounts by Werner Bickel and Gustav Brückmann were invaluable.

The chapter on U-boat transmissions, intercepts and decoding is based on background information primarily found in *Business in Great Waters*, also *The Critical Convoy Battles of March 1943,* and 'Translations of Intercepted Enemy Radio Traffic and the U-Boat Collateral File' from Records of Chief of Naval Operations (R G-38) reveals all too clearly how the Allies were privy to all German radio traffic.

The Allied Story
The torpedoing of S/S *Fort Rampart* is based mainly on Report of Master, Captain W Stein, OBE, Shipping Casualties-Trade Division, Report of Proceedings, Commanding Officer HMS *Arvida*, correspondence with former DEMS Gunner, Mr Charles Collis, DEMS Association Secretary, who joined *Fort Rampart* in New York and later served in

HMS *Penn* in the Southeast Asia C Zone; Mr R J Dickerson, ex-HMS *Impulsive*, and Mr Bill Robertson, ex- HMS *Offa* of the 3rd Support Group, as well as eye witness accounts of those on nearby ships of the convoy. The arrival of 3rd Support Group and its subsequent activities is from the Report of Proceedings by Senior Officer HMS *Offa*, while the final torpedoing of *Fort Rampart* is found in *Axis Submarine Successes 1939-45*, page 163, the war diaries of *U-226* and *U-628*, and Report of Proceedings from the commanding officers of HMS *Penn* and *Panther*.

The collision between *James Fenimore Cooper* and *Lena Luckenbach* is described by the two US Navy Armed Guard Commmanders aboard each vessel, and the subsequent fate of the latter vessel is found in *A Careless Word . . . A Needless Sinking* and in Report of Proceedings by the commanding officer of HMS *Dianthus*. Of particular help in describing events surrounding the salvage of damaged and abandoned *Lena Luckenbach* were Messers T F J Rogers, Jim Morris, Peter Bowen, and V A Whiteley of HMS *Bergamot*.

The chapter on air support drew heavily on the war diaries of *Spencer* and *Duane*, reports by the US Navy armed guard commanders, Report of Proceedings by escort commanders, and *The War at Sea Vol 2*.

Background to support groups is found in *The War at Sea Vol 2, The Battle of the Atlantic* and *Business in Great Waters*, while the activities of the Support Group dispatched to Convoy HX-233 was found in Reports of Proceedings for the four destroyers involved.

Background information on the US side of the story is found in *Operation Drumbeat, The U-Boat War in the Caribbean, Track of the Grey Wolf, Memoirs, The War at Sea*, and *Business in Great Waters*, as well as the author's personal participation and observations. The Allied views are also in *North Atlantic Run* (Toronto 1985) and *The Battle of the Atlantic 1939-45*, page 129.

The escape of the Norwegian vessels from Göteborg, Sweden is described in *The War at Sea, Vol 1*, page 391, and their descriptions may be found in *Die Handelsflotten der Welt 1941* (Munich 1941). The activities of *Spencer* and *Duane* are in deck logs, *War Diary*, and After Action Reports, as well as in the official histories and descriptions of both vessels. The actions of the S/S *James Jackson* is found in her armed guard commanders' reports and personal accounts by the former US Merchant Marine Academy Cadets. The armed guard commander reports when useful have been included *verbatim*. The descriptions of events aboard both cutters are from personal accounts of officers and crew as well as personal interviews with *U-175* survivors and contemporary photographs.

The arrival of the Convoy in the UK is based on the composition of the convoy, cargoes and destinations, plus the Report of Proceedings of the commanding officer of HMCS *Wetaskiwin*, who assumed the role of senior officer after the departure of *Spencer* and *Duane*.

Unpublished Sources / Official Documentation

Crown copyright material in the Public Record Office is reproduced by permission of the Controller of Her Majesty's Stationary Office.

Name / Title
Convoy Diagram: HX-233, sailed 6.4.43, ADM 199/576
Form for Reporting Submarine Attack, ADM 199/576
ID Form AC
(a) Attack report-Commodore Dawson

(b) Report on vessels requiring investigation: *Lena Luckenbach* and *James Fenimore Cooper* (to US Navy).

(c) List of stragglers and those who did not sail:

    (A) *Mosli* (Nor.)

    (B) *W R Keever* (US)

    (C) *Axel Johnson* (Sw.)

    (D) *Kaituna* (Br.)

    (E) *Egda* (Nor.)

    (F) *Yemassee* (Pan)

    (G) *Cape Howe* (Br.)

    (H) *Hannibal Hamlin* (US)

Track chart, HMS *Dianthus*, HX-233, ADM 199/575

    sailed St. John 12 April 1943 to overtake convoy.

Analysis of Operations of Support, ADM 199/2060

    Groups in North Atlantic 14 April to 11 May 1943 and Convoy HX-233 (Monthly Anti-submarine report May 1943, Section 4).

Narratives: History of *U-175*, ADM 199/2060

    (as above, Section 4)

U-boat incidents: Report No 1309, ADM 199/2049

    Anti-Submarine Warfare Division, Naval Staff, 17 April 1943

Report by Commodore, Convoy HX-233, ADM 199/576

    O H Dawson, RNR

    (a) Noon positions

    (b) Report by Master *Stiklestad* on submerged object sighted

    (c) Forwarding endorsement, (Ref. S. 352/6583)

Analysis Support Groups 14 April, ADM 199/2020

Shipping casualties – Trade Division, ADM 199/2145

    Report of Master *Fort Rampart* Captain W. Stein.

    (See also ADM 199/2145)

Third Support Group (EG-3), ADM 199/575

Second SO Report of Proceedings Covering Period 13.4.43 to 25.4.43, Convoy HX-233 and Convoy SC-126.

    (a) HMS *Offa*, Senior Officer, (A / sw 1467/43)

    (b) HMS *Impulsive*

    (c) HMS *Penn* (NB: includes *coup de grâce, Fort Rampart*)

    (d) HMS *Panther*

HMS *Bryony* (attack 18.4.43 on U-boat with endorsement by Captain Heineman)

Log book USCGC *Spencer*, April 1943

Log book USCGC *Duane*, April 1943

Report of Proceedings, HMCS *Arvida*, dated 21 April 1943

Report of Proceedings, HMCS *Wetaskiwin*, 17-20 April 1943

Report of Proceedings, HMS *Bergamot*, 11-18 April 1943

Report of Proceedings, HMS *Dianthus*, 17-21 April 1943

After Action Report, Commanding Officer, USCGC *Spencer*

War Diary, Commanding Officer, Task Unit 24.1.3, April 1943, Convoy ON-175, Convoy HX-233 (20) War Diary, USCGC *Spencer*, 12-20 April 1943

After Action Report, USCGC *Duane*

HF/DF Report and Log, 11–20 April 1943: U-boat transmissions with narrative, HX-233

NAVAL MESSAGE FILE-signals

Final Report, Captain P Heineman, USN, Escort Commander, Convoy HX-233, 21 April
   1943; also hand-written draft

Draft report of sinking of *U-175*

List of documents declassified 10 January 1977, including photo list

List of personal effects of POWs on USCGC *Spencer*, 19 April 1943, and list of POW's

USCGC *Spencer*, Questionnaire regarding *U-175*

US ATLANTIC FLEET, Escort Unit 24.1.3, USCGC *Spencer*, 11 April 1943, St Johns:
   Operation Plan No 5–43
   (a) Organisation and transmissions
   (b) Annexes: Communications with Appendix
   (c) Escort doctrine with formations and diagrams

British Intelligence, NND 750122; Reports CPM B, B 311–342 with CB 04051 (68):
   U-175-Interrogation of Survivors, June 1943, NID 03262/43 and excerpts.
   (a) NID – 03262/43, British.
   (b) Excerpts from above, American, mainly relates to anti-aircraft training by U-boat
   crews.

Kriegstagebuch (War Diary) *U-92* ADM PG/30086/1–10/NID

Kriegstagebuch (War Diary) *U-175*, commissioning and first two patrols: T1022, #4185,
   RG 242, US National Archives

Kriegstagebuch *U-226* ADM PG/30 213/1/NID

Kriegstagebuch *U-628*, T1022 #3385, US National Archives

Kriegstagebuch *U-262* ADM PG/30235/4/NID

Voyage Reports (RG 38 Armed Guard files 1940-45 CNO)
   (a) US Armed Guard Commander S/S *James Fenimore Cooper*
   (b) US Armed Guard Commander S/S *G Harrison Smith*
   (c) US Armed Guard Commander S/S *James Jackson*
   (d) US Armed Guard Commander S/S *Lena Luckenbach*
   (e) US Armed Guard Commander S/S *Alcoa Cutter*
   (f) US Armed Guard Commander S/S *Sun*
   (g) US Armed Guard Commander S/S *Roger Williams*
   (h) US Armed Guard Commander S/S *George Handley*
   (i) US Armed Guard Commander S/S *Jonathan Worth*
   (j) US Armed Guard Commander S/S *Wallace E Pratt*
   (k) US Armed Guard Commander S/S *William D Pender*

Signal file US Navy – collision of S/S *James Fenimore Cooper* and S/S *Lena Luckenbach*, 20
   to 23 April 1943

Signal intercept file, US Navy. Ktlt Heinrich Bruns, CO *U-175*, 3 January-25 April 1943
   (RG 38, Records of the CNO: Translations of Intercepted Enemy Radio Traffic) 1943
   complete

Information obtained from German naval prisoners, American summary, relates to AA
training of U-boat crews
   (a) British source: Information received in Britain 15 April through 23 May 1943 and
   22 April to 1 May 1943. Summary by Catesby ap G Jones, Colonel, G S C, Chief,
   Prisoner of War Branch
   (b) US National Archives, R G 165, Entry 179. (B-314, 4 June 1943; B-319, 16 June
   1943; and B-322, 5–19 May 1943

Lloyd's Captain's Register (Guildhall Ms 18.568/13b)

Naval Messages, RCN Serial 38–8440 MOEF 'A' (2) Department of National Defense (Naval Service) Ottawa, courtesy Directorate of History, Canada

Progress Report for Defense Council (Weekly) Most Secret RCN NSS 1000–5-19 V 3, CSC 190; Department of Defense (Naval Service) Weekly Summary of Information respecting Departmental Activities, Summary No 181, Report No 119, Ottawa, 23 April 1943; (Ottawa), courtesy Directorate of History, Canada

Merchant Shipping Casualties, Report No 16 for week ending 19 April 1943, RCN NS 1048–47-5; Secret Attacks of Trans-Atlantic Convoys during the Past Four Weeks April 17 HX-233, *Fort Rampart* (Ottawa) Courtesy Directorate History Canada

Brief History of HMCS *Skeena*; 8000, Directorate of History, Ottawa, Canada

NA *Convoy ops* 1650–239/15 Prior 1944: Summary of Trade Division April and May 1943; RCN Control of convoys. Merchant Shipping & Trade Summaries 1943; Courtesy Directorate of History, Ottawa Canada

RCN NA Convoy Ops Analyses of Support Group Operations Secret, Anti-U-boat Division, Admiralty 1. Support Groups 14 April-11 May 1943, Directorate of History, Ottawa, Canada

Publications

Bagnasco, Ermino, *Submarines of World War II* (Annapolis 1978)

Bekker, Cajus, *Verdammte See* (Oldenburg 1971)

Bickel, Werner, *Meine Erlebnisse im 2, Weltkrieg* (1996 unpublished)

British Vessels Lost at Sea 1939–1945 (Cambridge 1980)

Brown, David, *Warship Losses of World War Two* (Annapolis 1995)

Browning, Robert M, *U.S. Merchant Vessels War Casualties of World War II* (Annapolis 1996)

Brückmann, Gustav, *U-Boat Historie*. Revised (1994 unpublished)

Breyer, Siegfried, and Koop, Gerhard, *Die Deutsche Kriegsmarine 1935-1945*, Band 3 (Friedberg 1987)

Buchheim, Lothar-Günther, *The Boat* (New York 1976)

Bunker, John G, *The Liberty Ships* (Annapolis 1972) (convoy number incorrect)

———. *Heroes in Dungarees* (Annapolis 1995) (*U-175* not sunk 'by gunfire')

Colledge, J J, *Ships of the Royal Navy*, Vol I (Newton Abbot 1969)

Costello, John, and Hughes, Terry, *The Battle of the Atlantic* (London 1987) (Incorrectly reports 'straggler' sunk.)

Cremer, Peter, *U-333* (London 1984)

Delshall, Gaylord T M, *The U-Boat War in the Caribbean* (Annapolis 1994)

Dönitz, Admiral Karl, *Memoirs: Ten Years and Twenty Days* (London 1959) (pp 335-6, U-boat number incorrect.)

Fahey, James C, *Ships and Aircraft of the US Fleet* (New York 1946)

Franke, Fregatten Kapitän a D Heinz, Ritterkreuzträger, *Sonderunternehmung in den St. Lorenz-Golf als Komandant mit 'U-262' in den St, Lorens Strom!* (unpublished)

Gasaway, E B, *Grey Wolf, Grey Sea* (London 1972)

Gentile, Gary, *Track of the Gray Wolf* (New York 1989)

Gröner, Erich, *Die Handelsflotten der Welt: 1941* (Berlin 1941)

———. *Die Deutschen Kriegsschiffe 1815–1945, Band 2* (Koblenz, 1983)

Hadley, Michael L, *U-Boats against Canada* (Montreal and Kingston 1985)

Halpern, Prof Paul G *A Naval History of World War I* (London 1994)

Handbook on German Military Forces: War Department Technical Manual TM-E 30-451 (Washington 1945)

Haskell, W A. 'Battle of the Atlantic – Turning Point and Climax, March-April 1943.' *Island Ad-Vantages, COMPASS*, 29 April 1993

——. 'Eyewitness Account of the Loss of *U-175*, 17 April 1943.' *U-Boat War: International Journal of Submarine Warfare 1914-1945*, Vol 1 No 5, Spring 1992

Hastings, Max, *Bomber Command* (London 1979)

Herzog, Bodo, *Deutsche U-Boote 1906-1966* (Erlangen 1993)

Hessler, F/Kapt Günther F Hoschatt, K/Kapt Alfred; and Rohwer, Lt z Z Jürgen, *The U-Boat War in the Atlantic 1939–1945*, (HMSO 1989, three vols in one, (Produced for British Admiralty and US Navy, Primary author, Hessler, was Grand Admiral Dönitz's son-in-law who commanded *U-107* in 1940-41 then became Operations Staff Officer to Flag Officer of U-boats.)

Högel, Georg, *Embleme Wappen Malings deutscher U-Boote 1939-1945* (Hamburg 1996)

Kelshall, Gaylord T M, *The U-Boat War in the Caribbean*, (Annapolis 1994) (total *U-175* sinkings incorrect)

Kerr, J Lennox, *Touching the Adventures of Merchantmen in the Second World War* (London 1959)

Lenton, H T & Colledge, J J, *Warships of World War II* (Shepperton 1980)

Macintyre, Donald, *The Battle of the Atlantic* (London, 1961) (pp 169-70, wrong U-boat number.)

Masters, David, *In Peril on the Sea* (London 1960)

Merchant Navy at War, HMSO (London 1944)

Middlebrook, Martin, *Convoy* (New York 1976) (excellent report of convoys SC-122 and HX-229.)

Milner, Marc, *North Atlantic Run: the Royal Canadian Navy and the Battle for the Convoys* (Toronto 1985) (NB reports eight U-boats with four attacks.)

——. *The U-Boat Hunters: The Royal Canadian Navy and the Offensive against Germany's Submarines* (Annapolis 1994)

Mitchell, W H and Sawyer, L A, *The Oceans, the Forts & the Parks: Wartime Standard Ships, Vol II* (Stockport 1966)

Moore, Captain Arthur R, *A Careless Word . . . A Needless Sinking* (Farmington 1984)

Morison, Samuel E, 'Battle of the Atlantic,' *History of US Naval Operations in WW II*, Vol I. (NB allegedly official US Navy history, with access to official files and records; many errors.)

——. 'The Atlantic Battle Won,' *History of US Naval Operations in WW II*, Vol X (New York 1962)

——. *Two Ocean War* (Boston 1963)

Mulligan, Timothy P, *The Life and Death of U-boat Ace Werner Henke* (Norman 1995)

Noble, Dennis L 'CGC *Spencer* Rams, Sinks Nazi U-Boat,' *Commandant's Bulletin*, April 1993, (*Spencer* did not 'ram' *U-175*.)

Pallud, Jean Paul, 'U-Boat Bases,' *After the Battle*, No 55 (London 1987)

Pitt, Barrie, *Die Schlacht im Atlantik* (Eltville 1994) (pp84-93, wrong commander)

Price, Scott T, '*Spencer* Sinks the *U-175*,' *The Coast Guard and the North Atlantic Campaign*, Commandant Bulletin insert, November 1984.

Rohwer, Dr Jürgen, and Hümmelchen, Gerhard, *Chronology of the War at Sea 1939-1945* (Annapolis 1992)

Rohwer, Dr Jürgen, *Axis Submarine Successes 1939-1945* (Annapolis 1983)

——. *The Critical Convoy Battles of March 1943* (Annapolis 1977) (excellent coverage of convoy control and U-boat operations, supplements Martin Middlebrook's *Convoy*)

Roskill, Captain Steven E, DSC, RN, *The War at Sea 1939-1945*, Vol II (London 1956)

Ruegg, Bob, and Hague, Arnold, *Convoys to Russia 1941-45* (Kendal 1992)

Sawyer, L A, and Mitchell, W H, *The Liberty Ships* (London 1970)

Scheina, Robert L, *US Coast Guard Cutters & Craft of World War II* (Annapolis 1982)

——. *US Coast Guard Cutters and Craft 1946-1990* (Annapolis 1990)

Seidl, Edward H, 'Cameraman's Jackpot,' *Coast Guard Magazine* (date unknown)

Sellwood, A V, *The Warring Seas* (London 1956)

Showell, Jak P Mallmann, *U-Boat Command and the Battle of the Atlantic* (London 1989)

——. *U-Boats under the Swastika* (Exeter, 1973)

Silverstone, Paul H, *US Warships of World War II* (Sheperton 1968)

Slader, John, *The Fourth Service–Merchantmen at War 1939-45* (Corfe Mullen 1995)

'*Spencer* and *Duane* vs. German U-boat: What Really Happened,' *The Bulletin, US Coast Guard Academy Alumni Association*, Vol 13 No 2, March-April 1981.

Standard Oil Company of NJ, *Ships of the Esso Fleet in World War II* (1946)

Stern, Robert, *Type VII U-Boats* (Annapolis 1991)

Strobridge, Truman R and Noble, Dennis L, 'Deep Sea Duel,' *Sea Classics:* special issue; *US Coast Guard at War*, Vol 1, 1995

Tarrant, V E, *U-Boat Offensive 1914-1945* (Annapolis 1989)

Taylor, J C, *German Warships of World War II* (London 1966)

Terraine, John, *Business in Great Waters – The U-Boat Wars 1916-1945* (London 1989) (reports five U-boats present during attack on convoy HX-233)

The Battle of the Atlantic: The Official Account of the Fight Against the U-boats 1939-1945: (London HMSO 1946) (and the German translation by Korv Kpt d Res Hans Köberling, 1997, with pertinent German reports inserted.)

The Submarine Commanders' Handbook (*Befehlshaber der Unterseeboots*). U Kdt Hdb, 1943 with amendments nos 3, 1–11.

The United States Merchant Marine at War. WSA (Washington 1946)

U-Bootsmuseum U-995; Laboe, Deutscher Marinebund (Guidebook to the U-boat *U-995* by the German Naval Memorial Association.)

US Naval Intelligence, *Uniforms & Insignia of the Navies of the World* (Washington 1942)

Vause, Jordan, *U-Boat Ace: The Story of Wolfgang Lüth* (Annapolis 1990)

Waters, Captain John M, USCG, *Bloody Winter* (Annapolis 1967) (several errors, eg POWs not landed in Ireland).

Wells, Donald A, *The Laws of Land Warfare*: London, nd, Contributions to Military Studies, Number 132, pp 133-141 'The Care of Prisoners' (of War).

Werner, Herbert A, *Iron Coffins* (London 1975)

Williamson, Gordon, *Aces of the Reich* (London 1989)

Willoughby, Malcom F, *The US Coast Guard in World War II* (Annapolis 1989)

——. *U-Boat Krieg* (München 1976)

Index

Except for Convoy HX-233, *Spencer*, *Duane* and *U-175*, the index includes the names of all ships and individuals mentioned in the text. Individual convoys and U-boats are grouped under the entries 'Convoys' and 'U-boats'.